AF814173

QUE Bee

From Doubts to Distinction

Your ICSE 2026 Exams Partner

GIST OF THE TEXTBOOK
Crisp & Complete Theory - No need to go back to textbooks!

ALL TYPES OF LATEST PATTERN QUESTIONS
MCQs Including Statement Based, Arrange in Sequence Based Questions, Extract Based Questions, All in one place!

KEY WORDS HIGHLIGHTED
Important points neatly Underlined Never miss what matters

COUNCIL-STYLE ANSWERS
Write responses like an examiner expects

SAMPLE & SPECIMEN PAPER
Practice in real-exam mode. Perfect your timing, strategy and confidence.

ARIHANT PRAKASHAN

(School Division Series)

卐 **ADMINISTRATIVE & PRODUCTION OFFICES**

Regd. Office

'Ramchhaya' 4577/15, Agarwal Road, Darya Ganj, New Delhi -110002
Tele: 011- 47630600, 43518550; Fax: 011- 23280316

卐 **Head Office**

Kalindi, TP Nagar, Meerut (UP) - 250002, Tel: 0121-7156203, 7156204

卐 **SALES & SUPPORT OFFICES**

Agra, Ahmedabad, Bengaluru, Bareilly, Chennai, Delhi, Guwahati, Hyderabad, Jaipur, Jhansi, Kolkata, Lucknow, Nagpur & Pune.

PO No : TXT-XX-XXXXXXX-X-XX

Published By Arihant Publications (India) Ltd.

For further information about the books published by Arihant, log on to www.arihantbooks.com or e-mail at info@arihantbooks.com

Follow us on

卐 **PRICE** ₹200.00

PRODUCTION TEAM

Publishing Manager
Keshav Mohan

Project Head
Manju

Cover Designer
Bilal Hashmi

Inner Designer
Ankit Tyagi

Page Layouting
Lalit Chaprana

Proof Reader
Harsh Agarwal

QUE Bee

ICSE
LITERATURE IN ENGLISH (PAPER 2)
Class 9

Major Elements in the Book

Drama (Julius Caesar)	Prose (Treasure Chest)	Poetry (Treasure Chest)
About the Author	Introduction	Introduction
About the Drama	About the Story	About the Poem
Themes of the Drama	Character Introduction	Exploring the Stanzas
Actwise Plot of Julius Caesar	Story at a Glance	Theme of the Poem
Major & Minor Characters	Theme	Message Conveyed by the Story
Summary of the whole Drama	Message Conveyed by the Story	Style, Tone & Mode
Actwise Scenewise Summary of	Style, Tone & Mode	Title
the Drama	Title, Figures of Speech	Literary Devices
Multiple Choice Questions (107)	Multiple Choice Questions (116)	Multiple Choice Questions (124)
Extract Based Questions (23)	Extract Based Questions (28)	Extract Based Questions (28)

Created by

Gregory R. Raphael

MA, M Phill. (English)
HOD English
St. Thomas' English Medium School, Meerut

Contributors

Parneet Kaur, Vaishali Jaiswal, Saba

From Learner to Leader

Step-Into the Spotlight

QUE Bee is more than just a book - it's a platform for young achievers like you to guide future toppers. If you've cracked the code to smart study or have insights that can make learning easier for others, this is your moment to shine!

What Can You Share?

- Your study techniques, time management tips, or motivation hacks
- Feedback or suggestions to make QUE Bee even better
- Real experiences that can guide other students through the exam maze

What's in It for You?

- Your name will be featured in our exclusive Student Panel in the next edition
- Win exciting & surprise rewards for impactful suggestions
- **Get published** - your photo, Ideas-or even interviews can be featured in the book
- **Become a student icon** - recognized and followed by peers across schools

Let your learning become someone else's ladder.
Be remembered. Be featured. Be the guide.

SCAN TO SHARE YOUR IDEA

Index

TREASURE CHEST: PROSE

TREASURE CHEST: POETRY

Latest Course Structure

PAPER 2 - LITERATURE IN ENGLISH (Two hours) - 80 Marks

Candidates will be required to answer questions based on the prescribed textbooks, which include Drama, Prose (Short Stories) and Poetry.

DRAMA AND PROSE (SHORT STORIES)

Questions set will be central to the text. Candidates will be required to show that they have understood the passage and are able to clearly respond in their own words.

Excerpts may be given from the drama and prose texts leading to questions.

POETRY

A poem, or lines from poems, will be given and questions will be set to test the candidates' response. The questions will focus on the content, understanding and the personal response of candidates to the entire poem as a whole.

I. **DRAMA** : Julius Caesar - William Shakespeare (Acts I & II)

II. **TREASURE CHEST** : A Collection of ICSE Short Stories & Poems (Evergreen Publications (India) Ltd. New Delhi)

PROSE (Short Stories):

1. Bonku Babu's Friend – Satyajit Ray
2. Oliver Asks for More – Charles Dickens
3. The Model Millionaire – Oscar Wilde
4. Home-coming – Rabindranath Tagore
5. The Boy Who Broke the Bank – Ruskin Bond

POETRY

1. A Work of Artifice – Marge Piercy
2. Skimbleshanks: The Railway Cat – T.S. Eliot
3. I Remember, I Remember – Thomas Hood
4. A Doctor's Journal Entry for August 6, 1945 – Vikram Seth
5. The Night Mail – W.H. Auden

NOTE : *The Class IX Examination is to be conducted on the portion of the syllabus that is prescribed for Class IX.*

DRAMA : JULIUS CAESAR

Act 1 : Scene 1-3

Act 2 : Scene 1-4

JULIUS CAESAR

William Shakespeare

About the Author

An English playwright, actor and poet, William Shakespeare (1564-1616) is generally regarded as the greatest writer of the Elizabethan Era. His extensive work includes thirty-seven plays, one hundred and fifty-four sonnets and two long narrative poems.

Initially an actor, he started writing plays around 1589, with his early plays primarily being comedies and histories. He wrote mainly tragedies until, 1608 entering the last phase of his literary career with tragicomedies. His plays are marked with effective use of soliloquy, humour, clever rhetoric and double entendres (meaning). His works express the complete range of human experience with complex characters.

About the Drama

William Shakespeare's **Julius Caesar** was written in 1599 and is based on historical events surrounding the assassination of the Roman leader Gaius Julius Caesar in 44 BC.

The story begins with Cassius convincing Brutus, a noble Roman, to join a conspiracy against Caesar, fearing his ambition might lead to tyranny. Despite personal loyalty, Brutus agrees, believing it's for the greater good of Rome. Caesar ignores warnings and omens about his fate and is ultimately assassinated in the Senate by the conspirators.

Following Caesar's death, Mark Antony skilfully turns public opinion against the conspirators through a powerful funeral speech inciting a civil war. Brutus and Cassius face defeat on the battlefield, leading to their suicides. Antony and Octavius, Caesar's heir, emerge victorious, setting the stage for the rise of the Roman Empire.

Themes of the Drama

The play is rich in political intrigue and moral complexity exploring the themes of

Major Themes

Power | Ambition | Betrayal | Fate | Loyalty

- **Power and Corruption** The play examines the dangers of unchecked ambition and the corrupting influence of power. The fear that Caesar may become a tyrant drives the conspirators to assassinate him, showcasing how the pursuit and maintenance of power can lead to ethical compromises and destructive consequences.
- **Betrayal and Loyalty** Betrayal is a central theme with Brutus' betrayal of Caesar being the most significant. This theme underscores the tension between personal loyalty and public duty as Brutus justifies his actions as necessary for the republic's welfare despite his affection for Caesar.
- **Fate vs Free Will** Throughout the play, characters grapple with their ability to control their destinies. Caesar's dismissal of omens and prophecies highlights the tension between fate and human agency, suggesting that while fate may guide events, personal choices still play a crucial role.
- **Rhetoric and Manipulation** The power of language and rhetoric is vividly displayed in Mark Antony's funeral speech which manipulates the crowd's emotions and turns public opinion against the conspirators. This theme illustrates how persuasive speech can shape political outcomes and sway masses.
- **Public vs Private Self** Characters in the play often struggle with their public personas and private feelings. Brutus, in particular, embodies this conflict as he navigates his personal loyalty to Caesar and his perceived duty to Rome.

Actwise Plot of *Julius Caesar*

Act 1 : "The Seeds of Conspiracy"
This act sets the stage for the rising tension in Rome, with Caesar's growing power and the discontent among the conspirators.

Act 2 : "The Conspiracy Takes Shape"
Brutus wrestles with his conscience and ultimately joins the conspiracy as the plot to assassinate Caesar is finalised.

Act 3 : "The Fall of Caesar"
The pivotal act where Caesar is assassinated and the aftermath begins with the famous funeral orations.

Act 4 : "The Aftermath of Betrayal"
The power struggle continues as Brutus and Cassius face the consequences of their actions. The triad consolidates power.

Act 5 : "The Battle of Philippi"
The final act concludes with the battle, the deaths of key characters and the ultimate resolution of the conflict.

Major Characters

- **Julius Caesar** The leader of Rome whose assassination is the central event of the play
- **Brutus** A Roman senator and the main conspirator against Caesar, he is torn between loyalty to Caesar and his duty to Rome
- **Cassius** A senator who masterminds the plot to kill Caesar and a leader of the conspiracy
- **Mark Antony** A loyal friend of Caesar who seeks revenge for Caesar's assassination
- **Portia** Brutus' wife who is concerned about his secretive actions and she commits suicide because she relatises Brutus misfortunes
- **Calpurnia** Caesar's wife who has ominous dreams about Caesar's death
- **Octavius** Caesar's adopted son and heir who plays a role in the power struggle after Caesar's death

Minor Characters

- **Flavius** A tribune who opposes Caesar's rise to power
- **Marullus** A tribune who also opposes Caesar's ascent and is punished for removing decorations from Caesar's statues
- **Soothsayer** A mysterious figure who warns Caesar about the Ides of March
- **Artemidorus** A teacher of rhetoric who tries to warn Caesar of the conspiracy through a letter
- **Decius Brutus** A member of the conspiracy who persuades Caesar to go to the Senate on the day of his assassination
- **Metellus Cimber** A conspirator who asks for the repeal of his brother's banishment to create a reason for the assassination

- **Trebonius** A conspirator who leads Mark Antony away from Caesar at the Senate to help facilitate the assassination
- **Ligarius** A conspirator who joins Brutus and Cassius' cause despite initially being hesitant
- **Cicero** A respected Roman senator who is not involved in the conspiracy but is mentioned in passing
- **Cinna (the poet)** A poet who is mistaken for one of the conspirators and is killed by a mob
- **Varro and Claudius** Servants to Brutus
- **Strato** A servant to Brutus who assists in his final moments
- **Dardanius** Another servant of Brutus who is involved in his death
- **Aemilius Lepidus** He is a member of the second triumvirate and he basically does Antony's tasks.
- **Lucilius** He is a noble friend of Brutus (who pretends to be Brutus). He is captured by Antony's soldiers
- **Titinius** He is Brutus' servant who goes for a joy ride and ultimately commits suicide
- **Messala** He is a soldier of Brutus and Cassius and tells Brutus that his wife is dead

Summary of the Drama

The play begins with people celebrating Caesar's victory over Pompey. Flavius and Marullus, two tribunes, scold the citizens for changing their loyalty from Pompey to Caesar. Meanwhile, Cassius, a senator, is unhappy with Caesar's rise to power and begins plotting against him. He tries to persuade Brutus, Caesar's close friend, to join the conspiracy by playing on his love for Rome. Brutus is torn but agrees after thinking about Caesar's ambition.

Brutus decides to join the conspiracy believing that killing Caesar is the only way to save Rome from tyranny. Caesar's wife, Calpurnia, has a nightmare that Caesar will be killed and begs him not to go to the Senate. He initially agrees but is later persuaded by Decius who reinterprets the dream as a good omen. Caesar decides to go to the Senate. Brutus' wife, Portia, is anxious but is kept in the dark. Meanwhile, a man named Artemidorus tries to warn Caesar by giving him a letter but Caesar ignores it.

At the Senate, Caesar is assassinated by the conspirators. Brutus delivers the final blow claiming it was for Rome's good. After Caesar's death, Mark Antony, Caesar's loyal friend, pretends to accept the murder. However, he cleverly turns the people against the conspirators by showing them Caesar's will which leaves wealth to the people. The crowd becomes angry and starts hunting down the conspirators.

Antony, Octavius and Lepidus form a triad to rule Rome and punish Caesar's supporters. Brutus and Cassius, now in conflict, eventually reconcile. Brutus learns that his wife has died. Both sides prepare for battle with the stage set for a final confrontation.

The forces of Brutus and Cassius face off against those of Antony and Octavius in a final battle. Cassius believes his army is losing and asks his servant to kill him. However, Brutus' side continues fighting. Eventually, Brutus, realising defeat is near, asks his servant to hold his sword while he kills himself. Antony and Octavius emerge victorious. They mourn Brutus, calling him an honourable man, reflecting on the tragic events that unfolded.

ACT 1 : SCENE 1

Summary of Act 1 Scene 1

In Act 1, Scene 1 of *Julius Caesar*, two Roman tribunes, Flavius and Marullus, find the common people celebrating Caesar's victory over Pompey. The people are cheering for Caesar and wearing festive clothes. However, Flavius and Marullus are upset by the people's sudden change in loyalty. They were loyal to the Roman Senate and are concerned about Caesar's growing power. They scold the citizens for their fickleness and remind them of their past support for Pompey. They believe Caesar's growing power could lead to the end of the Roman Republic.

To further show their disapproval of Caesar, Flavius and Marullus decide to remove the decorations from Caesar's statues. They do so in hopes of preventing Caesar's image from becoming too prominent. Flavius argues that if Caesar continues to gain power, he might become a dictator, which would threaten the freedom of Rome.

This scene highlights the political tension in Rome and introduces the growing concern about Caesar's influence. It further sets the stage for the plot against Caesar as it introduces characters who are concerned about Caesar's rise.

Characters in the Scene

- **Flavius** Flavius is a Roman tribune who is concerned about Caesar's growing power. He criticises the people for their fickleness as they once supported Pompey but are now celebrating Caesar's victory. Flavius is deeply worried that Caesar may become a tyrant; so, he takes action to reduce Caesar's influence by removing decorations from Caesar's statues.
- **Marullus** Marullus is another Roman tribune working alongside Flavius. Like Flavius, he is upset with the citizens for switching their loyalty from Pompey to Caesar. He scolds the people for their disloyalty and participates in the decision to remove the decorations from Caesar's statues in an attempt to curb his rising power.
- **Commoners (Workers)** A group of Roman citizens who are celebrating Caesar's victory over Pompey. They are described as being easily swayed, having once cheered for Pompey but now showing their support for Caesar. They are scolded by Flavius and Marullus for their inconsistency and disloyalty.
- **Caesar** Caesar himself does not directly appear in the opening scene of the play. However, he is mentioned several times and is the cause of chaos and disorder that Flavius and Marullus are attempting to quell.

Vocab Vault

Knave A dishonest man

Beseech Request or implore

Wherefore For what reason or why

Tributaries A ruler or state that pays tribute to a conqueror

Replication Duplication or repetition

Exalted Glorious

Servile Submissive

EXAM ORIENTED QUESTIONS

TYPE - 1 Multiple Choice Questions

01 Mark

Q.1 Where does Act 1, Scene 1 of *Julius Caesar* take place?

(a) The Senate (b) The streets of Rome
(c) Caesar's palace (d) Pompey's house

Q.2 Who are the first characters introduced in Act 1, Scene 1?

(a) Brutus and Cassius
(b) Flavius and Marullus
(c) Caesar and Antony
(d) Portia and Calpurnia

Q.3 What are the commoners celebrating in Act 1, Scene 1? **(ICSE Specimen 2024)**

(a) Caesar's victory over the sons of Pompey
(b) Caesar's victory over Pompey
(c) The Feast of the Lupercal
(d) The Ides of March

Q.4 What sarcastic reason does the cobbler give Flavius for leading citizens on the street?

(a) To get himself more work
(b) To rejoice in Caesar's Triumph
(c) To celebrate the feast
(d) To quell the show

Q.5 What are the people in the street doing when Flavius and Marullus first appear?

(a) Listening to a speech by Caesar
(b) Preparing for a festival
(c) Cheering and celebrating Caesar
(d) Arguing over Caesar's rule

Q.6 Identify why Flavius and Marullus angry with the people?

(a) They are not supporting Caesar enough
(b) They are celebrating Caesar's victory after previously supporting Pompey
(c) They are supporting Pompey over Caesar
(d) They are celebrating too loudly

Q.7 What does Marullus tell the people about their behaviour?

(a) They should continue celebrating Caesar
(b) They are being disloyal and ungrateful
(c) They should support Pompey again
(d) They should be silent and not speak against Caesar

Q.8 What do Flavius and Marullus do to show their disapproval of Caesar?

(a) Attack the citizens
(b) Remove decorations from Caesar's statues
(c) Declare Caesar a tyrant
(d) Call for an election

Q.9 What is Flavius' concern about Caesar's growing power?

(a) Caesar might become too wealthy
(b) Caesar could become a dictator and end the Republic
(c) Caesar might start a war
(d) Caesar might ignore the Senate

Q.10 What does Marullus suggest will happen if Caesar becomes too powerful?

(a) Rome will be more peaceful
(b) Caesar will give all his wealth to the people
(c) The people will suffer
(d) Caesar will step down

Q.11 Which of the following lines reflects Flavius' patriotism?

(a) "What other bond/Than secret Romans that have spoke the word/And will not let their vows be broke?"
(b) "These growing feathers pluck'd from Caesar's wing/Will make him fly an ordinary pitch."
(c) "If Caesar live, he will have all his wants."
(d) "The people are a fickle, changeable crowd."

Q.12 Select the option that shows the correct relationship between statements (1) and (2). **(ICSE Specimen 2024)**

Statement 1 Flavius tells Marullus that they would have to take all the decorations off Caesar's statues.

Statement 2 Flavius fears that Caesar's growing powers would result in a life of servitude for all Romans.

(a) Statement 1 is true and Statement 2 is false
(b) Statement 2 is true and Statement 1 is false.
(c) Statement 2 is the cause for Statement 1.
(d) Statement 1 and Statement 2 are independent of each other.

Q.13 Arrange the following events from Act 1, Scene 1 of *Julius Caesar* in the correct sequence.

1. Flavius and Marullus meet the commoners celebrating Caesar's victory.

2. Flavius and Marullus decide to remove decorations from Caesar's statues.
3. Flavius criticises the people for being disloyal and fickle.
4. Flavius expresses his concern about Caesar's rising power.
5. The commoners explain they are celebrating Caesar's victory over Pompey.

(a) 1, 5, 3, 4, 2
(b) 5, 1, 3, 4, 2
(c) 1, 4, 3, 2, 5
(d) 3, 1, 4, 2, 5

Q.14 According to this scene, what central theme of the play is reflected here?
(a) Conflict between monarchists and republicans
(b) Conflict between anarchy and democracy
(c) Conflict between dictatorship and democracy
(d) None of the above

Q.15 What does Marullus compare the commoners to?
(a) Blocks and stones
(b) Senseless things
(c) Hard hearts and cruel men of Rome
(d) All of the above

Answers

1. (b)	2. (b)	3. (b)	4. (a)	5. (c)	6. (b)	7. (b)	8. (b)	9. (b)	10. (c)
11. (b)	12. (c)	13. (a)	14. (a)	15. (d)					

Explanations

11. By 'plucking the feathers', Flavius is symbolically trying to limit Caesar's rise. This reflects his desire to protect the Roman Republic. This, thus, demonstrates his patriotism.
12. Flavius' fear of Caesar's growing powers is the reason behind him removing the decorations. He believes that Caesar's increasing influence could lead to a loss of freedom for Romans.

TYPE - 2 Extract Based Questions — 16 Marks

Extract 1

Flavius - Hence! Home, you idle creatures, get you home!
Is this a holiday? What, know you not,
Being mechanical, you ought not walk
Upon a laboring day without the sign
Of your profession?-Speak, what trade art thou?

(i) **What does Flavius mean when he addresses the commoners as 'idle creatures' in this passage? How does it reflect his attitude toward the people of Rome?** **(3)**

Ans. Flavius refers to the commoners as 'idle creatures' to criticise their behaviour as they are not working. They are instead celebrating Caesar's victory. His use of the word 'idle' conveys his belief that the common people are lazy and unproductive.

This reflects Flavius' disapproval of the people's lack of commitment to their work as well as their celebration of Caesar's success. His attitude suggests that he is arrogant and harsh.

(ii) **How does Flavius' questioning of the commoners about their profession highlight the theme of social class in *Julius Caesar*?** **(3)**

Ans. Flavius' question 'What trade art thou?' underscores the division between the social classes in Rome.

By questioning the commoners about their profession, he is reminding them of their lower status as workers. Thus, suggesting that they have no right to partake in activities like celebration during a workday.

The question emphasises the societal expectations placed upon different classes. This moment reflects the tension between the ruling class and the common people.

(iii) **In what way do Flavius' remarks about the 'sign of your profession' reveal his views on Roman values and the role of the common people in society?** **(3)**

Ans. Flavius' reference to the 'sign of your profession' implies that the common people should be visibly engaged in their work instead of indulging in celebrations. He believes that every citizen has a role to play and the commoners should remain focused on their duties.

Flavius' words reflect his view that Roman society thrives on order, discipline and hard work. He feels that these values are being undermined by the people's idle behaviour.

(iv) **What is the significance of Flavius' reference to a 'laboring day' in this passage? How does it connect to the larger political context of the play? (3)**

Ans. Flavius' reference to a 'laboring day' highlights the importance of work and productivity in Roman society, especially in contrast to the celebratory mood of the common people. He is chastising the people for treating a workday like a holiday; thus, neglecting their civic duties.

This statement connects to the larger political context by underscoring the political divide between the elite and the common people. Flavius' concern is that the common people, distracted by such celebrations and are not paying attention to the political implications of Caesar's rise to power which threatens the Republic.

(v) **Important character traits of Flavius are revealed in this scene. Mention any two. What is your opinion of the man? Give a reason to justify your answer. (4)**

Ans. In Act 1, Scene 1 of *Julius Caesar*, Flavius displays two important traits - patriotism and disapproving attitude. He is deeply concerned about Caesar's rise to power, fearing the loss of Roman freedom, showing his loyalty to the Republic.

Additionally, he harshly criticises the commoners for abandoning Pompey and celebrating Caesar.

Flavius can be viewed as a well-intentioned character, committed to preserving the Republic. However, his rigid approach toward the common people makes him seem elitist. While his patriotism is admirable, his lack of empathy for the lower class makes his methods questionable.

Extract 2

Marullus-Wherefore rejoice? What conquest
brings he home?
What tributaries follow him to Rome
To grace in captive bonds his chariot wheels?
You blocks, you stones, you worse than
senseless things!
O you hard hearts, you cruel men of Rome,
Knew you not Pompey? Many a time and oft
Have you climbed up to walls and battlements,
To towers and windows, yea, to chimney tops,
Your infants in your arms, and there have sat
The livelong day, with patient expectation,
To see great Pompey pass the streets of Rome.

(i) **What is Marullus' main criticism of the Roman people in these lines? (3)**

Ans. Marullus criticises the Roman people for their fickle-mindedness and disloyalty. He accuses them of celebrating Caesar's triumph without considering the consequences while forgetting their former admiration for Pompey.

By calling them 'blocks', 'stones' and 'worse than senseless things', he expresses his frustration with their thoughtless behaviour and lack of true political conviction.

(ii) **What is the significance of Marullus' question 'What conquest brings he home'? How does it reflect his perspective on Caesar's victory? (3)**

Ans. Marullus' question 'What conquest brings he home?' challenges the legitimacy of Caesar's celebration. He questions whether Caesar's victory is truly deserving of such a grand celebration as it lacks the traditional elements of conquest.

This reflects Marullus' belief that Caesar's power is growing too quickly, without any clear justification, and that the people should not be celebrating what he views as a dangerous establishment of power.

(iii) **How does Marullus use the imagery of 'tributaries' and 'chariot wheels' to criticise the Roman people's support for Caesar? (3)**

Ans. Marullus uses the imagery of 'tributaries' and 'chariot wheels' to suggest that Caesar's victory is one of domination, not glory, as it involves bringing captives in chains to honour him. The idea of 'tributaries' following Caesar implies that he has subdued others.

Marullus' mention of 'gracing in captive bonds his chariot wheels' emphasises the humiliating nature of this triumph. He contrasted it with the pride and dignity that should be reserved for legitimate conquerors.

This imagery highlights his disapproval of the people's celebration of a leader whose victory may not be entirely just.

(iv) **In these lines, Marullus refers to the Roman people as 'hard hearts' and 'cruel men'. What do these phrases reveal about his attitude towards them? (3)**

Ans. The phrases 'hard hearts' and 'cruel men' reveal Marullus' anger and frustration toward the Roman people. He feels that they are insensitive and unfeeling for celebrating Caesar's rise to power, He sees this rise as a threat to Rome's republican values.

By calling them 'cruel', Marullus suggests that their actions have a negative impact on the future of the Republic.

(v) **Why does Marullus mention the common people's previous enthusiasm for Pompey? What does this reveal about their changing loyalties? (4)**

Ans. Marullus mentions the common people's previous enthusiasm for Pompey to highlight their inconsistency and fickleness. He recalls how, in the past, the people eagerly awaited Pompey's processions.

This serves as a contrast to their current behaviour of celebrating Caesar showing that their loyalties have shifted.

Marullus is angered by this change feeling that the people are disloyal and easily manipulated.

This reference reveals the impulsive nature of the common people's allegiances and underscores Marullus' frustration with their lack of political awareness.

Extract 3

It is no matter. Let no images
Be hung with Caesar's trophies. I'll about
And drive away the vulgar from the streets;
So do you too, where you perceive them thick.
These growing feathers plucked from
Caesar's wing
Will make him fly an ordinary pitch,
Who else would soar above the view of men
And keep us all in servile fearfulness.

(i) **Who is the speaker of the above lines? What is his main objective in saying 'Let no images / Be hung with Caesar's trophies'?** **(3)**

Ans. The speaker of the given lines is Flavius.

His main objective in saying 'Let no images / Be hung with Caesar's trophies' is to prevent Caesar from being glorified and idolised. He believes that they can limit the public's admiration for him and reduce his influence by removing these symbols of Caesar's triumphs.

This action is part of Flavius' larger effort to curb Caesar's rising power which he sees as a threat to the Republic.

(ii) **Why does the speaker intend to 'drive away the vulgar from the streets'?** **(3)**

Ans. The speaker, Flavius, intends to 'drive away the vulgar from the streets' to prevent the common people from celebrating Caesar's victory. He views the commoners as being easily manipulated.

By dispersing them, he hopes to stop them from further elevating Caesar's status.

(iii) **What does the speaker mean by 'These growing feathers plucked from Caesar's wing'?** **(3)**

Ans. The phrase 'These growing feathers plucked from Caesar's wing' is a metaphor by the phrase, the speaker means to diminish Caesar's increasing power. Flavius is suggesting that by removing the people's support and symbols of Caesar's glory, they can limit his rise to supremacy.

The 'feathers' symbolise the strength and potential of Caesar's growing influence and by 'plucking' them, Flavius hopes to reduce Caesar's power and prevent him from becoming too dominant.

(iv) **How does the speaker view Caesar's potential rise to power?** **(3)**

Ans. Flavius views Caesar's potential rise to power with great alarm. The phrase 'soar above the view of men' suggests that Flavius fears Caesar will become an autocratic ruler, beyond the control of the people.

The reference to 'servile fearfulness' indicates that Flavius believes Caesar's rule would lead to the people living in fear and subjugation, with their freedoms lost.

Flavius is deeply concerned that Caesar's growing power will result in tyranny and the destruction of the Republic.

(v) **What is the underlying political message in the speaker's statement, 'These growing feathers plucked from Caesar's wing / Will make him fly an ordinary pitch'?** **(4)**

Ans. The underlying political message in the given statement is that by reducing Caesar's power and influence, they can prevent him from becoming an exceptional leader who dominates over the people.

The 'growing feathers' represent Caesar's expanding influence and 'plucking them' symbolises the effort to diminish his political power.

Flavius believes that they can keep him at an 'ordinary pitch' by curbing Caesar's rise, meaning that he will not become a tyrant but remain within the bounds of a republic with shared power.

ACT 1 : SCENE 2

Summary of Act 1 Scene 2

The scene is set during the Feast of Lupercal, a festival held in a public space in Rome. Julius Caesar enters with his entourage (associates), including his wife and notable figures such as Brutus, Cassius and Mark Antony. Caesar asks Antony to touch Calpurnia in the race believing it will make her fertile. As the celebration begins, a soothsayer steps forward and warns Caesar to 'Beware the Ides of March'. Caesar dismisses the warning as nonsense and moves on with the festivities.

Once Caesar departs, Cassius engages Brutus in a private conversation. Cassius expresses his deep concern over Caesar's increasing power and influence implying that Caesar aspires to become a dictator. Cassius appeals to Brutus' sense of duty to Rome by suggesting that it is their responsibility to prevent Caesar from potentially becoming a tyrant. He flatters Brutus by asserting that the people of Rome hold him in high esteem and would support him over Caesar. This conversation plants the initial seeds of doubt in Brutus' mind setting the stage for the eventual conspiracy.

Brutus admits that he shares some of Cassius' concerns regarding Caesar's ambition. However, he remains conflicted about the idea of taking action against him.

Meanwhile, Caesar expresses suspicions about Cassius to Mark Antony noting that Cassius has a 'lean and hungry look' which he finds dangerous. Despite Antony's reassurances, Caesar remains uneasy about Cassius. While talking, Cassius and Brutus hear noise of people shouting. They are unaware of its source.

Casca enters and informs Brutus and Cassius about the source of the shouting. He explains that Antony offered Caesar the crown three times and each time, Caesar refused it.

Together, they discuss the events further, with Cassius continuing to manipulate the conversation to cast doubt on Caesar's intentions. Casca leaves and Cassius seizes the moment to solidify his influence over Brutus. He promises to forge letters from Roman citizens expressing concern over Caesar's power which he plans to plant in Brutus' house to sway him further.

This scene introduces key tensions and conflicts, highlighting the growing unease with Caesar's power and setting the groundwork for the subsequent betrayal.

Vocab Vault

Soothsayer Someone who makes predictions of the future
Ides of March 15th of March
Countenance The appearance conveyed by a person's face
Cogitation Attentive consideration and thought
Rout An overwhelming defeat
Gusty Blow in puffs or short blasts
Chafing Soreness or irritation of the skin caused by friction
Yonder Distant but within sight
Sinew A band of tissue connecting a muscle to its bony attachment
Luster The property of something that shines with reflected light
Conjure Summon into action or bring into existence
Encompassed Surround and have or hold within
Repute The state of being held in high esteem and honour
Rabblement A noisy disturbance or a rabble or mob
Amiss In an improper or mistaken manner
Infirmity The state of being weak in health or body
Wenches Young women
Mettle The courage to carry on
Tardy After the expected or usual time
Yoke A wooden frame across the shoulders for carrying buckets

Characters in the Scene

- **Julius Caesar** The central figure of the play, a successful Roman general and leader. In this scene, he dismisses the soothsayer's warning and expresses suspicion towards Cassius.
- **Calpurnia** Caesar's wife who appears briefly. Caesar instructs Mark Antony to touch her during the race at the Feast of Lupercal to cure her barrenness, as part of a Roman superstition.
- **Mark Antony** A loyal friend of Caesar, participating in the Lupercal festivities. Caesar confides in him about his distrust of Cassius.
- **Brutus** A respected Roman senator and close friend of Caesar. He is approached by Cassius who begins to sow seeds of doubt in his mind regarding Caesar's ambition.
- **Cassius** A senator deeply concerned about Caesar's rise to power. He is manipulative and persuasive working to convince Brutus to join the conspiracy against Caesar.
- **Soothsayer** A mysterious figure who delivers the famous warning to Caesar, 'Beware the Ides of March', which Caesar ignores.
- **Casca** A senator who reports to Brutus and Cassius about Caesar's reaction to the crown offered to him during the public festivities

EXAM ORIENTED QUESTIONS

TYPE - 1 Multiple Choice Questions

01 Mark

Q.1 What does Caesar ask Antony to do in this scene?
(a) Lead his army into battle
(b) Touch Calpurnia during the Lupercal race
(c) Speak to the Senate
(d) Speak to Brutus

Q.2 Who warns Caesar about 'the Ides of March'?
(a) Soothsayer
(b) Cassius
(c) Brutus
(d) Artemidorus

Q.3 What is Caesar's response to the Soothsayer's warning?
(a) He dismisses it
(b) He becomes worried
(c) He asks his advisors about it
(d) He takes immediate action

Q.4 What does Caesar say about his own nature in this scene?
(a) He is humble and wise
(b) He is unwilling to be controlled by others
(c) He is a slave to fate
(d) He is fearful of death

Q.5 Identify what Caesar's statement about death suggests about his character.
(a) He is afraid of death
(b) He is overconfident
(c) He fears nothing
(d) He is superstitious

Q.6 What does Cassius say about Caesar's power in this scene?
(a) He is a great leader
(b) He is too weak to rule Rome
(c) He has become too powerful for the good of Rome
(d) He is destined to be a God

Q.7 How does Brutus react to Caesar's increasing power?
(a) He is excited by it
(b) He is indifferent
(c) He is concerned and conflicted
(d) He is angry

Q.8 What is Cassius' main complaint about Caesar?
(a) He is too arrogant
(b) He is mentally unstable
(c) He is weak and unfit to rule
(d) He does not understand the needs of the people

Q.9 **Why does Cassius tell Brutus the story about saving Caesar from drowning?**
(a) To show how Caesar is ungrateful
(b) To make Brutus feel sorry for Caesar
(c) To suggest that Caesar is not deserving of power
(d) To make Brutus admire Caesar

Q.10 **How does Brutus feel about Caesar's rise to power?**
(a) He wants to help Caesar become king
(b) He fears what might happen if Caesar becomes too powerful
(c) He believes Caesar is a true leader
(d) He wants to distance himself from politics

Q.11 **Who tries to warn Caesar about the potential danger of trusting others in Act 1, Scene 2?**
(a) Brutus (b) Cassius
(c) Calpurnia (d) The Soothsayer

Q.12 **What does Caesar mean when he says 'Let me have men about me that are fat'?**
(a) He wants strong soldiers
(b) He dislikes lean men
(c) He wants men who are content and not ambitious
(d) He is looking for wealthy men

Q.13 **How does Cassius feel about the celebration in honour of Caesar?**
(a) He thinks it's a waste of time
(b) He is proud of Caesar
(c) He wishes to join it
(d) He dislikes the idea of Caesar's glory

Q.14 **What does Cassius want Brutus to believe about Caesar?**
(a) That Caesar is weak and incapable
(b) That Caesar is a tyrant
(c) That Caesar is benevolent
(d) That Caesar is beloved by all

Q.15 **Which theme is prominent in Act 1, Scene 2 of *Julius Caesar*?**
(a) Betrayal and loyalty (b) The dangers of ambition
(c) The power of women (d) The inevitability of fate

Q.16 **Select the option that shows the correct relationship between statements (1) and (2).**
Statement 1 Cassius tells Brutus the story of saving Caesar from drowning in the Tiber River.
Statement 2 Cassius wants to show Brutus that Caesar is weak and unworthy of ruling Rome.
(a) Statement 1 is true and Statement 2 is false
(b) Statement 2 is true and Statement 1 is false.
(c) Statement 2 is the cause for Statement 1.
(d) Statement 1 and Statement 2 are independent of each other.

Q.17 Arrange the following events from Act 1, Scene 2 of *Julius Caesar* in the correct sequence.
1. **Caesar is accompanied by his followers, including his wife Calpurnia, Antony and others.**
2. **The Soothsayer approaches Caesar and warns him to 'Beware the Ides of March'.**
3. **Caesar brushes off the soothsayer's warning, stating that he fears nothing and that danger is aware of his power.**
4. **Caesar tells Antony to touch Calpurnia during the Lupercal race to cure her barrenness which is a superstitious belief.**
5. **Cassius begins his attempt to sway Brutus by questioning Caesar's ambitions and telling him about how Caesar is not as powerful as he appears.**

(a) 1, 2, 3, 4, 5 (b) 1, 5, 3, 2, 4
(c) 2, 4, 3, 1, 5 (d) 4, 3, 1, 2, 5

Q.18 Arrange the following events from Act 1, Scene 2 of *Julius Caesar* in the correct sequence.
1. **Cassius tells Brutus about an event where he saved Caesar from drowning in the Tiber River emphasising Caesar's weaknesses.**
2. **Brutus expresses his inner conflict.**
3. **Cassius begins to plant the idea in Brutus's mind that Caesar is not fit to rule and that Brutus has the potential to lead Rome instead.**
4. **Brutus begins to question Caesar's power and is slowly persuaded by Cassius to join the conspiracy.**
5. **Caesar speaks about his own strength and invincibility, stating that he is not afraid of danger and that even danger fears him.**

(a) 1, 2, 3, 4, 5 (b) 1, 5, 3, 2, 4
(c) 2, 4, 3, 1, 5 (d) 4, 3, 1, 2, 5

Answers

1. (b)	2. (a)	3. (a)	4. (b)	5. (c)	6. (c)	7. (c)	8. (c)	9. (c)	10. (b)
11. (b)	12. (c)	13. (d)	14. (b)	15. (b)	16. (c)	17. (a)	18. (b)		

Explanations

11. It is Cassius who attempts to warn Caesar about the potential danger of trusting other, particularly those who might flatter him.
15. In this scene, Cassius expresses concerns about Caesar's growing power and ambition. The theme of ambition and its potential dangers is a key element that sets the stage for the conspiracy.

TYPE - 2 Extract Based Questions   16 Marks

Extract 1

"Beware the Ides of March"

(i) **What is the significance of the above phrase in the play? Who said it?** **(3)**

Ans. The phrase 'Beware the Ides of March' is a warning given to Caesar by a Soothsayer in Act 1, Scene 2. It foreshadows Caesar's assassination which is set to occur on March 15th (the Ides of March).

The warning signifies the danger Caesar faces and serves as a pivotal moment in the play highlighting the theme of fate versus free will.

(ii) **How does Caesar respond to the above warning? What does this reveal about his character?** **(3)**

Ans. Caesar dismisses the Soothsayer's warning by saying, 'He is a dreamer. Let us leave him. Pass.' This response reveals Caesar's arrogance and his sense of invincibility. He believes that he is too powerful to be harmed. Thus, no danger can threaten him. His dismissive attitude toward the warning highlights his hubris which ultimately leads to his tragic downfall.

(iii) **How does the above warning impact the audience's perception of Caesar's fate?** **(3)**

Ans. The Soothsayer's warning foreshadows Caesar's impending assassination. The audience knows that the Ides of March will be the day of Caesar's death but Caesar himself remains unaware of the danger.

This creates a sense of inevitability and tension as the audience watches Caesar continue on his path toward destruction despite being given an early warning.

The phrase deepens the tragic nature of Caesar's character.

(iv) **In what way does the above warning contribute to the themes of fate and free will in the play?** **(3)**

Ans. The Soothsayer's warning about the Ides of March introduces the theme of fate, suggesting that some events are predestined and cannot be avoided. Despite this, Caesar exercises his free will by dismissing the warning and continuing on his path.

This contrast between fate and free will is central to the play as characters struggle with the tension between what is fated to happen and the choices they make. Caesar's refusal to heed the warning shows a belief in his own agency and control. However, ultimately, he cannot escape the fate that awaits him.

(v) **How do the other characters react to the above warning? What does this reveal about their views on Caesar's leadership?** **(4)**

Ans. While Caesar dismisses the Soothsayer's warning, other characters, like Brutus and Cassius, are more aware of the potential dangers Caesar's growing power poses to Rome. Cassius, in particular, uses the warning as further justification for plotting against Caesar.

The Soothsayer's warning emphasises the growing concern among those who fear Caesar's ambition and potential tyranny. It also highlights Caesar's isolation as he is unwilling to listen to the voices of caution.

This reflects his disregard for the opinions of others and his belief in his own supremacy.

Extract 2

Cassius - 'Tis just.
And it is very much lamented, Brutus,
That you have no such mirrors as will turn
Your hidden worthiness into your eye,
That you might see your shadow. I have heard
Where many of the best respect in Rome,
Except immortal Caesar, speaking of Brutus
And groaning underneath this age's yoke,
Have wished that noble Brutus had his eyes.

(i) **What is the significance of Cassius' statement - 'Tis just' - in the context of his conversation with Brutus?** **(3)**

Ans. Cassius statement 'Tis just' acknowledges Brutus' concerns or thoughts as valid. It further marks the beginning of Cassius attempt to manipulate Brutus into believing that Caesar's growing power is a threat to Rome.

It is part of Cassius' strategy to build a understanding with Brutus by agreeing with him and using his doubts to further his own cause.

(ii) **How does Cassius use flattery to manipulate Brutus in this passage?** **(3)**

Ans. Cassius uses flattery by telling Brutus that many of the 'best respect in Rome' lament that Brutus cannot see his own worth. He claims that if Brutus could recognise his greatness, he would understand why others wish he had more influence in Rome.

This manipulative tactic is designed to make Brutus feel important and noble and to make him question why he is not using his potential to challenge Caesar; thus, persuading him to join the conspiracy.

(iii) **What is the role of 'shadow' in the line 'That you might see your shadow'? How does it contribute to the overall meaning of the passage?** **(3)**

Ans. The 'shadow' in the given line symbolises Brutus true character and potential. Cassius suggests that Brutus' noble qualities are hidden from him, just like a person's shadow is often not fully visible. The use of 'shadow' implies that Brutus has greatness within him that he is not fully aware of.

Cassius wants him to recognise it. This idea of the 'shadow' is part of Cassius attempt to flatter Brutus and encourage him to challenge Caesar's rule.

(iv) What does Cassius mean by groaning underneath this age's yoke'? How does this phrase help to convince Brutus? (3)

Ans. By saying that 'many of the best respect in Rome, except immortal Caesar' are 'groaning underneath this age's yoke', Cassius is emphasising people's suffering under Caesar's growing power. The 'yoke' represents the burden or oppression of Caesar's rule.

This phrase is designed to make Brutus feel that there is widespread discontent with Caesar's leadership and that, as a noble and respected Roman, Brutus has a responsibility to oppose Caesar for the good of Rome. Cassius is using this rhetoric to appeal to Brutus's sense of honour and duty.

(v) How does Cassius describe Brutus in comparison to Caesar in this extract? (4)

Ans. In this passage, Cassius describes Brutus as noble, respected and virtuous suggesting that Brutus is worthy of greater recognition and power. He contrasts Brutus' hidden greatness with Caesar's 'immortality' positioning Caesar as the established, yet oppressive, ruler of Rome.

While Caesar is referred to as 'immortal', Cassius implies that Brutus has untapped potential and noble qualities that people in Rome admire. However, Brutus himself cannot see them.

Cassius wants to make Brutus feel that he is more deserving of power and influence than Caesar thus, using flattery to encourage Brutus to act against Caesar.

Extract 3

Brutus: What means this shouting?
I do fear the people
Choose Caesar for their king.
Cassius: Ay, do you fear it?
Then must I think you would not have it so.
Brutus: I would not, Cassius; yet I love him well.

(i) Where are Brutus and Cassius?
What does Brutus 'fear' is the reason for 'this shouting'?
Later in the scene, Brutus hears a second shout. What does he think this is about? (3)

Ans. Brutus and Cassius are in a public place in Rome, likely on the streets or near the Senate, as they are observing the people's reactions and the events around them.

Brutus fears that the shouting is a sign that the people are cheering for Caesar to be crowned king. He is concerned that Caesar's rise to power may signal the end of the Roman Republic and the beginning of tyranny.

When Brutus hears the second shout, he initially believes it is related to Caesar being crowned king.

(ii) Later in the scene, how do Brutus and Cassius come to know of the actual reason for all the shouting? Who gives them the details?
How had they drawn this man's attention? (3)

Ans. They learn that the shouting is in celebration of Caesar being offered the crown by Mark Antony. The news is brought to them by Casca who provides the details of what happened during the ceremony.

They drew Casca's attention by asking him directly about the cause of the shouting as they were curious about the event taking place with Caesar and the crowd.

(iii) 'I would not Cassius, yet I love him well.' What does this line reveal about Brutus's mental state?
How did Brutus describe his state of mind earlier in the scene? (3)

Ans. This line reveals Brutus' internal conflict. He loves Caesar but fears that Caesar's ambition will lead him to become a tyrant. Brutus is torn between his affection for Caesar and his fear for Rome's future. This reflects his deep moral and emotional struggle.

Earlier in the scene, Brutus describes his state of mind as troubled and conflicted. This indicates that he feels uneasy about Caesar's growing power and the implications it has for Rome, even though he holds personal affection for Caesar.

(iv) What does Cassius say to prove that Caesar was as weak as any other human being?
State any one physical disability of Caesar's that is mentioned in this scene. (3)

Ans. Cassius tells Brutus that Caesar is not as powerful or divine as people think. He recounts how Caesar once fell ill and had to be physically supported showing that Caesar has the same human frailties as anyone else. He also criticises the idea that Caesar is 'immortal' or invincible.

One physical disability mentioned is Caesar's epilepsy, referred to when Cassius describes how Caesar had a fever while in Spain which made him appear weak and vulnerable.

(v) Important character traits of Cassius are revealed in this scene. Mention any two. (ICSE Specimen 2024, 4)
What is your opinion of the man? Give a reason to justify your answer.

Ans. Cassius reveals two important traits in this scene - manipulation and cynicism.

Cassius is a highly ambitious and manipulative character who is willing to use others, including Brutus, to achieve his own goals. His cynicism and disdain for Caesar's power reflect his belief in his own superiority but his manipulative nature makes him a dangerous figure. His actions demonstrate a lack of integrity as he seeks to manipulate Brutus into a conspiracy for personal gain, using flattery and deceit rather than moral reasoning.

Extract 4

Cassius - With lusty sinews, throwing it aside
And stemming it with hearts of controversy.
But ere we could arrive the point proposed,
Caesar cried 'Help me, Cassius, or I sink!'
I, as Aeneas, our great ancestor,
Did from the flames of Troy upon his shoulder
The old Anchises bear, so from the waves of Tiber
Did I the tired Caesar.

(i) What is meant by the phrase 'With lusty sinews, throwing it aside / And stemming it with hearts of controversy'? (3)

Ans. The phrase 'lusty sinews' refers to strong muscles, symbolising physical strength, while 'hearts of controversy' implies a spirited determination. Together, these phrases convey the image of men using both physical and emotional strength to oppose or resist a challenge. This refers to the physical and political struggle in Rome, particularly against Caesar's rise to power, with Cassius and others trying to counter Caesar's ambitions.

(ii) What is the significance of Caesar crying 'Help me, Cassius, or I sink!' in this passage? (3)

Ans. This cry highlights Caesar's vulnerability despite his apparent strength and power. It shows that even Caesar, seen as invincible by many, has moments of weakness. His call for help from Cassius contrasts with the image of the all-powerful leader and serves as a reminder that Caesar is still human, prone to moments of weakness and in need of assistance.

(iii) What is the connection between Cassius' actions and Aeneas from Greek mythology in this passage? (3)

Ans. Cassius compares himself to Aeneas, a Trojan hero from Greek mythology, who carried his father Anchises out of the burning city of Troy. By making this comparison, Cassius elevates his own actions of helping Caesar out of the Tiber River to the level of a heroic act. It implies that, like Aeneas, Cassius is saving a person who is in a weakened state and can be seen as playing the role of a saviour.

(iv) What does Cassius' comparison to Aeneas reveal about his attitude toward Caesar? (3)

Ans. Cassius' comparison of himself to Aeneas reveals a complex attitude toward Caesar. While he is helping Caesar, he is also subtly suggesting that Caesar is not as strong or divine as he is made out to be. Cassius' reference to the myth of Aeneas hints at his own belief in his own heroic qualities and subtly underscores the idea that Caesar, despite his great power, is still a vulnerable figure who requires aid from others.

This is part of Cassius' ongoing effort to diminish Caesar's image and build himself up in the eyes of others.

(v) How does this passage contribute to the theme of power and weakness in the play *Julius Caesar*? (4)

Ans. This passage highlights the theme of power and weakness by showing that even the mighty Caesar is not invincible. His cry for help reveals his vulnerability contrasting with the perception of him as an all-powerful leader.

By drawing comparisons to heroic figures like Aeneas, Cassius not only elevates his own actions but also shows how Caesar's supposed strength can be questioned.

This underscores the central tension in the play where Caesar's rise to power is met with both admiration and fear and where characters like Cassius question whether Caesar's power is deserved or sustainable.

Extract 5

Casca - I can as well be
hanged as tell the manner of it.
It was mere foolery; I did not mark it.
I saw Mark Antony offer him
a crown (yet 'twas not a crown
neither; 'twas one of these coronets),
and, as I told you, he put it by once;
but for all that, to my thinking,
he would fain have had it.
Then he offered it to him again;
then he put it by again;
but to my thinking, he was very
loath to lay his fingers off it.

(ii) Why does Casca describe the event of Antony offering the crown to Caesar as 'mere foolery'? (3)

Ans. Casca refers to the event as 'mere foolery' because he sees it as a ridiculous and theatrical display, not a serious or genuine moment.

He is cynical about the whole situation. It implies that the offer and rejection of the crown were orchestrated to manipulate public perception and make Caesar appear humble and reluctant to accept power, even though he might have desired it.

(ii) **What does Casca suggest about Caesar's true feelings towards the crown? How did the crowd react each time Caesar refused the crown according to Casca?** **(3)**

Ans. Casca implies that Caesar's reluctance to take the crown was insincere and that he was merely playing to the crowd. This is further evidenced by his observation that Caesar seemed very hesitant to let go of the coronet each time it was offered.

According to Casca, the crowd reacted with loud cheering and applause each time Caesar refused the crown. Casca describes their enthusiastic reaction as overwhelming and suggests that the crowd was easily manipulated by Caesar's actions.

(iii) **What physical reaction did Caesar have after the third refusal of the crown?** **(3)**

Ans. After the third refusal of the crown, Caesar swooned and fell down, possibly due to an epileptic seizure. Casca mentions that the overwhelming reaction of the crowd, with their shouting and cheering, might have contributed to Caesar's physical collapse. He seemed almost choked by their breath.

(iv) **How does Casca's tone reflect his attitude toward Caesar and the event?** **(3)**

Ans. Casca's tone is sarcastic and dismissive. He mocks the event as foolish and insincere and he shows a clear disdain for both Caesar and the crowd's gullibility.

Casca's description implies that he sees the whole spectacle as manipulative and absurd, reflecting his cynical view of Caesar's ambitions and the people's adoration of him.

(v) **What does this passage reveal about the relationship between Caesar and the Roman populace?** **(4)**

Ans. This passage reveals a complex relationship between Caesar and the Roman populace. Caesar appears to manipulate public opinion by refusing the crown in a way that makes him seem humble and reluctant to take power.

Meanwhile, the crowd's enthusiastic response shows their adoration for Caesar yet their reactions are based on his calculated actions.

The scene illustrates how public perception can be influenced by political theatrics and how leaders like Caesar can use such displays to solidify their power.

ACT 1 : SCENE 3

Summary of Act 1 Scene 3

In Act 1, Scene 3 of *Julius Caesar*, a fierce storm rages over Rome symbolising the chaos and unrest in the city. Cicero and Casca meet in the streets, discussing the strange and ominous events: a lion roaming the Capitol, an owl seen during the day and men on fire walking the streets. Casca interprets these unnatural occurrences as bad omens forewarning danger.

Cassius soon arrives and uses the storm as a metaphor for the political turmoil in Rome. He expresses contempt for Caesar calling him a threat to Rome's freedom. Cassius blames the Roman people for their meekness and willingness to submit to Caesar's rule. He declares that he would rather die than live under Caesar's tyranny.

Cassius then persuades Casca to join the conspiracy against Caesar. He shares his plan to recruit Brutus by planting forged letters. These letters suggest widespread support for their cause. Cinna, another conspirator, joins them. They believe that his involvement will legitimise their efforts.

This scene underscores the themes of fate, political manipulation and the brewing conspiracy setting the stage for Caesar's eventual downfall.

Characters in the Scene

- **Cassius** Cassius is one of the leading conspirators against Caesar. In this scene, he is a key figure in stirring up concern and fear about Caesar's growing power. He actively works to recruit others to join the conspiracy, particularly seeking to win over Brutus. Cassius is manipulative and persuasive using rhetoric to appeal to others' fears and ideals, especially appealing to Brutus' sense of honour and patriotism.
- **Casca** Casca is another conspirator who plays a significant role in this scene. He describes the strange and ominous events that he witnessed in Rome, such as a slave with a burning hand and a lion that did not attack him. Casca's descriptions of these supernatural occurrences set the tone for the scene and contribute to the sense of foreboding.
- **Cinna** Cinna is a minor but important character in this scene. He is another conspirator who is involved in the plot against Caesar. Cinna's main role here is to convey Cassius's message to Brutus urging him to join the conspiracy. He is also a figure who helps to strengthen the conspiracy by participating in the recruitment of key figures like Brutus.
- **Cicero** A Roman senator and renowned orator.

Vocab Vault

Tempest A violent commotion or disturbance
Portentous Of momentous or ominous significance
Perilous Dangerous
Prodigious Great in size, force, extent or degree
Conceited Having an exaggerated sense of self-importance

EXAM ORIENTED QUESTIONS

TYPE - 1 Multiple Choice Questions

01 Mark

Q.1 What unusual event does Casca describe first?
(a) A lion roaming in the Capitol
(b) An owl hooting during the day
(c) Men on fire walking the streets
(d) A tempest dropping fire

Q.2 Which animal does Casca mention seeing in the Capitol?
(a) A wolf (b) A lion
(c) An eagle (d) A serpent

Q.3 What does Casca think the storm and strange occurrences symbolise?
(a) The gods are pleased with Rome
(b) The gods are angry and something bad will happen
(c) Caesar's rise to power
(d) Natural weather patterns

Q.4 What is Cassius' attitude toward the storm?
(a) He is fearful and wants to take shelter
(b) He sees it as a sign of Caesar's greatness
(c) He interprets it as a reflection of the political chaos in Rome
(d) He is indifferent to it

Q.5 What does Cassius do to show his contempt for Caesar during the storm?
(a) He curses the gods
(b) He bares his chest to the storm and invites the lightning to strike him
(c) He hides in fear
(d) He prays for the storm to end

Q.6 Identify why Cassius wants Brutus to join the conspiracy.
(a) Because Brutus is a strong warrior
(b) Because Brutus is Caesar's enemy
(c) Because Brutus is loved by the people and his involvement will lend credibility to their cause
(d) Because Brutus is easily manipulated

Q.7 What task does Cassius assign to Cinna?
(a) To gather weapons
(b) To spread rumours about Caesar
(c) To plant forged letters in places where Brutus will find them
(d) To assassinate Caesar

Q.8 What is Cassius' primary motivation for conspiring against Caesar?
(a) Personal envy of Caesar's power
(b) Love for Rome and fear of tyranny
(c) Desire for wealth and position
(d) Loyalty to Brutus

Q.9 How does Casca view the strange occurrences happening in Rome?
(a) As meaningless coincidences
(b) As signs of divine anger and impending doom
(c) As a test of Caesar's leadership
(d) As a sign of prosperity

Q.10 What does Cassius believe about the role of fate in the events unfolding in Rome?
(a) Fate controls everything
(b) The gods favour Caesar
(c) People control their own fate
(d) Fate is irrelevant

Q.11 How does Cassius plan to manipulate Brutus into joining the conspiracy?
(a) By threatening him
(b) By offering him a bribe
(c) By showing him the forged letters from 'the people of Rome'
(d) By appealing to his sense of honour

Q.12 What does the storm symbolise in this scene?
(a) The anger of the gods
(b) Caesar's internal conflict
(c) The political turmoil in Rome
(d) Natural disaster

Q.13 What does Casca think of the common people's reaction to the omens and Caesar's actions?
(a) They are wise and understanding
(b) They are easily manipulated and foolish
(c) They are indifferent
(d) They are supportive of Caesar's rise

Q.14 Why does Cassius send notes through Cinna at the end of Act I? **(ICSE Specimen 2024)**
(a) To warn Caesar about Brutus' betrayal so that he could take necessary action

(b) To assure Brutus that plans for the conspiracy were in place

(c) To remind Caesar to meet at the Capitol at the appointed time

(d) To convince Brutus that the Romans needed him to join the conspiracy

Q.15 Identify the tone of the Act 1, Scene 3 of *Julius Caesar*.

1. Ominous
2. Celebratory
3. Conspiratorial
4. Supportive
5. Furious

(a) 1 and 3 (b) 2 and 4

(c) 1 and 4 (d) 3 and 5

Q.16 Select the option that shows the correct relationship between statements (1) and (2).

Statement 1 Casca interprets the strange occurrences in Rome as mere coincidences.

Statement 2 Casca is skeptical of omens and believes they have no real significance.

(a) Statement 1 is true and Statement 2 is false.

(b) Statement 2 is true and Statement 1 is false.

(c) Statement 2 is the cause for Statement 1.

(d) Both statements are false.

Q.17 Select the option that shows the correct relationship between statements (1) and (2).

Statement 1 Casca joins the conspiracy against Caesar.

Statement 2 Casca is convinced by Cassius' arguments about Caesar's ambition and the danger it poses to the Republic.

(a) Statement 1 is true and Statement 2 is false

(b) Statement 2 is true and Statement 1 is false.

(c) Statement 2 is the cause for Statement 1.

(d) Both statements are false.

Q.18 Arrange the following events from Act 1, Scene 2 of *Julius Caesar* in the correct sequence.

1. A violent storm rages over Rome, symbolising the chaos and political unrest.
2. Cicero leaves after a brief conversation, not sharing Casca's alarm over the omens.
3. Casca agrees to join Cassius and the conspirators, expressing his willingness to resist Caesar's rise to power.
4. Cinna arrives and the three conspirators discuss their plan.

(a) 1, 2, 3, 4 (b) 1, 3, 2, 4

(c) 2, 4, 3, 1 (d) 4, 3, 1, 2

Answers

1. (d)	2. (b)	3. (b)	4. (c)	5. (b)	6. (c)	7. (c)	8. (b)	9. (b)	10. (c)
11. (c)	12. (c)	13. (b)	14. (d)	15. (a)	16. (d)	17. (c)	18. (a)		

Explanations

16. Casca describes the strange occurrences as signs of something ominous.
17. Casca joins the conspiracy against Caesar. Cassius' persuasion plays a direct role in his decision. Thus statement 2 is the cause for statement 1.

TYPE - 2 Extract Based Questions

16 Marks

Extract 1

Casca - A common slave
(you know him well by sight)
Held up his left hand, which did flame and burn
Like twenty torches joined; and yet his hand,
Not sensible of fire, remained unscorched.
Besides (I ha' not since put up my sword),
Against the Capitol I met a lion,
Who glazed upon me and went surly by
Without annoying me. And there were drawn
Upon a heap a hundred ghastly women,
Transformèd with their fear,
who swore they saw
Men all in fire walk up and down the streets.

(i) How does Casca's description of the common slave contribute to the themes of fate and supernatural omens in *Julius Caesar*? **(3)**

Ans. Casca's description of the slave - with a hand that burns like twenty torches but remains unscorched - symbolises the unnatural, mysterious events in Rome.
It suggests that the natural order is disrupted.
He thinks that the gods may be sending ominous signs about the fate of the republic.
This reflects the theme of fate and the tension between human agency and supernatural forces foreshadowing the tragic events to come.

(ii) What is the significance of Casca's encounter with the lion near the Capitol? How does it relate to the political atmosphere in Rome? **(3)**

Ans. The lion, which gazes at Casca but does not harm him, represents both danger and restraint. The Capitol, as a symbol of Roman power, is an ironic setting for such an encounter. The lion's surly but non-aggressive behaviour may symbolise the tension between Caesar and those who challenge him, as well as the growing unrest among the people.

The lion could be seen as a metaphor for Caesar's power which seems uncontrollable yet not immediately threatening.

(iii) In what way does Casca's report of the 'hundred ghastly women' contribute to the play's atmosphere of fear and forewarning? (3)

Ans. Casca's report of the hundred terrified women who claim to have seen men on fire walking through the streets heightens the atmosphere of fear and chaos in Rome.

These ghastly visions are portrayed as signs of an impending disaster. They suggest that the very fabric of reality is coming undone.

The transformation of the women into figures of fear emphasises the widespread anxiety in Rome. It further foreshadows the larger political upheaval that will result from Caesar's rise to power.

(iv) What is the symbolic significance of the strange phenomena in this extract in relation to the theme of omens and fate in the play? (3)

Ans. The strange phenomena (the fiery hand, the lion and the ghastly women) serve as omens that signal the disturbance in the natural and social order. They symbolise the turmoil and destruction that is to come.

These supernatural occurrences reflect the play's exploration of fate and free will, suggesting that the forces beyond human control are reacting to the political events unfolding in Rome. The constant presence of omens signals that something catastrophic is imminent.

(v) How does Casca's statement that he has 'not since put up my sword' reflect his state of mind and his perception of the political situation in Rome? (4)

Ans. Casca's remark that he has 'not since put up my sword' illustrates his heightened sense of fear and alertness to the growing threat in Rome. His sword remains drawn as a symbol of his readiness to defend himself against the dangers he perceives in the political climate.

This constant state of readiness also suggests his belief that the republic is on the brink of collapse and that violence is pending. Casca's personal fear reflects the wider anxiety of the Roman citizens and the conspirators as they anticipate the consequences of Caesar's increasing power.

Extract 2

Cassius - Their natures,
and preformèd faculties,
To monstrous quality-why,
you shall find
That heaven hath infused
them with these spirits
To make them instruments of fear
and warning Unto some monstrous state.
Now could I, Casca, name to thee a man
Most like this dreadful night,
That thunders, lightens,
opens graves, and roars
As doth the lion in the Capitol;

(i) What is the significance of the phrase 'heaven hath infused them with these spirits' in the context of the political situation in Rome? (3)

Ans. The phrase suggests that the unnatural occurrences and omens are divinely intended. These 'spirits' are not random but are sent to serve as instruments of fear and caution signalling that something catastrophic is about to occur.

This links the supernatural events to the political chaos surrounding Caesar's rise, suggesting that his ambition and potential tyranny are seen as offenses against natural and divine order.

(ii) How does the metaphor of the lion in the Capitol reflect the political tension and foreshadow events in *Julius Caesar*? (3)

Ans. The metaphor of the lion in the Capitol evokes imagery of both strength and danger. In the play, Caesar is often compared to a lion symbolising his power, dominance and authority. The lion in the Capitol, associated with the heart of Roman power, is a foreboding symbol of Caesar's growing influence.

The roar of the lion and its place in the Capitol foreshadow the looming political turmoil and the tension between Caesar and those who oppose him, particularly the conspirators.

(iii) How does Cassius' rhetoric about the monstrous nature of the night reflect his worldview and his feelings about Caesar? (3)

Ans. Cassius uses the 'monstrous' qualities of the night-thunder, lightning and graves opening as metaphors for the unnatural state of Rome under Caesar's rule. By likening the night to a 'monstrous' entity, he implies that Caesar's ambition and power have distorted the natural order and that the republic is in danger. Cassius views the events in Rome as signs of a catastrophic change.

His belief that the world is descending into chaos shapes his resolve to act against Caesar.

(iv) **What is the significance of the reference to 'preformèd faculties' in understanding Cassius' perception of human nature and power?** **(3)**

Ans. The term 'preformèd faculties' refers to the inherent qualities or characteristics of individuals, especially those with power. Cassius suggests that certain individuals are born with the potential to shape events.

However, these potentialities are being distorted by unnatural forces. In the context of the play, Cassius sees Caesar as a man whose natural abilities and ambitions are being corrupted by his desire for absolute power.

This view of human nature is key to understanding Cassius' motivation to remove Caesar from power.

(v) **In what ways do the references to 'thunder', 'lightning' and 'opening graves' symbolise the tension between fate and free will in *Julius Caesar*?** **(4)**

Ans. The references to 'thunder', 'lightning' and 'opening graves' symbolise the overwhelming and uncontrollable forces at work in Rome. These natural phenomena are typically seen as signs from the gods, suggesting that fate is inescapable and that events in the republic are being guided by supernatural forces beyond human control.

At the same time, Cassius' actions-attempting to manipulate Brutus and gather support for the conspiracy-represent the exercise of free will.

This tension between fate and free will is central to the play as the characters struggle to determine whether they are acting out of their own agency or if they are merely pawns in a larger game.

Extract 3

Nor stony tower, nor walls of beaten brass,
Nor airless dungeon, nor strong links of iron,
Can be retentive to the strength of spirit;
But life, being weary of these worldly bars,
Never lacks power to dismiss itself.
If I know this, know all the world besides,
That part of tyranny that I do bear
I can shake off at pleasure.

(i) **How does the imagery of 'stony tower', 'walls of beaten brass' and 'strong links of iron' contribute to the theme of freedom and captivity in this extract?** **(3)**

Ans. The imagery of 'stony tower', 'walls of beaten brass' and 'strong links of iron' emphasises the physical barriers and limitations that may confine the body.

However, the speaker argues that these external forces are powerless against the strength of the spirit.

This contrast between physical confinement and spiritual freedom reinforces the theme that the human spirit can transcend even the most oppressive physical restraints.

(ii) **What does the phrase 'life, being weary of these worldly bars, never lacks power to dismiss itself' suggest about the speaker's attitude towards life and death?** **(3)**

Ans. The given phrase suggests that the speaker views life as a temporary condition that can be rejected when the spirit grows tired of worldly limitations. The 'worldly bars' represent the constraints and suffering of life.

The speaker implies that when life becomes unbearable, the individual has the power to choose death as a form of escape.

This reveals a dark and nihilistic attitude toward existence, suggesting that life is not inherently valuable but can be discarded when it becomes intolerable.

(iii) **How does the speaker's declaration that 'I can shake off at pleasure' reflect their perception of power and control?** **(3)**

Ans. The speaker's declaration that they can 'shake off at pleasure' the tyranny they bear reveals a profound sense of personal independence and control over their fate.

The ability to 'shake off' tyranny suggests that the speaker does not perceive themselves as helpless under oppressive forces but as someone who can choose to free themselves from them at will.

This attitude reflects a belief in the ultimate power of the individual to transcend external control.

(iv) **What is the significance of the contrast between external confinement and internal freedom in this extract?** **(3)**

Ans. The contrast between external confinement and internal freedom emphasises the idea that while physical limitations can imprison the body, they cannot imprison the spirit. The external barriers (such as stone, brass or iron) represent the oppressive forces that try to limit or control individuals but the 'strength of spirit' symbolises inner resilience, willpower and independence.

The passage suggests that true freedom lies not in the absence of external constraints but in the capacity of the human spirit to remain independent and unbroken.

(v) **What is the philosophical implication of the statement 'That part of tyranny that I do bear I can shake off at pleasure'?** **(4)**

Ans. The philosophical implication of this statement is that the speaker views tyranny not as an inevitable force but as something that can be discarded by an individual if they choose to do so.

This reflects the idea of personal sovereignty and a belief in the individual's capacity to resist oppression. The statement suggests a philosophical stance that values self-sufficiency and self-determination, implying that, while external circumstances may impose tyranny, the individual retains the power to reject and overcome it at will.

This also touches on themes of existential freedom, where one's choices define their experience, regardless of external conditions.

Extract 4

I am glad on 't. What a fearful night is this!
There's two or three of us have
seen strange sights.
Cassius - Am I not stayed for? Tell me.
Cinna - Yes, you are. O Cassius, if you could
But win the noble Brutus to our party.

(i) How does Cassius' question 'Am I not stayed for? Tell me' reveal his sense of urgency and his role in the conspiracy? (3)

Ans. Cassius' question reveals his anxiety and impatience, reflecting his eagerness to act and move forward with the conspiracy against Caesar. By asking, 'Am I not stayed for?', he seeks confirmation that the necessary plans are in motion and that his involvement is awaited. This shows his leadership role in the plot as he is ready to push the conspiracy into action.

His urgency also suggests the high stakes of the situation, highlighting his belief that time is of the essence and that delay could jeopardise their plans.

(ii) What is the significance of Cinna's statement, 'O Cassius, if you could but win the noble Brutus to our party'? (3)

Ans. Cinna's statement underscores the importance of Brutus in the conspiracy. Brutus is seen as a highly respected figure. His support would lend sincerity and legitimacy to the plot against Caesar.

This moment emphasises the political strategy behind the conspiracy where the conspirators are trying to balance moral, political and personal considerations in their quest to undermine Caesar.

(iii) How does the mention of 'strange sights' contribute to the atmosphere of the scene? Who mentions the 'straight sights' in the second line of the extract? (3)

Ans. The mention of 'strange sights' contributes to the sense of unease and foreboding in the scene. This phrase, combined with the reference to a 'fearful night', sets the tone of uncertainty and impending danger.

The strange occurrences that are observed in the city-likely omens or supernatural events-serve to heighten the tension and reinforce the idea that something unnatural or catastrophic is on the horizon.

Cinna mentions the 'straight sights' in the second line of the extract.

(iv) What does Cinna's statement about Brutus suggest about the nature of the conspiracy and its members' motivations? (3)

Ans. Cinna's statement about Brutus reveals the conspirators' strategic approach to undermining Caesar's power. They believe that Brutus' involvement would not only make the conspiracy more formidable but also morally justifiable in the eyes of the Roman people.

The conspirators seek his support not merely for his personal abilities but for the symbolic weight his name carries in Rome. Cinna's plea underscores the tension between personal loyalty and political calculation.

(v) What role does Cassius play in the unfolding events of the play as suggested by his interactions with Cinna in this passage? (4)

Ans. Cassius plays the role of the instigator and the primary architect of the conspiracy against Caesar. His interaction with Cinna in this passage highlights his leadership in rallying others to oppose Caesar.

He is portrayed as someone who actively seeks to recruit key figures, such as Brutus, to lend moral and political weight to their cause. Cassius' focus on persuading Brutus suggests his recognition of the importance of securing influential support for the conspiracy.

His role in the play is pivotal in driving the plot forward; and, his interactions here demonstrate his tactical thinking and the strategic nature of the conspiracy.

ACT 2 : SCENE 1

Summary of Act 2 Scene 1

The scene takes place in Brutus' orchard late at night. Brutus is alone and deeply troubled. He considers the consequences of Caesar being crowned king fearing that absolute power may corrupt him. Despite his love for Caesar, Brutus believes that it is his duty to act in the best interest of Rome, even if it means assassinating Caesar. Lucius, Brutus' servant, enters and hands him a letter he found. The letter, secretly planted by Cassius, urges Brutus to take action against Caesar. Brutus interprets the letter as a call from the Roman people reinforcing his resolve to join the conspiracy.

Cassius arrives with the other conspirators including Casca, Decius, Cinna, Metellus Cimber and Trebonius. They discuss their plan to assassinate Caesar. Cassius suggests that they also kill Mark Antony but Brutus opposes this idea. He argues that their cause must appear noble, not driven by bloodlust. He reasons that killing Antony, would make their actions seem too violent. It would further undermine their purpose of protecting Rome.

Portia, Brutus' wife, enters looking concerned about his behaviour. She notices his distress and implores him to confide in her. Portia emphasises her loyalty and strength and argues that, as his wife, she deserves to know his secrets. Brutus, touched by her concern, promises to share his troubles with her later. The scene concludes with Ligarius, another conspirator, arriving at Brutus' house, eager to join the plot against Caesar despite being ill. The conspirators finalise their plans and Brutus toughens himself for the grim task ahead.

This scene is crucial in showcasing Brutus' internal conflict, his sense of honour and the moral dilemma he faces. It also highlights the conspirators' resolve and the pivotal role Brutus plays in legitimising their cause.

Characters in the Scene

- **Brutus** One of the conspirators against Caesar, he struggles with his conscience about assassinating Caesar
- **Lucius** Brutus' servant who brings messages and lights a candle for his master
- **Cassius** The leader of the conspiracy who persuades Brutus to join the plot
- **Casca** A conspirator, known for his blunt and somewhat cynical nature
- **Cinna** A conspirator, involved in planning the assassination
- **Metellus Cimber** A conspirator, later uses a plea to Caesar as a distraction
- **Trebonius** A conspirator, plays a role in luring Antony away from Caesar before the assassination
- **Portia** Brutus' wife, concerned about his secrecy and his inner turmoil
- **Decius Brutus** A Roman senator who is a member of conspiracy against Caesar

Vocab Vault

Taper A candle or a slender wax candle
Adder A small venomous snake, often symbolising deceit or treachery
Augmented Made greater in size, number or value; increased
Exhalation In the context of the play, it refers to meteors or luminous bodies seen in the sky, but can also mean the act of breathing out
Insurrection A violent uprising against authority or government
Visage The face or facial expression of a person
Cautelous Cautious, wary or deceitful
Watchful cares Worries that keep them up at night
Phantasma An hallucination
Carrions Dead and decaying flesh of animals; used metaphorically to refer to something repulsive or corrupt
Dismember To cut off the limbs of a body; metaphorically, to divide or tear apart
Ruddy Having a healthy red colour, often used to describe someone's complexion

EXAM ORIENTED QUESTIONS

TYPE - 1 Multiple Choice Questions

01 Mark

Q.1 What is Brutus contemplating at the beginning of the scene?
(a) Whether he should assassinate Caesar
(b) How to confront Cassius
(c) Whether to flee Rome
(d) How to persuade Antony to join the conspiracy

Q.2 Why does Brutus believe Caesar must be killed?
(a) Caesar has already become a tyrant.
(b) He might become a tyrant if given too much power.
(c) Caesar is conspiring against the Senate.
(d) Caesar has insulted Brutus.

Q.3 Who visits Brutus at his home during the night?
(a) Cassius and other conspirators
(b) Caesar
(c) Calpurnia
(d) Mark Antony

Q.4 What does Cassius propose regarding Mark Antony?
(a) To invite him to join the conspiracy
(b) To ignore him
(c) To kill him along with Caesar
(d) To exile him from Rome

Q.5 What is Brutus' opinion on killing Mark Antony?
(a) He agrees with Cassius.
(b) He refuses saying it would be too bloody.
(c) He wants to imprison Antony instead.
(d) He is undecided.

Q.6 What does Brutus believe will happen if they kill only Caesar?
(a) The people will revolt
(b) Rome will be saved without unnecessary bloodshed
(c) Antony will become the next dictator
(d) The Senate will lose power

Q.7 How does Decius plan to convince Caesar to go to the Capitol?
(a) By threatening him
(b) By flattering him and reinterpreting Calpurnia's dream
(c) By offering him money
(d) By telling him the Senate is in danger

Q.8 Why does Brutus oppose the idea of including Cicero in their group? **(ICSE Specimen 2024)**
(a) Brutus dislikes Cicero although the people respect him a lot.
(b) He knows Cicero loves Caesar unconditionally.
(c) Cicero never follows anything that other people begin.
(d) Cicero would not like to be included in a bloody conspiracy.

Q.9 What does Portia do to prove her strength and loyalty to Brutus?
(a) She refuses to eat.
(b) She wounds herself in the thigh.
(c) She writes a letter of support.
(d) She threatens to expose the conspiracy.

Q.10 How does Portia feel about Brutus' behaviour?
(a) She is indifferent.
(b) She is concerned and feels excluded.
(c) She is supportive without question.
(d) She is angry and confrontational.

Q.11 What does Brutus promise Portia regarding his secret?
(a) He will reveal it soon.
(b) He will never tell her.
(c) He will leave her if she insists on knowing.
(d) He has no intention of revealing it.

Q.12 Who is Ligarius and why does he visit Brutus?
(a) A conspirator who is sick but loyal to Brutus
(b) A Roman senator seeking protection
(c) A servant delivering a message
(d) A soldier warning about an attack

Q.13 What motivates Ligarius to join the conspiracy?
(a) His hatred for Caesar.
(b) His respect and loyalty to Brutus.
(c) His desire for personal power.
(d) A promise of wealth and status.

Q.14 What does Brutus tell Ligarius about the plan?
(a) He hints at the assassination of Caesar.
(b) He gives detailed instructions.
(c) He refuses to disclose any details.
(d) He tells Ligarius to wait for further orders.

Q.15 How does Brutus feel about the conspiracy by the end of the scene?
(a) Conflicted but determined
(b) Overjoyed and confident
(c) Regretful and hesitant
(d) Indifferent and detached

Q.16 What does the presence of thunder and lightning in this scene symbolise?
(a) The wrath of the gods
(b) Caesar's impending death
(c) Political turmoil and danger
(d) Brutus' inner conflict

Q.17 What does Brutus' soliloquy reveal about his character?
(a) He is power-hungry and ruthless.
(b) He is deeply introspective and morally conflicted.
(c) He is indifferent to the consequences of his actions.
(d) He is easily manipulated and weak-willed.

Q.18 What does Cassius represent in the conspiracy?
(a) The mastermind and motivator
(b) The reluctant follower
(c) The moral compass
(d) The peacemaker

Q.19 Why does Brutus refuse to take an oath with the conspirators?
(a) He believes their cause is righteous enough not to need one.
(b) He distrusts the other conspirators.
(c) He fears legal repercussions.
(d) He wants to avoid suspicion.

Q.20 How does Brutus justify the assassination of Caesar?
(a) As a pre-emptive strike to protect the Republic
(b) As a personal vendetta
(c) As an act of revenge
(d) As a way to gain power

Q.21 Which theme is prominently explored in this scene?
(a) The corrupting influence of power.
(b) The conflict between personal loyalty and public duty.
(c) The inevitability of fate.
(d) The power of persuasion.

Q.22 How does the scene end?
(a) The conspirators leave and Brutus prepares for the next day.
(b) Caesar arrives at Brutus' house.
(c) The conspirators fight among themselves.
(d) Brutus decides to abandon the conspiracy.

Q.23 Select the option that shows the correct relationship between statements (1) and (2).
Statement 1 Brutus decides to join the conspiracy against Caesar.
Statement 2 Brutus believes that Caesar's ambition will lead to tyranny and harm Rome.
(a) Statement 1 is true and Statement 2 is false
(b) Statement 2 is true and Statement 1 is false.
(c) Statement 2 is the cause for Statement 1.
(d) Statement 1 and Statement 2 are independent of each other.

Q.24 Select the option that shows the correct relationship between statements (1) and (2).
Statement 1 All the conspirators stand against killing Mark Antony along with Caesar.
Statement 2 Cassius fears that Antony might seek revenge and become a threat to their plans.
(a) Statement 1 is true and Statement 2 is false
(b) Statement 2 is true and Statement 1 is false.
(c) Statement 2 is the cause for Statement 1.
(d) Statement 1 and Statement 2 are independent of each other.

Q.25 Arrange the following events from Act 2, Scene 4 in the correct sequence.
1. Cassius discusses the need to kill Antony.
2. Brutus insists that they should not swear an oath.
3. The conspirators discuss whether to include Cicero.
4. Ligarius is brought into the conspiracy.

(a) 3, 2, 1, 4 (b) 2, 1, 4, 3
(c) 1, 3, 4, 2 (d) 4, 3, 2, 1

Q.26 Which of the following is not true about Brutus' feelings for Caesar?
(a) He loves Caesar
(b) Caesar's death will be for the good of Rome
(c) He has a personal grudge against Caesar
(d) None of the above

Q.27 Which literary device is used in this scene to reveal Brutus' confused state of mind?
(a) Anaphora (b) Soliloquy
(c) Personification (d) Irony

Answers

1. (a)	2. (b)	3. (a)	4. (c)	5. (b)	6. (b)	7. (b)	8. (c)	9. (b)	10. (b)
11. (a)	12. (d)	13. (b)	14. (a)	15. (a)	16. (c)	17. (b)	18. (c)	19. (a)	20. (a)
21. (b)	22. (a)	23. (c)	24. (b)	25. (a)	26. (c)	27. (b)			

Explanations

21. Brutus struggles with his loyalty to Caesar as a friend versus his perceived duty to Rome. He convinces himself that assassinating Caesar is necessary for the good of the Republic, even though Caesar has not yet abused his power. This internal conflict between personal emotions and civic responsibility is a key theme in the scene.

23. Brutus decides to join the conspiracy. His justification for the assassination is based on the idea that Caesar might become a tyrant, even though he has not shown such behaviour yet.

24. Most of the conspirators, including Brutus, argue against killing Antony. They believe that doing so would make their cause look too bloody and dishonourable.
Furthermore, Cassius fears that Antony might retaliate and seek revenge for Caesar's murder. Thus, statement 2 is true while statement 1 is false.

27. In the scene, Brutus delivers a soliloquy in which he wrestles with his thoughts about Caesar's rise to power. He is torn between loyatly to Caesar and his duty to Rome. it revials Brutus' internal confliet, reasoning and confusion without the influence of other characters.

TYPE - 2 Extract Based Questions

16 Marks

Extract 1

It must be by his death. And for my part
I know no personal cause to spurn at him,
But for the general. He would be crowned:
How that might change his nature, there's the question.

(i) How does Brutus' declaration 'It must be by his death' reflect his internal conflict between personal loyalty and political responsibility? (3)

Ans. Brutus' declaration reveals his deep internal struggle. He feels no personal animosity toward Caesar.

However, his sense of duty to Rome compels him to consider Caesar's assassination. Brutus believes that Caesar's potential rise to absolute power could endanger the republic. This suggests that his political responsibility outweighs personal feelings.

This conflict between personal loyalty and political duty underscores the tragic nature of Brutus' character, torn between love for his friend and his commitment to Rome's welfare.

(ii) Discuss the significance of Brutus' reasoning for Caesar's death 'for the general' and not from 'personal cause'. What does this reveal about his character and motivations? (3)

Ans. Brutus' reasoning for considering Caesar's death 'for the general' rather than from any 'personal cause' reveals his self-perception as a selfless and patriotic individual. It underscores his commitment to the welfare of Rome over personal emotions.

This reasoning showcases Brutus as an idealistic and honourable figure who prioritises the common good, even at the cost of personal loyalty.

However, it also hints at a potential flaw in his character - his naivety or idealism - which may blind him to the complexities and potential consequences of his actions.

(iii) Analyse the significance of the phrase 'He would be crowned' in the context of Roman political culture. How does this phrase underscore Brutus' fears? (3)

Ans. The phrase 'He would be crowned' signifies the possibility of Caesar attaining absolute power, akin to a monarch. Brutus' fear is that Caesar, once crowned, would become a tyrant undermining the democratic structures of Rome.

This anticipation of absolute power transforming Caesar's nature is central to Brutus' justification for his drastic actions.

(iv) What does Brutus' contemplation of 'How that might change his nature' suggest about his views on human nature and power? Do you think his fears are justified? (3)

Ans. Brutus' contemplation reflects a philosophical concern about the corrupting influence of power. He fears that crowning Caesar could fundamentally alter his character leading him to act tyrannically. This view aligns with the classical notion that power tends to corrupt.

While Brutus' fears are speculative, they underscore his caution about the potential dangers of concentrated power. Whether his fears are justified is subjective; historically, leaders with unchecked power have both fulfilled and defied such concerns.

(v) In what ways do these lines foreshadow the eventual consequences of Brutus' decision, both for himself and for Rome? (4)

Ans. These lines foreshadow the tragic consequences of Brutus' decision to join the conspiracy against Caesar. By pondering the potential change in Caesar's nature due to power, Brutus sets the stage for the eventual fallout of the assassination which leads to civil war and the downfall of the Republic he seeks to protect.

For Brutus personally, his decision results in immense personal turmoil, guilt and ultimately, his downfall. This foreshadowing highlights the tragic irony of Brutus' intentions and the unintended consequences of his actions.

Extract 2

No, not an oath. If not the face of men,
The sufferance of our souls, the time's abuse-
If these be motives weak, break off betimes,
And every man hence to his idle bed.
So let high-sighted tyranny range on
Till each man drop by lottery.

(i) Why does Brutus reject the idea of an oath? How does this decision reflect his views on honour and integrity? (3)

Ans. Brutus rejects the idea of an oath because he believes that their shared sense of duty and the moral gravity of their cause should be sufficient to bind them together.

His decision reflects his high regard for honour and integrity. It suggests that he values genuine commitment over formal pledges. He views an oath as unnecessary and perhaps even dishonourable. This stance emphasises Brutus' idealism and his belief in the nobility of their mission.

(ii) What does Brutus mean by 'the sufferance of our souls, the time's abuse'? How do these phrases convey the justification for the conspiracy? (3)

Ans. The phrase 'the sufferance of our souls' refers to the collective moral and emotional burden the conspirators feel due to the perceived tyranny of Caesar. 'The time's abuse' suggests the corruption and moral decay of the current era under Caesar's influence.

These phrases convey that the conspirators are motivated by a profound sense of duty to address the injustices and abuses of their time.

Brutus is arguing that their suffering and the moral degradation of Rome provide sufficient justification for their drastic actions.

(iii) Analyse how the phrase 'So let high-sighted tyranny range on' reflects Brutus' perception of the potential consequences of inaction. (3)

Ans. The given phrase reflects Brutus' fear of unchecked tyranny if they fail to act. He envisions a scenario where, without intervention, Caesar's ambition and authoritarian tendencies will lead to widespread oppression.

Brutus suggests that inaction would allow tyranny to flourish. It would further result in a grim fate where people suffer and die randomly ('each man drop by lottery').

(iv) How do these lines illustrate Brutus' leadership style and his influence on the conspirators? (3)

Ans. Brutus' rejection of an oath and his appeal to moral and philosophical reasons for their actions illustrate a leadership style that relies on persuasion, ethical reasoning and a shared sense of purpose.

He seeks to inspire the conspirators through appeals to their honour and duty rather than coercion or formal agreements.

(v) What does the reference to 'each man drop by lottery' suggest about Brutus' view of fate and the randomness of tyranny? (4)

Ans. The reference to 'each man drop by lottery' suggests Brutus' view that under tyranny, lives are at the mercy of arbitrary power and death or suffering can strike unpredictably.

This highlights his belief that tyranny creates a chaotic and unjust world where fate is no longer guided by merit or justice but by the whims of an authoritarian ruler.

Brutus uses this imagery to underscore the existential threat posed by Caesar's potential rule. It reinforces the idea that action is necessary to restore order and protect the lives and freedoms of the Roman people.

Extract 3

But it is doubtful yet
Whether Caesar will come forth today or no,
For he is superstitious grown of late,
Quite from the main opinion he held once
Of fantasy, of dreams, and ceremonies.
It may be these apparent prodigies,
The unaccustomed terror of this night,
And the persuasion of his augurers
May hold him from the Capitol today.

(i) How does Cassius' view of Caesar's superstitions in these lines reflect his perception of Caesar as a leader? (3)

Ans. Cassius' observation of Caesar's newfound superstition reveals his contempt toward Caesar's leadership. For Cassius, Caesar's reliance on these superstitions makes him seem weak, indecisive and susceptible to manipulation.

(ii) What does Cassius' reflection on Caesar's change in behaviour (his superstition) reveal about the theme of fate versus free will in the play? (3)

Ans. Cassius' reflection on Caesar's superstition highlights the theme of fate versus free will in the play. Caesar, once portrayed as a man who dismisses superstition, is now swayed by omens and prophecies.

This suggests that his fate is no longer entirely under his control. This marks a significant turning point in the play, where Caesar's belief in his own invincibility begins to falter and his decisions may be influenced by forces beyond his understanding or desire.

(iii) **How does the reference to 'the unaccustomed terror of this night' contribute to the sense of foreboding and inevitability in the play? (3)**

Ans. The reference to 'the unaccustomed terror of this night' heightens the sense of foreboding and inevitability in the play by evoking an atmosphere of fear and unnatural disturbance. This 'terror' suggests that something is deeply wrong with the world.

The phrase intensifies the tension, hinting at the disruption of the natural order and foreshadowing the violence that will soon unfold. This sense of dread contributes to the overall mood of impending doom, reinforcing the idea that significant, irreversible events are at hand.

(iv) **Why does Cassius consider the 'persuasion of his augurers' as a potential factor that could prevent Caesar from going to the Capitol? What does this reveal about the influence of religion and prophecy in the play? (3)**

Ans. Cassius considers the 'persuasion of his augurers' as a potential factor that could prevent Caesar from going to the Capitol. As per him, it underscores the power of religious and prophetic figures in shaping Caesar's decisions. The augurers' influence reflects the broader theme of religion and prophecy in *Julius Caesar* where supernatural forces and omens are seen as crucial determinants of action.

This highlights the vulnerability of even the most powerful individuals to forces they cannot fully control. Caesar's susceptibility to the augurers, despite his previous dismissal of such beliefs, reveals the tension between his personal ambition and the inevitable influence of fate and the supernatural in shaping human affairs.

(v) **What does Cassius' focus on Caesar's superstition and the 'apparent prodigies' suggest about his understanding of power and leadership? (4)**

Ans. Cassius' focus on Caesar's superstition and the 'apparent prodigies' suggests that he understands power and leadership as fragile and susceptible to external influences.

For Cassius, true power lies in the ability to maintain control over one's destiny. He sees Caesar's growing reliance on omens as a sign of weakness. Cassius' emphasis on these supernatural signs suggests that he believes leaders should be unshaken by such forces and should act with unwavering confidence.

Extract 4

You have some sick offence within your mind,
Which, by the right and virtue of my place,
I ought to know of: and, upon my knees,
I charm you, by my once-commended beauty,
By all your vows of love, and that great vow
Which did incorporate and make us one,
That you unfold to me, yourself, your half,
Why you are heavy, and what men to-night

(i) **What does Portia's statement, 'You have some sick offence within your mind', suggest about her perception of Brutus' emotional state and his secretive behaviour? (3)**

Ans. Portia's statement suggests that she perceives Brutus as troubled and mentally burdened, likely by something he is concealing.

The word 'sick' implies that whatever is on his mind is affecting his well-being potentially causing him inner turmoil.

Her use of 'offence' hints at a moral or emotional transgression, suggesting that Brutus' secrecy may involve something morally questionable.

This line reveals Portia's acute perception of her husband's state of mind and foreshadows her growing awareness of the conspiracy against Caesar as she senses a deeper issue at play.

(ii) **How does Portia's invocation of 'my once -commended beauty' reflect her understanding of the dynamics between herself and Brutus? (3)**

Ans. Portia's invocation of 'my once-commended beauty' reflects her attempt to appeal to Brutus' affection and the emotional bond they share.

By mentioning her beauty, she is reminding him of the love and admiration he once expressed for her. She is further suggesting that this past devotion should compel him to trust her with his secret.

This line reveals Portia's understanding of the power she holds over Brutus through their shared intimacy and her sense that she deserves to be included in his thoughts. It also highlights her vulnerability as she relies on their past emotional connection to encourage transparency.

(iii) **What does Portia's insistence on knowing 'why you are heavy' reveal about her character and her role in Brutus' life? (3)**

Ans. Portia's insistence on knowing 'why you are heavy' reveals her caring and attentive nature as well as her desire to be an active participant in her husband's life. Rather than being passive or distant, she wishes to share in his burdens.

This line also suggests that Portia sees herself as more than just a wife but as a friend and an equal partner in their marriage.

Her insistence reflects her emotional maturity and her belief that trust and openness are essential in their relationship.

This reveals her inner strength and determination to support Brutus through his challenges.

(iv) **Why does Portia refer to the men who 'did hide their faces even from darkness'? What does this suggest about her awareness of the conspiracy? (3)**

Ans. Portia's reference to the men who 'did hide their faces even from darkness' suggests that she is becoming suspicious of the secretive and covert nature of the actions surrounding Brutus.

These men, who have been visiting Brutus while hiding their identities, seem to be engaged in activities of questionable morality.

This reference shows that she is increasingly aware that something secretive and dangerous is occurring. Her ability to notice these signs and her awareness of the hidden actions of others indicate that she is perceptive and growing increasingly concerned about her husband's involvement in treason.

(v) **How does Portia's plea to Brutus reflect the broader themes of secrecy, loyalty and betrayal in the play? (4)**

Ans. Portia's plea to Brutus reflects the broader themes of secrecy, loyalty and betrayal that run throughout the play. Her desire for him to 'unfold to me, yourself, your half' speaks to the tension between personal loyalty and the secrets that threaten to erode trust in relationships. Portia's request to be included in Brutus' burdens highlights her loyalty to him.

However, Brutus' refusal to confide in her-out of both necessity and caution-reflects the theme of secrecy that pervades the play.

The secrecy surrounding the conspiracy is a key element in the drama. Portia's plea for transparency illustrates the personal cost of betrayal not only on a political level but also in intimate, personal relationships.

Extract 5

Soul of Rome,
Brave son derived from honorable loins,
Thou like an exorcist hast conjured up
My mortifièd spirit. Now bid me run,
And I will strive with things impossible,
Yea, get the better of them. What's to do?

(i) **How does Ligarius' description of Brutus as 'Soul of Rome' reflect his view of Brutus' character and his leadership role? (3)**

Ans. Ligarius' description of Brutus as 'Soul of Rome' emphasises his admiration for Brutus' character and the vital role he plays in the Roman state. By calling him the 'soul', Ligarius elevates Brutus to a nearly mythical status suggesting that Brutus embodies the essence of Rome itself.

This portrayal implies that Brutus represents Roman virtue, honour and justice. His leadership is seen as essential for the preservation of the republic.

(ii) **What is the significance of Ligarius describing Brutus as 'an exorcist' who has 'conjured up my mortifièd spirit'? (3)**

Ans. Ligarius' description of Brutus as 'an exorcist' who has 'conjured up my mortifièd spirit' reflects the transformative and almost supernatural influence Brutus has on him. The use of 'exorcist' implies that Brutus has the power to rid Ligarius of his emotional or spiritual paralysis ('mortifièd spirit') and awaken him to action.

This evokes the idea that Ligarius, before Brutus' intervention, was mentally or morally 'dead' but Brutus' call to arms has revived him.

It signifies Brutus' powerful, inspiring presence and the ability to rally others to his cause, even when they may have been previously disillusioned or inactive.

(iii) How does Ligarius' willingness to 'strive with things impossible' reflect his commitment to the conspiracy? (3)

Ans. Ligarius' statement that he will 'strive with things impossible' reflects his intense commitment to the conspiracy and his belief in the righteousness of their cause.

His willingness to challenge seemingly impossible odds demonstrates both his dedication and his confidence in the success of their mission.

It reveals a sense of urgency and determination suggesting that Ligarius is prepared to overcome any challenge in order to achieve their goal.

(iv) What does Ligarius' question 'What's to do'? reveal about his readiness and eagerness to join the conspiracy? (3)

Ans. Ligarius' question 'What's to do'? reveals his eagerness and readiness to take immediate action in support of the conspiracy. Having been inspired by Brutus' leadership, Ligarius is now fully committed and asking for the next steps.

His quick response indicates that he is no longer hesitant or questioning the moral implications of their plans. However, he is instead focused on executing their mission.

(v) How does Ligarius' speech, particularly his reference to 'honourable loins', contribute to the play's exploration of honour and lineage? (4)

Ans. Ligarius' reference to 'honourable loins' emphasises the importance of family honour and noble lineage in the play.

By invoking Brutus' ancestry, he highlights the notion that Brutus is a product of a distinguished lineage.

This suggests that his actions are rooted in a sense of honour and duty passed down through generations.

This aligns with the broader theme in *Julius Caesar* of the weight of familial and ancestral expectations, particularly regarding one's role in upholding Roman virtues.

Ligarius' praise of Brutus' heritage further glorifies him as a figure whose personal honour is intricately linked to the well-being of Rome.

ACT 2 : SCENE 2

Summary of Act 2 Scene 2

The scene begins with Calpurnia waking up Caesar. She is deeply troubled by ominous dreams she had during the night. She dreams of Caesar's statue spouting blood while Romans wash their hands in it, a vision she interprets as a warning of his impending death. Calpurnia pleads with him to stay home and avoid going to the Capitol. Instead, she asks him to send Antony to the Senate House.

A servant enters to inform Caesar that the priests don't want him to go out that day. When they pulled out the insides of the holy sacrifice, they found no heart within the animal.

Caesar interprets this as Gods telling him that he would be a coward if he stays home. However, Calpurnia's persistent concern convinces him to stay home.

Decius Brutus, one of the conspirators, arrives to escort Caesar to the Capitol. He skilfully reinterprets Calpurnia's dream, suggesting that it signifies Caesar's strength and the rejuvenation of Rome. He flatters Caesar's ego and also informs him that the Senate plans to offer him the crown that day. Persuaded by Decius's manipulation and not wanting to appear cowardly, Caesar decides to go to the Capitol despite Calpurnia's warnings.

The scene ends with Caesar, confident and unaware of the conspirators' true intentions, preparing to leave for the Senate.

Characters in the Scene

- **Julius Caesar** The most popular leader of Rome who is troubled by his wife's ominous dreams but is eventually persuaded to go to the Senate
- **Calpurnia** Caesar's wife who is deeply disturbed by her prophetic dream and urges Caesar to stay home to avoid danger
- **Servant** A household servant who brings news from the priests about their sacrifices, advising Caesar not to go out
- **Decius Brutus** One of the conspirators who cunningly reinterprets Calpurnia's dream in a positive way and convinces Caesar to go to the Senate
- **Publius** A senator who arrives to accompany Caesar to the Senate
- **Mark Antony** Caesar's loyal friend and supporter who enters as part of Caesar's entourage but does not play a major role in this scene

Vocab Vault

Whelped Born, especially used for animals

Squadrons Groups or divisions of soldiers, usually a tactical unit in military terms

Hurtled To move or throw with great force or speed

Entrails The internal organs, especially the intestines, of a person or animal

Portents Signs or warnings that something significant or ominous is about to happen, often referring to supernatural or divine messages

Tinctures Dyes or pigments used to colour something, or in a more metaphorical sense, a trace or slight infusion of a quality or feeling

Cognizance Awareness or recognition of something, often referring to understanding or consciousness of an event, fact or idea

Murther Murder

Opportune Occuring at a convenient time

EXAM ORIENTED QUESTIONS

TYPE - 1 Multiple Choice Questions

01 Mark

Q.1 Why is Calpurnia troubled at the beginning of the scene?
(a) She has heard rumours of a conspiracy.
(b) She had a dream about Caesar's death.
(c) She received a letter warning of danger.
(d) She saw an ominous bird outside their house.

Q.2 What does Calpurnia dream about?
(a) Caesar being crowned king.
(b) A lion roaming the streets of Rome.
(c) Caesar's statue spouting blood.
(d) The Capitol burning down.

Q.3 How does Caesar initially react to Calpurnia's concerns?
(a) He agrees to stay home.
(b) He dismisses her fears as foolish.
(c) He decides to consult a soothsayer.
(d) He plans to call off the Senate meeting.

Q.4 What does Calpurnia urge Caesar to do?
(a) Consult the soothsayer again.
(b) Go to the Capitol.
(c) Stay home and avoid the Senate.
(d) Pray to the gods for protection.

Q.5 Which of the following lines reflects Caesar's arrogance? **(ICSE Specimen 2024)**
(a) Danger knows well Caesar is more dangerous.
(b) Go, bid the priest do present sacrifice.
(c) For thy humour, I shall stay at home.
(d) I am ashamed, I did yield to them.

Q.6 How does Decius Brutus interpret Calpurnia's dream?
(a) As a warning of Caesar's death.
(b) As a vision of Caesar's strength and Rome's revival.
(c) As an omen of civil war.
(d) As a sign of divine punishment.

Q.7 What reason does Decius Brutus give to convince Caesar to go to the Capitol?
(a) The Senate plans to offer him the crown.
(b) The people are rioting.
(c) A conspiracy has been uncovered.
(d) The gods have sent a favourable omen.

Q.8 What does Decius say the Senate might think if Caesar does not show up?
(a) He is plotting against them.
(b) He is afraid or weak.
(c) He is unwell.
(d) He is arrogant and dismissive.

Q.9 What is Caesar's response to Decius's interpretation of the dream?
(a) He decides to stay home anyway.
(b) He becomes convinced and agrees to go.
(c) He asks for more time to think.
(d) He consults with another advisor.

Q.10 What does Caesar say about death?
(a) It is inevitable and should not be feared.
(b) It can be avoided with caution.
(c) It is a punishment from the gods.
(d) It is a sign of weakness.

Q.11 What does Caesar decide at the end of the scene?
(a) To stay home and avoid the Capitol.
(b) To attend the Senate meeting despite Calpurnia's fears.
(c) To send someone else in his place.
(d) To postpone the meeting until the omens are clear.

Q.12 What is the overall mood of Calpurnia in this scene?
I. Calm II. Fearful III. Anxious
IV. Indifferent V. Detached
(a) I and II (b) II and III (c) III and IV (d) IV and V

Q.13 Select the option that shows the correct relationship between statements (1) and (2).
Statement 1 Caesar dismisses Calpurnia's warnings and decides to go to the Senate despite her pleas.
Statement 2 Caesar believes that he is invincible and that no harm can come to him, as he views himself as more dangerous than danger itself.
(a) Statement 1 is true and Statement 2 is false
(b) Statement 2 is true and Statement 1 is false.
(c) Statement 2 is the cause for Statement 1.
(d) Statement 1 and Statement 2 are independent of each other.

Answers

1. (b) 2. (c) 3. (b) 4. (c) 5. (a) 6. (b) 7. (a) 8. (b) 9. (b) 10. (a)
11. (b) 12. (b) 13. (c)

TYPE - 2 Extract Based Questions

16 Marks

Extract 1

The gods do this in shame of cowardice.
Caesar should be a beast without a heart
If he should stay at home today for fear.
No, Caesar shall not. Danger knows full well
That Caesar is more dangerous than he.
We are two lions littered in one day,
And I the elder and more terrible.
And Caesar shall go forth.

(i) Analyse the significance of the phrase 'The gods do this in shame of cowardice.' What does this suggest about the Roman perception of bravery? (3)

Ans. This phrase implies that the gods disapprove of cowardice, associating it with dishonour. In Roman culture, bravery and courage were highly valued, and any form of fear was seen as shameful, especially for someone in power like Caesar.

The line suggests that Caesar must demonstrate his courage to maintain his honour and reputation.

(ii) What does Caesar mean when he says, 'Caesar should be a beast without a heart' ? (3)

Ans. When Caesar says, 'Caesar should be a beast without a heart' , he means that if he allows fear to prevent him from going to the Senate, he would be acting disgraceful and dishonourable.

In Roman culture, bravery and courage were highly valued, and to stay home out of fear would make him less than a man-more like a beast which is driven by instincts rather than reason or courage. He implies that his identity as a leader requires him to face danger without hesitation.

(iii) In what way does Caesar's statement 'Danger knows full well that Caesar is more dangerous than he' reflect his arrogance? (3)

Ans. Caesar's statement showcases his overconfidence and arrogance, suggesting that he is not afraid of danger but in fact, more dangerous than any threat.

This belief in his invulnerability and superiority reveals his inflated sense of self-worth and hubris.

(iv) How does the metaphor of 'We are two lions littered in one day' reflect Caesar's view of himself and others? (3)

Ans. The given metaphor reflects Caesar's view of himself as powerful and dominant, equating himself to a lion, a symbol of strength and authority. It also suggests that he recognises the strength in others, but places himself above them.

By calling himself the 'elder and more terrible' lion, Caesar emphasises his superiority, portraying himself as the more formidable force, both in experience and strength.

(v) What does Caesar's refusal to stay at home despite his wife's warnings suggest about his character? How does Caesar's decision to go forth foreshadow his eventual fate? (4)

Ans. Caesar's refusal demonstrates his pride, arrogance and unwillingness to appear weak or fearful. It reveals a character driven by an overwhelming desire to assert control, maintain his reputation and avoid showing vulnerability even in the face of potential danger.

Caesar's decision to ignore warnings and push forward reflects his tragic flaw of arrogance which ultimately leads to his downfall. His belief in his invincibility and disregard for omens foreshadows his tragic death as his overconfidence blinds him to the danger around him.

Extract 2

Calpurnia : Alas! my Lord. Your wisdom is
consum'd in confidence.
Do not go forth today: call it my fear
That keeps you in the house, and not your own.
We'll send Mark Antony to the Senate House

(ICSE Specimen 2024)

(i) Where are the speakers? Describe the weather outside. What is Calpurnia trying to prevent Caesar from doing? (3)

Ans. The speakers, Calpurnia and Caesar are inside Caesar's house in Rome.

The weather outside is stormy, with ominous signs and unnatural occurrences being reported, which contribute to Calpurnia's fear.

Calpurnia is trying to prevent Caesar from going to the Senate House because she fears for his safety based on her ominous dream and strange reports.

(ii) State two unusual things Calpurnia had heard of that made her fearful. What nightmare had she had? (3)

Ans. Calpurnia had heard of unnatural occurrences such as a lioness giving birth in the streets, graves opening and warriors fighting in the clouds.

Calpurnia dreamt that Caesar's statue was spouting blood like a fountain and Romans were washing their hands in it.

(iii) How did Caesar calm his wife's fears? What does Calpurnia mean by 'Your wisdom is consum'd in confidence'? (3)

Ans. Caesar tried to calm Calpurnia by asserting that death is inevitable and it is cowardly to fear it. He also downplayed the significance of the omens.

Calpurnia means that Caesar's overconfidence is clouding his judgement, making him dismissive of the warnings and the potential danger.

(iv) How does Decius interpret Calpurnia's dream? (3)

Ans. Decius reinterprets Calpurnia's dream positively, suggesting that the blood flowing from Caesar's statue symbolises Rome drawing strength and vitality from him, indicating that Caesar is a life-giving force.

(v) What does Caesar finally decide to do? **(ICSE Specimen 2024, 4)**

What can you infer about his character from this decision?

Mention two aspects of Calpurnia's character revealed in this scene.

Ans. Caesar ultimately decides to go to the Senate, persuaded by Decius's flattering interpretation of the dream and his fear of appearing cowardly.

Caesar's decision reveals his arrogance, desire for control, and fear of seeming weak or superstitious, which makes him susceptible to flattery.

Calpurnia is shown to be deeply caring and protective of Caesar, as well as intuitive and fearful of the omens, reflecting her strong belief in supernatural warnings.

Extract 3

This dream is all amiss interpreted.
It was a vision fair and fortunate.
Your statue spouting blood in many pipes,
In which so many smiling Romans bathed,
Signifies that from you great Rome shall suck
Reviving blood, and that great men shall press
For tinctures, stains, relics, and cognizance.
This by Calpurnia's dream is signified.

(i) Who is the speaker? How does the speaker reinterpret Calpurnia's dream? What is his motive for doing so? (3)

Ans. The speaker, Decius, reinterprets Calpurnia's dream as a positive omen, suggesting that Caesar's blood symbolises vitality and rejuvenation for Rome.

The speaker reinterprets Calpurnia's dream by implying that great Romans will seek to honour Caesar by associating themselves with him.

His motive is to persuade Caesar to go to the Senate, furthering the conspirators' plan.

(ii) Analyse the rhetorical strategies the speaker uses to convince Caesar that the dream is favourable. (3)

Ans. Decius uses flattery, reinterpreting the dream in a way that appeals to Caesar's vanity and desire for legacy.

He presents the imagery of Romans bathing in Caesar's blood as a metaphor for their reverence and dependence on him; thus, appealing to Caesar's ego and sense of importance.

(iii) What does the speaker's reinterpretation of the dream reveal about his character and his role in the conspiracy? (3)

Ans. Decius' reinterpretation reveals his cunning, manipulative nature, and his ability to use persuasive language to influence others.

His role in the conspiracy is pivotal as he skilfully convinces Caesar to ignore the warnings and attend the Senate.

(iv) How does the speaker's explanation contrast with Calpurnia's interpretation? What impact does this have on Caesar's decision? (3)

Ans. Calpurnia's interpretation is fearful and cautionary, viewing the dream as a dire warning of danger to Caesar. In contrast, Decius' explanation is optimistic and glorifying.

This stark contrast sways Caesar to dismiss his wife's fears leading him to attend the Senate where he ultimately meets his demise.

(v) Important character traits of Decius are revealed in this scene. Mention any two. What is your opinion of the man? Give a reason to justify your answer. (4)

Ans. Decius displays two important traits in this scene- manipulativeness and persuasiveness. He skilfully reinterprets Calpurnia's dream to appeal to Caesar's vanity convincing him to attend the Senate.

His cunning use of flattery and rhetorical tactics shows his ability to influence and deceive effectively.

Decius appears as a cunning and opportunistic individual willing to manipulate others for personal and political gain. His lack of moral integrity, evident in his deceitful actions, highlights his dangerous nature as he prioritises the conspiracy's success over honesty or loyalty.

ACT 2 : SCENE 3

Summary of Act 2 Scene 3

Artemidorus enters with a letter in hand which he has written to warn Caesar about the conspiracy against him. The letter specifically names Brutus and the other conspirators. Artemidorus plans to present the letter to Caesar as he passes by. He is hoping that if Caesar reads it and takes the warning seriously, he will avoid his impending death. However, Artemidorus fears that if Caesar ignores the letter and continues to trust the wrong people, then 'the Fates with traitors do contrive' suggesting that fate itself is plotting with the conspirators to bring about Caesar's demise.

This scene emphasises the theme of fate versus free will as Artemidorus tries to intervene but Caesar's refusal to heed warnings from others ultimately leads to his downfall.

Character in the Scene

- **Artemidorus** A Roman teacher and supporter of Caesar. He represents common citizens.

EXAM ORIENTED QUESTIONS

TYPE - 1 Multiple Choice Questions — 01 Mark

Q.1 What is the purpose of the letter Artemidorus has written?
(a) To warn Caesar about the conspiracy against him
(b) To invite Caesar to a banquet
(c) To ask Caesar for a political favour
(d) To threaten Caesar

Q.2 What does Artemidorus plan to do with the letter?
(a) Deliver it to Caesar personally
(b) Leave it at Caesar's house
(c) Send it with a messenger
(d) Read it aloud in the Senate

Q.3 What does Artemidorus say about fate in relation to the conspirators?
(a) Fate is on Caesar's side
(b) The Fates are conspiring with the traitors
(c) Fate will punish the conspirators
(d) Fate has no role in the conspiracy

Q.4 What does Artemidorus believe about the importance of timing in delivering the letter?
(a) Timing is irrelevant; the message is what matters
(b) Caesar must read the letter immediately to save his life
(c) The letter should be delivered after the Senate meeting
(d) It is too late to change the outcome

Q.5 What is the tone of Artemidorus' speech in this scene?
I. Fearful — II. Confident
III. Hopeful — IV. Determined
V. Indifferent
(a) I and II
(b) II and III
(c) III and IV
(d) IV and V

Q.6 Select the option that shows the correct relationship between statements (1) and (2).
Statement 1 Artemidorus plans to give Caesar the letter in public.

Statement 2 Artemidorus believes that Caesar will only read the letter if it appears important and urgent.

(a) Statement 1 is true and Statement 2 is false

(b) Statement 2 is true and Statement 1 is false.

(c) Statement 2 is the cause for Statement 1.

(d) Statement 1 and Statement 2 are independent of each other.

Answers

1. (a) 2. (a) 3. (b) 4. (b) 5. (c) 6. (a)

TYPE - 2 Extract Based Questions

16 Marks

Extract 1

Here will I stand till Caesar pass along,
And as a suitor will I give him this.
My heart laments that virtue cannot live
Out of the teeth of emulation.
If thou read this, O Caesar, thou mayest live;
If not, the Fates with traitors do contrive.

(i) What is Artemidorus' purpose for standing in this spot? How does he plan to deliver his message to Caesar? (3)

Ans. Artemidorus' purpose for standing in this spot is to intercept Caesar as he passes by. His purpose is to warn Caesar about the conspiracy against him. Disguising himself as a common suitor, Artemidorus plans to hand Caesar a letter detailing the names of the conspirators and their plot. He hopes that by reading this letter, Caesar will be alerted to the danger and take necessary precautions to save himself from the impending assassination.

(ii) Analyse the meaning of the line "My heart laments that virtue cannot live out of the teeth of emulation". What does this reveal about Artemidorus' view of the situation? (3)

Ans. The given line reflects Artemidorus' sorrow that virtuous leaders like Caesar are often targets of envy and rivalry.

He believes that Caesar's goodness and leadership provoke jealousy leading to his downfall.

This reveals Artemidorus' view that in a corrupt and competitive political environment, even the most virtuous individuals are vulnerable to destruction by those driven by ambition and envy.

(iii) Discuss the significance of the phrase 'the Fates with traitors do contrive' in the context of Artemidorus's mission. (3)

Ans. Through this phrase, Artemidorus implies that if Caesar does not heed his warning, his fate will be decided by the conspirators. This highlights the inevitability of Caesar's downfall if he remains unaware of the plot.

(iv) What does Artemidorus' statement about virtue and emulation suggest about the political environment in Rome? (3)

Ans. Artemidorus' statement suggests that the political environment in Rome is fraught with jealousy and rivalry, where virtue and noble qualities are overshadowed by personal ambition and envy. It implies a corrupt and dangerous atmosphere where even the most virtuous leaders are not safe from betrayal and conspiracy. It further highlights the unevenness of moral integrity in the face of political manipulation and the thirst for power.

(v) Evaluate Artemidorus' role in the narrative. How does his attempt to warn Caesar contribute to the tension of the scene? (4)

Ans. Artemidorus' role in the narrative is pivotal as he serves as the last line of defense for Caesar. His attempt to warn Caesar by presenting the letter containing the names of the conspirators heightens the tension of the scene. It introduces a glimmer of hope for Caesar's survival.

His failure or success in delivering the message directly impacts the outcome of the assassination plot. The suspense of whether Caesar will heed the warning or ignore it amplifies the dramatic irony and deepens the tragedy as the audience knows the conspirators' intentions.

ACT 2 : SCENE 4

Summary of Act 2 Scene 4

In Act 2, Scene 4 of *Julius Caesar*, Portia, Brutus' wife, is anxious and worried about the conspiracy. She has been trying to convince Brutus to reveal his plans to her but he has kept his secret. Portia is deeply concerned for him.

Portia sends her servant to the Senate to find out what is happening as she anxiously awaits news of Caesar's fate. She remains hopeful that Brutus will act honourably but her worry grows as she waits for any word from him. Portia, thereafter, encounters the Soothsayer. She questions him about Caesar's fate.

The Soothsayer expresses his fear that something harmful may happen to Caesar but is unsure of the specifics. He plans to go to the Capitol to warn Caesar again.

This scene illustrates Portia's devotion to Brutus and her concern for his well-being. It also underscores the personal stakes for the conspirators, showing that their actions are not only political but also deeply connected to their personal relationships.

Characters in the Scene

- **Portia** Brutus' wife who is deeply worried about him and the conspiracy. She is anxious to learn what is happening at the Senate and whether Brutus is safe
- **Lucius** Portia's servant who is tasked with going to the Senate to gather news about Brutus and what is happening there
- **Soothsayer** A character who briefly appears, warning Caesar of his fate but is not involved in the main action of this scene

Vocab Vault

Errand A task or mission

Constancy The quality of being unchanging, steadfast or loyal

EXAM ORIENTED QUESTIONS

TYPE - 1 Multiple Choice Questions

01 Mark

Q.1 'I would have had thee there and here again
Ere I can tell thee what thou shouldst do there.'
These lines tell us that Portia is feeling ....
(ICSE Specimen 2024)

(a) angry
(b) weak
(c) sad
(d) anxious

Q.2 What does Portia ask her servant, Lucius, to do?

(a) Go to the Senate House and observe what happens
(b) Deliver a letter to Caesar
(c) Prepare a meal for Brutus
(d) Find Brutus and bring him home

Q.3 Why is Portia so concerned about Brutus?

(a) She knows about the conspiracy against Caesar
(b) She fears Brutus is ill
(c) She thinks Brutus is planning to leave Rome
(d) She suspects Brutus is unfaithful

Q.4 What does the Soothsayer plan to do in this scene?

(a) Warn Caesar again
(b) Deliver a message to Brutus
(c) Pray at the temple
(d) Join the conspirators

Q.5 What is Portia's reaction to the Soothsayer's plan?
(a) She is reassured
(b) She remains anxious and fearful
(c) She ignores it
(d) She becomes angry

Q.6 What does the Soothsayer say about Caesar's future?
(a) He is safe from harm
(b) He is in great danger
(c) He will be crowned king
(d) He will leave Rome

Q.7 What does Portia's concern for Brutus reveal about her character?
(a) She is indifferent to political matters
(b) She is deeply loyal and supportive
(c) She is manipulative and deceitful
(d) She is self-centered and uncaring

Q.8 What is the tone of Act 2, Scene 4 of *Julius Caesar* where Portia is worried about Brutus and the conspiracy?
(a) Confident and calm
(b) Anxious and tense
(c) Optimistic and joyful
(d) Sarcastic and mocking

Q.9 Select the option that shows the correct relationship between statements (1) and (2).
Statement 1 Portia is confident about Brutus' success in the conspiracy.
Statement 2 Portia has strong faith in Brutus' abilities and moral judgment.
(a) Statement 1 is true and Statement 2 is false
(b) Statement 2 is true and Statement 1 is false.
(c) Statement 2 is the cause for Statement 1.
(d) Statement 1 and Statement 2 are independent of each other.

Q.10 Arrange the following events from Act 2, Scene 4 in the correct sequence.
1. Portia sends Lucius to the Capitol.
2. The Soothsayer plans to warn Caesar again.
3. Portia shows her anxiety and speaks to herself.
4. Portia asks Lucius about Brutus' whereabouts.

(a) 4, 1, 2, 3 (b) 3, 4, 1, 2
(c) 1, 3, 4, 2 (d) 2, 3, 1, 4

Answers

1. (d) 2. (a) 3. (a) 4. (a) 5. (b) 6. (b) 7. (b) 8. (b) 9. (b) 10. (b)

TYPE - 2 Extract Based Questions

16 Marks

Extract 1

Lucius - Madam, what should I do?
Run to the Capitol, and nothing else?
And so return to you, and nothing else?
Portia - Yes, bring me word, boy,
if thy lord look well,
For he went sickly forth. And take good note
What Caesar doth, what suitors press to him.
Hark, boy, what noise is that?

(i) What is the significance of Lucius' confusion in his dialogue with Portia? How does it reflect the urgency of the situation? **(3)**

Ans. Lucius' confusion highlights his uncertainty about the importance of his task. His questions reflect the doubt at the gravity and urgency of Portia's request. This shows that she is deeply concerned about Caesar's actions and state of health.

This moment underscores the tense atmosphere as Portia desperately seeks information, unaware of the conspiracy's unfolding.

(ii) How does Portia's command to Lucius to observe Caesar's behaviour indicate her concern for her husband's safety? **(3)**

Ans. Portia's request for Lucius to monitor Caesar's interactions and health shows her deep concern for her husband's well-being. She is anxious about Caesar's vulnerability may impact Brutus.

Her focus on what Caesar does and who approaches him reflects her intuition about the danger he faces despite not being fully aware of the conspiracy.

(iii) Why does Portia emphasise that Lucius should observe what Caesar does and which suitors approach him? What might this reveal about her understanding of Caesar's political position? **(3)**

Ans. Portia emphasises these actions because she understands Caesar's high political status and the importance of his interactions with others.

She wants Lucius to note any signs of distress or unusual behaviour as well as who is seeking his attention.

This suggests that Portia is aware of the power struggles and intrigues surrounding Caesar highlighting her awareness of the political complexities at play.

(iv) Analyse Portia's reaction to hearing a noise after sending Lucius on his mission. How does this contribute to the tone of the scene? (3)

Ans. Portia's reaction to the noise reflects her heightened anxiety and suspicion. The sudden sound intensifies the tense atmosphere as she is already nervous about Caesar's safety.

This moment adds to the sense of impending danger, making the tone of the scene one of urgency, fear and anticipation.

(v) What does Portia's command to Lucius, 'bring me word, boy, if thy lord look well', reveal about her relationship with Brutus and her role in the domestic sphere? (4)

Ans. Portia's command shows her role as a concerned wife, deeply invested in Brutus's welfare. It also highlights the trust and communication within their relationship as she seeks information about his health.

Her concern for his physical state reflects her protective nature. Her desire to stay informed about his activities suggests a deep emotional involvement in his life, even as political tensions rise around them.

Extract 2

None that I know will be, much that
I fear may chance.
Good morrow to you. Here the street is narrow.
The throng that follows Caesar at the heels,
Of senators, of praetors, common suitors,
Will crowd a feeble man almost to death.
I'll get me to a place more void, and there
Speak to great Caesar as he comes along.

(i) How does the description of the crowded street reflect the political climate in Rome? (3)

Ans. The crowded street, filled with senators, praetors and common suitors following Caesar, symbolises the power dynamics and political tension in Rome.

It suggests that Caesar's influence is immense as people from all walks of life are drawn to him.

The crowd's overwhelming presence represents both Caesar's control over Rome and the danger of political manipulation where the common people and politicians alike are closely following his every move.

(ii) What does the speaker's decision to find a quieter place to speak to Caesar reveal about his character and the challenges he faces? (3)

Ans. The speaker's decision to move to a quieter place reflects his awareness of the dangers and challenges of approaching Caesar in such a crowded and chaotic setting. It shows that the speaker is cautious and strategic understanding the physical and political risks involved.

His need for a less crowded space suggests a desire for clarity and direct communication with Caesar, free from distractions and threats.

(iii) What is the significance of the line, 'The throng that follows Caesar at the heels, / Of senators, of praetors, common suitors', in understanding the power structure in Rome? (3)

Ans. This line emphasises Caesar's central position in Roman politics, with all manner of individuals-senators, praetors and suitors-flocking to him. It highlights the hierarchical nature of Roman society and politics, where Caesar is the focal point, and everyone, regardless of rank, feels compelled to seek his attention.

This line underscores Caesar's influence and the political climate where power and patronage are concentrated around him.

(iv) How does the speaker's mention of the 'feeble man' in the crowd suggest the physical and metaphorical risks associated with Caesar's rise to power? (3)

Ans. The 'feeble man' in the crowd suggests both the literal danger of being crushed in a crowd and the vulnerability of those who are powerless in the face of Caesar's overwhelming influence.

This phrase reflects how Caesar's rise to power creates an environment where weaker individuals are at the mercy of the powerful. It symbolises the marginalisation of the less influential in Caesar's world.

(v) In what way does the speaker's attempt to avoid the crowd and find a 'place more void' demonstrate the tension between public and private action in the context of the play? (4)

Ans. The speaker's desire to find a quieter, less crowded place to speak to Caesar reflects the tension between public spectacle and private, more intimate actions. Caesar's public persona and the political rituals surrounding him create an environment where individual action is often drowned out by the throng.

The speaker's need for solitude to speak to Caesar highlights the contrast between the spectacle of public life and the private decisions that shape the course of events, particularly in the context of the conspiracy.

TREASURE CHEST: PROSE

01

BONKU BABU'S FRIEND

Satyajit Ray

Introduction

Bonku Babu's Friend is a short story by Satyajit Ray, a renowned Indian filmmaker and writer. This story blends science fiction with humour and social commentary, making it both entertaining and thought-provoking. Written in a simple language, the story highlights several significant ideas of self-discovery, transformation, and social prejudice. It mixes mundane life with an extraordinary event to underline the power of unexpected events in shaping human confidence and self-worth.

About the Story

The story **Bonku Babu's Friend** revolves around a school teacher Bonku Babu. He is shy and meek in nature. This is why, often teased and disrespected by the naughty students and fellow villagers. One evening when Bonku Babu is on his way home he unexpectedly meets Ang, an alien from another planet. He advises Bonku Babu to be confident and to stand for himself.

Character Introduction

- **Bonku Babu** A quiet teacher who is transformed after meeting Ang. He is simple, timid and soft-spoken.
- **Ang** An extraterrestrial being from the planet Craneus. He is an intelligent being who acts as a catalyst for Bonku's transformation.
- **Sripati Babu** A respected figure in the village.
- **Villagers** The men who frequently tease and belittle Bonku Babu.

Story at a Glance

Bonku Babu, a calm and kind teacher, had taught geography and Bengali for 22 years at Kankurgachhi Village Primary School. Despite his students' pranks, he never got angry and often invited good students to his home to share stories of foreign adventures.

On weekends, he attended gatherings hosted by Sripati Majumdar, a respected person in village. However, the men there teased him, which hurt him more than his students' tricks. One night, after Bonku Babu claimed he wasn't afraid of ghosts, they played a prank on him–a figure jumped from a tree, tearing his kurta and injuring his neck.

Another time, a debate about aliens began. Bonku Babu suggested aliens might visit their village but the men mocked him, joking that he could be taken as a 'specimen'. He left the gathering, feeling hurt.

As he walked home, a strange light appeared and a shiny pink alien named Ang from the planet Craneus greeted him. Ang claimed to be highly advanced, spoke thousands of languages and froze Bonku Babu in place with a pebble. He showed Bonku Babu amazing sights, like the Northern Lights and fierce wildlife in Brazil.

Ang advised Bonku Babu to be confident and stand up for himself. Inspired, Bonku Babu shocked the villagers the next day by criticising their behaviour and announcing he would never attend their gatherings again, leaving with newfound confidence.

Vocab Vault

Pique A sudden feeling of irritation or resentment.
Humbug Nonsense or something deceptive.
Feign To pretend or fake something.
Flittermouse Another word for a bat.
Irrepressible Impossible to control or restrain.
Veered off Changed direction suddenly
Aurora Borealis A natural light display seen in high-latitude regions, also known as the Northern Lights.
Walrus A large marine mammal with long tusks, found in the Arctic.
Piranhas A type of carnivorous fish known for its sharp teeth and aggressive nature.
Impenetrable Impossible to pass through or enter; inaccessible.
Foliage The leaves of plants, collectively.
Appetite A strong desire for something, often related to food or other needs.
Implications The possible effects or consequences of an action or event.
Guffaw A loud and boisterous laugh.
Uproariously In a very noisy, loud, or uncontrollable manner.
Sycophants People who seek to gain advantage by flattering.

Theme

The theme of this story revolves around self-realisation empowerment and transformation. The story highlights the importance of recognising self-worth and asserting individuality. It highlights the idea of breaking free from inferiority complexes and raising voice against prejudice and injustices.

Message Conveyed by the Story

The message of the story is about self-confidence and personal growth. After meeting Ang, Bonku Babu learns the value of speaking up against injustice, being assertive and not letting anyone insult him. The story encourages individuals to break free from meekness and learn the power of self confidence.

Style, Tone and Mood

- **Style** The writing is quite descriptive and interesting, using vivid language.
- **Tone** The tone starts humorous and light and becomes assertive towards the end.
- **Mood** The mood is curious and surprising.

Title

The title 'Bonku Babu's Friend' highlights the importance of a good friend, Ang, the alien, in Bonku Babu's life. Despite being from another planet, Ang becomes Bonku Babu's friend, offering him advice and helping him shape his confidence and self-worth. The title emphasises the importance of true friendship in helping one transform.

Figures of Speech

- **Metaphor** "Bonku Babu was fetched, even if he tried to keep away." *Compares Bonku Babu to an object that can be fetched, implying his lack of control.*
  "It was essential to have a butt of ridicule in the group." *Compares Bonku Babu to a 'butt of ridicule', meaning he was the target of mockery.*
- **Simile** "His chin was so much like a camel's." *Direct comparison using 'like'.*
  "His eyes were like the eyes of a tortoise." *Comparison of Bhairav Chakravarty's eyes to a tortoise's.*
- **Personification** "The crickets were silent." *Gives human-like quality (silence) to crickets, making it eerie.*
  "Not even in his wildest dreams had Bonku Babu witnessed such a strange scene." *Dreams are given the ability to be 'wild', making them seem alive.*
- **Hyperbole** *(Exaggeration for effect)* "There isn't a single language in your solar system that I do not know." *Ang exaggerates his linguistic ability.*
  "Nothing can be more effective than this in making an enemy utterly powerless." *Overstatement of the power of the pebble-like object.*
- **Irony** "A far superior being than man." *Ironic, as the alien appears physically unimpressive.*
  "According to Sripati Majumdar, it was essential to have a butt of ridicule in the group." *Ironic, as it highlights the cruelty of the so-called 'friendly' meetings.*
- **Symbolism** "A little while ago, you could not move an inch." *The paralysis represents Bonku Babu's helplessness, not just physically but socially.*
  "The creature's eyes were round and bright yellow." *The glowing yellow eyes symbolise otherworldliness and knowledge.*

EXAM ORIENTED QUESTIONS

TYPE - 1 Multiple Choice Questions

01 Mark

Q.1 Bonku Babu's personality before meeting Ang was ....

(a) confident and assertive.
(b) shy and easily influenced by others.
(c) very rebellious and outspoken.
(d) overly ambitious.

Q.2 The unusual event that occurred in Poncha Ghosh's bamboo grove.

(a) All the bamboo leaves turned yellow overnight.
(b) All the bamboo around the pond lost their leaves suddenly.
(c) The pond froze solid in winter.
(d) Strange footprints were found around the pond.

Q.3 The phrase 'He felt all his hair rise' presents a feeling of ....

(a) curiosity (b) fear or surprise
(c) happiness (d) calmness

Q.4 What does Bonku Babu's initial meekness symbolise in the story?

(a) The power of silence and patience.
(b) His reluctance to engage with others.
(c) The societal pressure to follow and not speak up.
(d) His natural behaviour is to be quiet.

Q.5 Ang used .... to show Bonku Babu the Arctic and Brazil.

(a) a telescope
(b) a small tube with a glass end
(c) a holographic projector
(d) a magical mirror

Q.6 Why does Bonku Babu become confident after meeting Ang?

(a) Ang gives him a magical power.
(b) Ang offers him a job.
(c) Ang teaches him to stand up for himself.
(d) Ang gives him a gift.

Q.7 How did Bonku Babu behave at the villagers' meeting after his encounter with Ang?

(a) He remained quiet and observant.
(b) He argued with the villagers about their opinions on aliens.
(c) He apologised for being late and stayed silent throughout.
(d) He laughed loudly, criticised the villagers, and shared his experience with Ang.

Q.8 Ang advised Bonku Babu ....

(a) to be more assertive and protest against injustice
(b) to ignore societal norms
(c) to leave the village and explore the world
(d) to become a scientist and study space

Q.9 The feeling the story has when Bonku Babu first meets Ang and is amazed by the alien's wisdom.

(a) Scary and tense
(b) Mysterious and interesting
(c) Fun and funny
(d) Sad and gloomy

Q.10 'He was actually dancing.' What does this phrase indicate about Bonku Babu's mood?

(a) He is celebrating (b) He is confused
(c) He is upset (d) He is relaxed and content

Q.11 What reaction did the villagers have when Bonku Babu shared his story?

(a) They were shocked and silent.
(b) They believed him immediately.
(c) They laughed and teased him.
(d) They left the meeting in anger.

Q.12 What lesson can be learned from the fact that Bonku Babu's newfound confidence made him stand out in the village?

(a) That standing out is always the best approach, regardless of the situation.
(b) That conforming to societal norms leads to a better life.
(c) Following others' opinions is the safest path.
(d) That individuality can sometimes be terrifying but it can also lead to personal growth.

Q.13 The tone changes when Bonku Babu speaks to the villagers at the meeting from .... to ....

(a) serious to quiet (b) angry to confrontational
(c) to happy to humorous (d) calm to composed

Q.14 Select the option that shows the correct relationship between statement (1) and (2).

Statement 1 The villagers react with surprise and shock when Bonku Babu announces he will no longer attend their meetings.

Statement 2 Bonku Babu criticises their actions and reveals his encounter with Ang, an alien.

(a) Statement 1 is true, and Statement 2 is false.
(b) Statement 1 is false, and Statement 2 is true.
(c) Both statements are true.
(d) Both statements are false.

Q.15 How do the villagers react to Bonku Babu's sudden change in behaviour?

(a) They are supportive and proud of him.
(b) They are shocked, confused and silent.
(c) They ignore him and continue talking.
(d) They start laughing at him.

Q.16 Why does Bonku Babu laugh uproariously after meeting Ang?

(a) He is nervous and unsure of how to react.
(b) He is mocking the villagers and their way of thinking.
(c) His laughter represents his newfound freedom and confidence after realising his potential.
(d) He is embarrassed by his previous behavior and wants to cover it up with laughter.

Q.17 Complete the sentence with the appropriate phrase: Bonku Babu was left in awe after his meeting with Ang, as he realised that his life had been transformed. He no longer felt .... when facing challenges or criticism.

(a) like an outsider (b) overconfident
(c) meek and mild (d) lost and confused

Q.18 What role do the villagers play in the story, and what does their reaction to Bonku Babu's change suggest?

(a) They represent the traditional, conservative mindset of society, resistant to change.
(b) They serve as a source of encouragement and support for Bonku Babu.
(c) They represent individuals who are always looking for entertainment.
(d) They show the importance of listening to others' opinions.

Q.19 Satyajit Ray used the character of Ang, an alien, to deliver the message of self-empowerment ....

(a) to create a fantastical setting for entertainment
(b) to highlight the conflict between humans and aliens
(c) to show that wisdom and guidance can come from unexpected sources
(d) to create a sense of mystery and confusion

Q.20 What could Bonku Babu's encounter with Ang teach you about the importance of challenging societal expectations and norms?

(a) Society's expectations are always right and should never be challenged.
(b) It's important to challenge societal norms when they limit personal growth and self-expression.
(c) Society's expectations should always be followed without question.
(d) Society's norms do not affect individual progress.

Q.21 Select the option that shows the correct relationship between statements (1) and (2).

Statement 1 Bonku Babu's transformation into a confident person is triggered by his encounter with Ang.

Statement 2 Ang, an alien from another planet, encourages Bonku Babu to speak up and not accept injustice.

(a) Statement 1 is true, and Statement 2 is false.
(b) Statement 1 is false, and Statement 2 is true.
(c) Both statements are true.
(d) Both statements are false.

Q.22 The author uses Bonku Babu's meeting with Ang to explore themes of societal expectations and self-identity by ....

(a) by showing Bonku Babu's escape from societal pressure
(b) by depicting the villagers' ignorance and insensitivity
(c) by focusing on Bonku Babu's discomfort in the meeting
(d) by showing the importance of pleasing others

Q.23 Bonku Babu's transformation in the story symbolises

(a) his desire for revenge
(b) the awakening of his inner strength
(c) his need for approval from others
(d) the escape from reality

Q.24 The central theme of Bonku Babu's Friend.

(a) The importance of maintaining social status
(b) The value of questioning societal norms and standing up for oneself
(c) The significance of remaining silent in the face of injustice
(d) The benefits of avoiding new experiences and change

Q.25 Identify the correct sequence of events that happen when Bonku Babu meets Ang?

1. Bonku Babu shares his experience with the villagers.
2. Ang gives Bonku Babu advice on standing up for himself.
3. Bonku Babu leaves the meeting with newfound confidence.
4. Bonku Babu sees the strange creatures and the Aurora Borealis.

(a) 1, 2, 3, 4 (b) 2, 1, 3, 4
(c) 4, 2, 3, 1 (d) 1, 3, 2, 4

Q.26 **Identify the figure of speech used in the phrase 'Bonku Babu was fetched, even if he tried to keep away'?**
(a) Simile (b) Personification
(c) Metaphor (d) Irony

Q.27 **In your opinion, what was the most important lesson Bonku Babu learned from Ang?**
(a) That extraterrestrial life exists
(b) That intelligence is not about appearance but about curiosity and confidence
(c) That society never changes
(d) That fear should guide human actions

Q.28 **If you were to rewrite the ending, how would you make Bonku Babu use his newfound confidence?**
(a) He would prove his encounter by bringing Ang back
(b) He would challenge his bullies and inspire his students
(c) He would leave his village and work for space research
(d) He would become a writer documenting alien encounters

Answers

1. (b)	2. (b)	3. (b)	4. (c)	5. (b)	6. (c)	7. (d)	8. (a)	9. (b)	10. (a)
11. (a)	12. (d)	13. (b)	14. (c)	15. (b)	16. (c)	17. (c)	18. (a)	19. (c)	20. (b)
21. (c)	22. (b)	23. (b)	24. (b)	25. (c)	26. (c)	27. (b)	28. (b)		

TYPE - 2 Extract Based Questions

16 Marks

Extract 1

"All at once, his ears began ringing. He felt as if someone was humming loudly --- a long, steady noise ---- there was no way he could stop it."

(i) **Where was Bonku Babu at this point in the story? An object came into view as he moved forward. Describe what he saw.** **(3)**

Ans. Bonku Babu was deep inside the bamboo grove owned by Poncha Ghosh. As he moved forward, he saw a strange object that looked like a giant glass bowl.

The entire area was illuminated by its pinklight. The object appeared to be 'breathing'. Soon after, he saw the alien, Ang, who started speaking to him.

(ii) **A weird creature soon began talking to Bonku Babu. What did he say to Bonku about having made a mistake?** **(3)**

Ans. The creature, Ang, told Bonku Babu that he had made a mistake by being too meek and mild in his life. Ang criticised him for not standing up for himself which has led him to live a life without much progress.

Ang advised him that it was wrong for anyone to tolerate insult or harm without protest.

(iii) **In what way did the creature prove that he was superior to humans?** **(3)**

Ans. The creature proved his superiority through advanced technology and wisdom. He showed Bonku Babu extraordinary sights, like foreign lands and natural phenomena, through a tube.

Ang also displayed his intelligence by understanding Bonku Babu's character and offering advice to help him improve. Ang also immobilised him and thereby showcased his advanced power.

(iv) **How did Bonku Babu's dreams of visiting foreign lands come true? Describe any one such land that he 'saw'.** **(3)**

Ans. Bonku Babu's dreams of visiting foreign lands came true when Ang used a magical tube to show him different parts of the world.

One of the lands he saw was covered in snow where he witnessed the vibrant Aurora Borealis. He spotted igloos, polar bears and walruses fighting, with blood staining the soft white snow.

This was an extraordinary experience that Bonku Babu could not have imagined in reality.

(v) **How did the creature's advice affect Bonku Babu? Comment on his transformation at the end of the story. What do you like about the way the story ends?** **(4)**

Ans. The creature's advice deeply affected Bonku Babu.

It gave him the confidence to stand up for himself and speak out against those who insulted him.

By the end of the story, he confronted the villagers boldly.

The ending is satisfying because it shows Bonku Babu's personal growth and newfound courage.

His transformation inspires readers to believe in their potential to change and overcome self-doubt.

Extract 2

"It was December, and Bonku Babu was looking at an area hidden under layers of snow. Still, he broke out into a sweat. 'What about Brazil? Don't you wish to go there?' asked Ang. Bonku Babu remembered instantly-piranhas, those deadly carnivorous fish! Amazing. How did this Ang know what he would like to see?

(i) **Describe the forest Bonku Babu saw through the tube. What details stood out to him? (3)**

Ans. Bonku Babu saw a dense forest with very little sunlight filtering through the thick foliage. The forest appeared dark and almost impenetrable, suggesting it was difficult to pass through or explore.

(ii) **How does the description of the "dense forest" and "impenetrable foliage" help us understand Bonku Babu's feelings in this scene? (3)**

Ans. The description of the dense forest and impenetrable foliage reflects Bonku Babu's sense of being unsure in an unfamiliar environment. The words make the place seem mysterious and dangerous, which matches Bonku Babu's feeling of fear. This helps us understand his inner confusion and hesitation as he sees something new.

(iii) **Do you think Bonku Babu's first reaction to Brazil (thinking of piranhas) makes it harder for him to enjoy new experiences? (3)**

Ans. Yes, Bonku Babu's focus on piranhas suggests that he might have a hard time enjoying new experiences because he's so focused on potential dangers.

He might miss out on the good parts because he's too worried about the risks. This is something many people can relate to.

(iv) **What does the description of Bonku Babu 'breaking out into a sweat' despite the cold December setting suggest about his emotional state? (4)**

Ans. The description of Bonku Babu sweating in the cold December setting suggests that he is feeling anxious or frightened.

Though the weather is cold, his emotional response is intense. The scenes he is seeing through the tube, like the walruses fighting and the blood on the snow are shocking.

This highlights his nervousness or stress and shows conflict between the physical environment and his internal emotional turmoil.

Extract 3

"However, as human beings go, you are not too bad. I mean, you are a good man. But you have a major fault. You are much too meek and mild. That is why you have made so little progress in life. You must always speak up against injustice, and protest if anyone hurts or insults you without any provocation. To take things quietly is wrong, not just for man, but for any creature anywhere."

(i) **What does Ang think about Bonku Babu as a person? (3)**

Ans. Ang thinks that Bonku Babu is a good man but he is too meek and mild, which is why he has not made much progress in life.

(ii) **Identify the major fault that Ang points out about Bonku Babu? What does this suggest about personal growth? (3)**

Ans. Ang points out that Bonku Babu is too meek and mild, and does things that other people say without asking questions.

This suggests that personal growth requires confidence, the ability to voice ones thoughts, and the courage to challenge injustice. Ang suggests that without this, one might be unable to make progress in life.

(iii) **What does Ang advise Bonku Babu to do when someone insults or hurts him? (3)**

Ans. Ang advises Bonku Babu to speak up against injustice and protest if anyone hurts or insults him, instead of taking things quietly.

(iv) **According to Ang, why is it wrong to take things quietly? (3)**

Ans. According to Ang, it is wrong to take things quietly because it is not just humans but all creatures who should stand up against injustice and not accept being wronged without protest.

(v) **How does Ang's advice aim to change Bonku Babu's attitude towards life? (4)**

Ans. Ang's advice aims to help Bonku Babu become more assertive and confident, encouraging him to stand up for himself and not let others treat him unfairly. This would lead to Bonku Babu making more progress in life.

Extract 4

'There were billions and billions of people in the world. But who got the chance to have this wonderful experience? Bonkubihari Datta, teacher of geography and Bengali in the Kankurgachhi Village Primary School. No one else. From today, at least in this particular matter, he was unique, in the whole wide world. Bonku Babu realised that he was no longer walking. With a spring in every step, he was actually dancing.'

(i) **Analyse why Bonku Babu feels unique after his experience with Ang? (3)**

Ans. Bonku Babu felt unique because, out of billions of people, he was the only one who had the chance to experience the extraordinary adventure with Ang, making him feel special and different from everyone else.

(ii) **How did Bonku Babu's physical movement change after meeting Ang? (3)**

Ans. After meeting Ang, Bonku Babu's physical movement changed from walking to dancing. He felt full of energy and was more confident and joyful.

(iii) **Bonku Babu's physical movement changed. What does suggest about his emotional state? (3)**

Ans. Bonku Babu's change in physical movement suggests that he was feeling energised and confident after his unique experience with Ang. His lively and joyful steps reflect his newfound self-confidence and happiness.

(iv) **How does Bonku Babu's sense of being special relate to the theme of the story? (3)**

Ans. Bonku Babu's sense of uniqueness highlights the theme of personal transformation.

His feeling of being special represents how his encounter with Ang has positively changed his perception of himself.

(v) **Explore how the creature's advice affected Bonku Babu? (4)**

How does this moment in the story contribute to Bonku Babu's character development?

Ans. Ang's advice made Bonku Babu realise the importance of standing up for himself, being confident, and speaking out against injustice.

This moment makes a significant shift in Bonku Babu's character development.

His meeting with Ang leads to his transformation and he now feels self empowered. He goes from being a quiet, self-doubting person to someone who is confident and assertive.

Extract 5

"Friends! I have great pleasure in telling you that this is the last time you will see me at your meetings. The only reason I am here today is simply that I would like to tell you a few truths before I go. Number one - this is for all of you - you all speak a great deal of absolute rubbish. Only idiots talk of things they don't know anything about. Number two - this is for Chandi Babu - at your age, hiding other people's shoes and umbrellas is not just childish, but totally stupid and wrong."

(i) **What is Bonku Babu announcing to his friends in the extract? (3)**

Ans. Bonku Babu is announcing that he will no longer attend their meetings and is saying goodbye to them. This shows a major shift in his behaviour, as he is usually a quiet and reserved person.

(ii) **Explain how Bonku Babu describes the conversations at the meetings. (3)**

Ans. Bonku Babu describes the conversations at the meetings as 'absolute rubbish'. He criticises villagers for talking about things they don't understand, calling them idiots for discussing topics without knowledge or proper understanding.

(iii) **Why does Bonku Babu call Chandi Babu's actions childish and wrong? (3)**

Ans. Bonku Babu calls Chandi Babu's actions childish and wrong because at his age, it is immature to be involved in such acts. Bonku Babu believes that such actions are not only foolish but also morally wrong, reflecting his newfound assertiveness and confidence.

(iv) **Describe the attitude the Bonku Babu has towards the villagers in this extract? What is the change in his behaviour? (3)**

Ans. Bonku Babu's attitude towards the villagers in this extract is one of criticism. Bonku Babu has moved from being a quiet, reserved man to someone who speaks for himself confidently. He boldly criticises his friends for their meaningless conversations and even calls out Chandi Babu for his childish behaviour.

His speech reflects his transformation from being meek and mild to someone who is willing to stand up for what he believes is right.

(v) **How does Bonku Babu's speech reflect his transformation? (4)**

Ans. Bonku Babu's speech shows a significant transformation in his character. Previously he was a meek and mild person. However, he now speaks out with confidence, criticising the behaviour of the villagers.

His transformation is a result of the advice given by Ang which encouraged him to speak up against injustice and not tolerate insults. This change reflects his newfound self-confidence and independence.

Extract 6

"In the same instant, the cup fell from Ramkanai's hand, shattering to pieces, and splattering hot tea on most of the others."

(i) How does Ramkanai's reaction to Bonku Babu's speech reflect the mood of the villagers? (3)

Ans. Ramkanai drops the cup because he is surprised and shocked by Bonku Babu's sudden confidence. This shows how the villagers are not used to Bonku Babu speaking up.

(ii) What does the moment when the cup shatters symbolise about Bonku Babu's transformation? (3)

Ans. The broken cup represents a change. Just like the cup breaks, Bonku Babu's new confidence shakes up the village. It challenges the villagers to think differently.

(iii) Analyse the tone of the story when Bonku Babu first encounters Ang. How does it change as the story progresses? (3)

Ans. The tone is initially mysterious and curious when Bonku Babu first meets Ang.
As the story progresses, it becomes more intense and assertive after he learns to speak for himself.

(iv) How does the mood shift when Bonku Babu sees the strange creature? (3)

Ans. The mood changes from calm to eerie and tense.
Bonku Babu feels strange experiences, like the ringing in his ears and the sensation of being immobile. This creates a sense of unease and mystery in the atmosphere.

(v) What is the atmosphere like when Bonku Babu realises the importance of standing up for himself? (4)

Ans. The atmosphere becomes strong and empowering.
After receiving advice from Ang, Bonku Babu feels more confident. The mood shifts from confusion to clarity as he understands his own potential to stand up against injustice.

02

OLIVER ASKS FOR MORE

Charles Dickens

Introduction

Oliver Asks for More is an excerpt from Charles Dickens' novel Oliver Twist, which was published in 1838. The story is set in Victorian England, a time when poor children suffered terrible hardships, especially in workhouses. This story symbolises resistance against oppression and highlights the inhumanity of the workhouse system. It marks the beginning of Oliver's struggles and sets the tone for the exploration of ideas of poverty, injustice and resilience.

About the Story

This story is based on the classic story 'Oliver Twist'. Oliver Twist is born in a workhouse which is a sad and cold place. His mother dies moments after his birth, leaving him without love or care. The boys in the workhouse, including Oliver, were treated badly. They were not given proper food.

One day, when Oliver asks for more food, he is punished severely. He was locked in a dark room and beaten up by the officer. The boy is offered for adoption to anyone willing to pay five pounds.

Character Introduction

- **Oliver Twist** An orphan born in a workhouse, treated badly when he asked for more food.
- **Mr. Bumble** A strict workhouse official, who punishes Oliver for asking for more food and gives him the name 'Oliver Twist'.
- **The Doctor** A detached figure who attends to Oliver's dying mother and confirms her death shortly after giving birth.
- **The Old Woman** A kind but resigned figure who takes care of Oliver after his mother dies and dresses him in worn clothes.
- **Mr. Sowerberry** A coffin maker.

Story at a Glance

Oliver Twist is born in a workhouse in a small English town. Oliver's young mother, whose name is unknown, came to the workhouse in very poor condition. She gave birth to Oliver but sadly died. The doctor and an old woman observe that she has no wedding ring, thereby concluding her unmarried status. Oliver is left an orphan as they couldn't identify the background of the mother.

The orphaned Oliver is named by Mr. Bumble, an officer. He says he follows a strict alphabetical system for naming orphans. He named the last one Swubble. Oliver grows up pale as he is malnourished. He is made to live under harsh conditions in the workhouse. The children receive limited portions of food, which leaves them hungry. They clean their soup bowls with spoons until they shine, emphasising their desperate state.

One evening, the starving boys decide that someone should ask for more food. They choose Oliver to do the same. After finishing their meal, Oliver approaches the master and says, "Please, sir, I want some more." This bold request shocks the master, who hits Oliver and calls for Mr. Bumble. Oliver is accused of not following orders.

Oliver is locked in a dark room for a week as punishment and is beaten daily by Mr. Bumble. The workhouse officials put up a notice offering five pounds to anyone willing to take Oliver off their hands. Oliver feels scared, hungry and lives in sadness.

Outside the workhouse, Mr. Bumble encounters Mr. Sowerberry, a coffin-maker who supplies coffins for the workhouse's deceased. Mr. Bumble inquires if Mr. Sowerberry knows anyone willing to adopt Oliver. He indirectly suggests that the Coffin maker should adopt the boy.

Vocab Vault

Workhouse A place where poor people who had no money or home lived and worked in exchange for food and shelter.

Seize Take hold of something suddenly or forcefully.

Coffins Boxes in which dead bodies are placed for burial or cremation.

Theme

One of the central themes of the story is the exploitation and mistreatment of the poor in society. The atmosphere of the workhouse is presented as harsh where basic needs like food are not provided adequately, highlighting themes of social injustice and class divide. Other themes such as injustice and cruelty of the workhouse system, lack of morality, dehumanisation and struggle for survival are presented.

Message Conveyed by the Story

The story highlights that society often neglects and mistreats the poor and vulnerable. However, even in the face of hardship, innocent people like Oliver, deserve kindness and a chance for a better life. The story highlights the importance of compassion, justice, and the need for a change in society.

Style Tone and Mood

- **Style** The writing is clear and direct and use simple words to explain the story.
- **Tone** The tone is sympathetic and sorrowful for Oliver and rest of the kids.
- **Mood** The mood is melancholic, reflecting the harsh conditions Oliver faces. No trace of monotonous.

Title

The title 'Oliver Asks for More' is appropriate as it shows a key moment when Oliver, an orphan, asks for more food in the workhouse. He is punished for the same. It highlights how he's just trying to survive in a world that doesn't care about him. The title also symbolises Oliver's innocence and his desire for something in the unjust world.

Figures of Speech

- **Hyperbole** *(Exaggeration)* 'He asked for more? I cannot believe it. One day, they will hang the boy.' 'The master hit Oliver with his spoon!'. 'They posted a notice on the workhouse gate saying that if anyone wanted the boy, they could take him.'
- **Imagery** 'The doctor put the child's cold white lips onto the woman's face and she held the child one last time in her arms before passing away.' 'She had walked a lot and her shoes were in bad shape with holes.' 'He was taken away and shut in a dark room.'
- **Metaphor** 'The world would have no pity or love for him.' 'His life in the workhouse was miserable.' 'The workhouse was a prison without bars.'
- **Personification** 'The master's face went very pale.' 'The fire crackled as the old woman sat down on a chair in front of it.' 'The notice on the gate called out to anyone willing to take the boy.'
- **Irony** 'The master was a fat, healthy man but he went very pale.' 'They gave the boys just three meals of thin soup every day-and a small piece of bread on Sundays.' 'A big pot of soup stood in the hall, but each boy could only have one small bowl.'
- **Symbolism** 'The large hall with a big pot where soup was served.' 'Mr. Bumble's stick, raised towards the notice.' 'Oliver was dressed in very old clothes reserved for babies born in the workhouse.'

EXAM ORIENTED QUESTIONS

TYPE - 1 Multiple Choice Questions

01 Mark

Q.1 Oliver Twist was born ....
(a) in a hospital (b) in a castle
(c) in a workhouse (d) in a church

Q.2 Oliver's mother said .... before she died?
(a) "Take care of my child"
(b) "Let me see the child and die."
(c) "I want to live for my child."
(d) "Where is the doctor?"

Q.3 Why did the doctor think Oliver's mother was unmarried?
(a) She was too young.
(b) She had no wedding ring.
(c) She admitted it before dying.
(d) The old woman told him.

Q.4 Identify the tone of the story during Oliver's birth scene.
(a) Joyful and celebratory (b) Somber and melancholic
(c) Hopeful and optimistic (d) Energetic and lively

Q.5 The absence of Oliver's mother's wedding ring symbolises ....
(a) society's judgement of unmarried mothers
(b) ger poverty and desperation
(c) the mystery of her background
(d) her rejection of marriage

Q.6 Who named Oliver Twist?
(a) The old woman (b) Mr. Sowerberry
(c) Mr. Bumble (d) The doctor

Q.7 What system did Mr. Bumble use to name the workhouse children?
(a) By their date of birth (b) By their appearance
(c) Alphabetical order (d) Random names

Q.8 Identify what the line "Let me see the child and die" imply about Oliver's mother.
(a) She was hopeful about her future.
(b) She had accepted her death and wanted to see her child before passing.
(c) She wanted to name her child before dying.
(d) She was determined to recover and raise her child.

Q.9 "The child was an orphan, born into a world which had no love or pity for him"
What does this line imply about Oliver's circumstances?
(a) He was cared for by kind strangers.
(b) He was expected to find his own way.
(c) Society was supportive of orphaned children.
(d) His life would be filled with hardship and suffering.

Q.10 Explore what the treatment of Oliver in the workhouse reveals about society's attitude toward the poor in the 19th century?
(a) Sympathy and support for the poor
(b) Respect and admiration for the poor
(c) A desire to uplift the poor through education
(d) Indifference and neglect of the poor

Q.11 The master's reaction to Oliver's request for more soup criticises the authority figures.
(a) By portraying the master as a kind but firm leader
(b) By showing the master's calm and rational response
(c) By emphasising the master's cruelty and lack of compassion.
(d) By depicting the master as a victim of the system

Q.12 If Mr. Sowerberry adopts Oliver, how might his life change?
(a) He would have a chance to live a better life outside the workhouse.
(b) He would face more hardships as an apprentice to a coffin-maker.
(c) He would become a wealthy and respected citizen.
(d) He would immediately find a loving family.

Q.13 Select the option that shows the correct relationship between statements (1) and (2).
Statement 1 Oliver's mother arrived at the workhouse in good health.
Statement 2 The doctor and the old woman were present during Oliver's birth.
(a) Both statements are true.
(b) Both statements are false.
(c) Statement 1 is true, and Statement 2 is false.
(d) Statement 1 is false, and Statement 2 is true.

Q.14 Select the option that shows the correct relationship between statements (1) and (2).
Statement 1 Mr. Bumble named the workhouse children using an alphabetical system.
Statement 2 Oliver's name was chosen randomly by the old woman.
(a) Both statements are true.
(b) Both statements are false.

(c) Statement 1 is true, and Statement 2 is false.
(d) Statement 1 is false, and Statement 2 is true.

Q.15 What does Mr. Bumble's naming system for orphaned children suggests about his character?
(a) He is highly empathetic toward the children.
(b) He views the children as insignificant.
(c) He is deeply concerned about the children's future.
(d) He is creative and thoughtful in his approach.

Q.16 What does the line "Please, sir, I want some more" imply about Oliver's character?
(a) He was a rebellious and bold child.
(b) He was brave enough to challenge authority despite his fear.
(c) He wanted to cause trouble in the workhouse.
(d) He believed the workhouse would give him more food.

Q.17 The punishment for Oliver after he asked for more food was?
(a) He was locked in a dark room.
(b) He was expelled from the workhouse.
(c) He was given extra chores.
(d) He was denied food.

Q.18 Why is Oliver locked in a dark room after asking for more food?
(a) To punish him for breaking the workhouse rules.
(b) To protect him from the other boys.
(c) To give him time to reflect on his actions.
(d) Because there was no space in the dining hall.

Q.19 Highlight the significance of Oliver being offered for adoption with a five-pound reward.
(a) It shows that the workhouse is generous with its funds.
(b) It highlights how little value is placed on Oliver's life.
(c) It demonstrates that Oliver is seen as a valuable member of society.
(d) It suggests that many people are eager to adopt children.

Q.20 How does the atmosphere in the workhouse dining hall reflect the boys' living conditions?
(a) Cheerful and supportive, showing the boys are well cared for.
(b) Gloomy and oppressive, reflecting hunger and neglect.
(c) Chaotic and disorganised, showing a lack of rules.
(d) Warm and inviting, representing community and friendship.

Q.21 Identify the theme that is evident in Mr. Bumble's attitude while offering Oliver for adoption with five pounds?
(a) Treating people like objects that can be bought.
(b) The importance of kindness and generosity.
(c) The value of children in society.
(d) The rise of hope in bleak circumstances.

Q.22 What is the correct sequence of events in Oliver Twist after he asks for more food?
1. Oliver is taken away and locked in a dark room.
2. Mr. Bumble offers Oliver for adoption with a five-pound reward.
3. The master is shocked and calls for help.
4. Oliver asks for more soup in front of the master.
(a) 1, 2, 3, 4 (b) 3, 4, 1, 2
(c) 4, 3, 1, 2 (d) 2, 4, 3, 1

Q.23 'The bowls never needed washing, because the boys cleaned them with their spoons until they shone.'
This line means that ....
(a) the boys enjoyed washing their bowls
(b) the boys never got enough to eat
(c) the boys wanted to keep their bowls shiny
(d) the boys did not enjoy washing bowls

Q.24 Which of the following statements best reflects the irony in Oliver's request for more?
(a) The workhouse was meant to help the poor but it denied them food.
(b) The workhouse master expected gratitude but received a complaint.
(c) Oliver's request was reasonable but it was treated as a crime.
(d) All of the above

Answers

1. (c)	2. (b)	3. (b)	4. (b)	5. (a)	6. (c)	7. (c)	8. (b)	9. (d)	10. (d)
11. (c)	12. (b)	13. (d)	14. (c)	15. (b)	16. (b)	17. (a)	18. (a)	19. (d)	20. (b)
21. (a)	22. (c)	23. (b)	24. (d)						

TYPE - 2 Extract Based Questions

16 Marks

Extract 1

"Oliver Twist's mother, a young woman, lay ill in bed. A doctor and an old woman stood by her side. She lifted her head from the pillow. "Let me see the child and die." **(ICSE Specimen 2024)**

(i) **Who is the 'child' referred to in the above extract? What might have been the young woman's feelings when she said this?** **(3)**

Ans. The child referred to in the above extract is Oliver Twist, the newborn son of the young woman.

When the young woman said, "Let me see the child and die," she might have been feeling a mixture of emotions such as love, sorrow and despair.

Her words suggest she had accepted her destiny and felt deeply sad about leaving her child behind in a harsh world.

(ii) **How did the young woman who gave birth to the child end up in the workhouse?** **(3)**

Ans. The young woman who gave birth to Oliver Twist ended up in the workhouse due to poverty. In the 19th-century Victorian society, the poor often had no other option but to go to the workhouse for shelter and support. Her situation reflects the harsh conditions faced by many poor people during that time.

(iii) **Who named the young child? What method did he use to do this?** **(3)**

Ans. The young child was named by Mr. Bumble, the workhouse official. Mr. Bumble followed a specific procedure for naming the babies in the workhouse, where each new child was given a name in order from A to Z.

When asked about the naming, Mr. Bumble casually mentioned that he had named the previous child 'Swubble'. This shows that orphan children were treated as mere numbers rather than humans.

(iv) **How did the old woman take care of the child? What does this tell us about her nature?** **(3)**

Ans. The old woman took care of the child by dressing him in very old clothes used for babies born in the workhouse. She dressed him carefully after his mother passed away.

This tells us that the old woman was helpless in the situation. Her actions reflect a sense of duty rather than emotional attachment, as she did what was expected in taking care of the child.

(v) **At the end of the story, a notice was posted outside the workhouse gate. What did it say?**

Why do you think the reward was mentioned on the notice? **(4)**

Ans. The notice posted outside the workhouse gate offered a reward of five pounds to anyone who would take Oliver Twist. The reward was mentioned on the notice because Oliver was seen as a burden to the work house and they were looking to get rid of him.

The five pounds was a bribe to encourage someone to take the child away from the workhouse, despite the fact that he was an orphan. It reflects the harsh nature of the society at the time where orphans were treated as commodities.

Extract 2

"The doctor put the child in her arms. She pressed her cold white lips to its face, and then fell back. She is dead, said the doctor. 'Yes, poor dear,' said the old woman, as she took the child away from its dead mother, Poor dear!"

(i) **Who is 'her' in the extract? What happens to 'her' after the child is placed in her arms?** **(3)**

Ans. 'Her' refers to the woman who is the mother of the child. After the child is placed in her arms, she presses her 'cold white lips' to its face, indicating a final moment of love or connection.

This suggests that the woman dies shortly after holding her child, as indicated by the doctor's statement, 'She is dead'.

(ii) **What do the doctor's and the old woman's responses to the woman's death reveal about their attitudes toward her death?** **(3)**

Ans. The doctor's response, 'She is dead', is a very direct and clinical response. It shows a detached and professional attitude towards death. In contrast, the old woman's response, 'Poor dear', shows a sense of sympathy and compassion.

The old woman seems to feel sorrow for the woman, but the doctor remains emotionless and focused on the practical aspect of the situation.

(iii) **Comment on the author's narration based on the story.** **(3)**

Ans. The author's narration in the story is very straightforward. The way the doctor reacts with a simple 'She is dead' creates a sense of emotional distance, while the old woman's 'Poor dear' adds a touch of sympathy.

The author uses simple but powerful imagery, like 'cold white lips' and 'fell back', to show the death of the woman.

The tone of the narration is direct and to-the-point, reflecting the cold reality of the situation, while still hinting at the sorrow and helplessness of the people around her.

(iv) **What does the extract indicate about the condition of Victorian society? (3)**

Ans. The extract highlights the harsh and indifferent nature of Victorian society, particularly their behaviour towards the poor. The doctor's clinical response to the woman's death reflects the lack of compassion and dehumanising attitude towards the lower section of the society.

The mention of the workhouse and the fact that the woman was in such a poor situation shows how society failed to support individuals who were in poverty, especially women.

(v) **What does the old woman's words 'Poor dear' suggest about her understanding of the situation? (4)**

Ans. The old woman's words 'Poor dear' show that she feels sorry for the woman who has died. However, her response suggests that she is helpless.

She understands that the woman's situation is sad, but she might not be able to do anything to help. The words could also reflect that death is common in the workhouse.

Extract 3

"The child was an orphan, born into a world which had no love or pity for him. No one was able to discover who the baby's father was, or what his mother's name was."

(i) **What does the phrase "born into a world which had no love or pity for him" suggest? (3)**

Ans. The phrase suggests that the child's life began in a cold and uncaring environment. It refers to the society where he is born and likely to face neglect and hardship. It highlights the lack of compassion or support for him in the world he was born into. It conveys a sense of abandonment, not only from his family but also from society at large.

(ii) **Why is the child's identity described as unknown? What does it indicate? (3)**

Ans. The child's identity is described as unknown because his father was never identified and his mother died shortly after his birth. The description emphasises the child's abandonment. The fact that no one knows his parents' identities reflects the deprivation he would face in this world.

(iii) **How does the child's lack of identity and family background reflect the social conditions of the time? (3)**

Ans. The child's lack of identity and family background reflects the harsh social conditions of the time, particularly for orphans and the poor. It shows that society was having no sympathy for the needs of the poor, and orphans were often left without care or hope, mirroring the coldness of Victorian society.

Although the ones in power created provisions such as workhouses, the condition was miserable.

(iv) **Dickens attempts to present the class difference of the 19th century Victorian society. Justify. (3)**

Ans. Dickens highlights the harsh reality of class differences of 19th century Victorian society. He portrays the child as an orphan, with no known father and a dead mother. The child's identity being unknown reflects how the lower class, especially orphans, were forgotten.

The workhouse, where the child is born and the lack of sympathy shown by the characters reflect the social divide of that time.

(v) **Describe the intention of Dickens behind this story. (4)**

Ans. The intention of Charles Dickens behind this story is to throw light on the social injustices faced by the poor in Victorian society. Dickens attempts to critique the indifference and neglect shown by society towards the poor.

By highlighting the class divide, the exploitation of the poor, and the lack of compassion, Dickens aims to make the readers empathise. He uses his characters and their experiences to emphasise the need for change and a more compassionate society.

Extract 4

"In the evening, the boys sat down at the tables. The master stood by the pot, and the soup was served. It disappeared quickly. The boys whispered and made signs to Oliver. He stood up from the table and went to the master, with his bowl and spoon in his hands. 'Please, sir,' he said, 'I want some more!'

The master was a fat, healthy man, but he went very pale. He looked with surprise at the small boy.

(i) **Where were the boys sitting when the soup was served? What did Oliver do after the soup was served? Were the boys well fed? (3)**

Ans. The boys were sitting at tables in the workhouse when the soup was served.

After the soup was served, Oliver stood up from the table, went to the master with his bowl and spoon, and asked for more soup.

The boys at the workhouse were not well fed and were given a small portion that wasn't enough.

(ii) **Why do you think Oliver chose to ask for more soup despite knowing the consequences? (3)**

Ans. Oliver may have been so hungry and desperate that he took the risk of asking for more soup, knowing it could lead to punishment.

The other children had decided to ask for more, and Oliver was chosen to speak on behalf of all of them. It reflects his desire for something better, even at the cost of punishment.

(iii) **What does the reaction of the other boys to Oliver's actions suggest about their situation? (3)**

Ans. The other boys whispering and making signs to Oliver indicates that they are accustomed to the harsh conditions of the workhouse and are perhaps too fearful to ask for more themselves.

It shows their deprivation. Their lives are governed by fear and survival. The workhouse was like a prison where children feared to speak anything.

(iv) **How does the master's reaction to Oliver's request for more soup reflect the attitudes of the authorities in the workhouse? (3)**

Ans. The master's reaction, which is to look at Oliver with surprise and then react with anger, reflects the lack of compassion and authority's harshness toward the poor.

It shows how the authorities in the workhouse viewed the children as undeserving of any kindness or care. The children were not even fed properly and the authorities didn't seem to care.

(v) **Draw a contrast between the appearance of the authority and that of the children at the workhouse. What does it indicate? (4)**

Ans. The contrast between the master and the children in the workhouse highlights the social inequality.

The master is depicted as a 'fat, healthy man', symbolising his comfort and authority, while the children, like Oliver, are malnourished and pale.

This contrast emphasises the harsh class divide and exploitation of the poor in Victorian society.

Extract 5

"He took Oliver away and shut him in a dark room. The next morning a notice appeared on the workhouse gate. Five pounds were offered to anybody who would take Oliver Twist. Oliver was a prisoner in that cold, dark room for a whole week. Every morning he was taken outside to wash, and Mr. Bumble beat him with a stick."

(i) **Where was Oliver taken? What was his condition during the week? (3)**

Ans. Oliver was taken to a dark room where he remained locked up for a whole week. He was kept as a prisoner in the cold and dark room, only being taken outside in the mornings to wash.

(ii) **What action was taken by the authorities regarding Oliver? (3)**

Ans. The authorities took the step of posting a notice on the workhouse gate, offering a reward of five pounds to anyone who would take Oliver Twist away. They did not care about the well-being of the child, treating him like an object to be sold.

It reflects a cold, heartless system where children were not seen as individuals, but rather as commodities.

(iii) **The way Oliver is treated in the dark room shows how harsh life is in the workhouse. Justify. (3)**

Ans. A workhouse was a type of institution in 19th century Britain where poor people, including orphans and the elderly, were sent to live and work. Oliver's time in the dark room and the beatings he received from Mr. Bumble show how badly he was treated in the workhouse.

It highlights how cruel and harsh life was for children in workhouses. They were often punished and neglected, with little care or kindness, reflecting the unfair and tough conditions of that time.

(iv) **What does Mr. Bumble's behaviour toward Oliver indicate about his character? (3)**

Ans. Mr. Bumble's behaviour of locking Oliver in a dark room and beating him with a stick suggests that he is a cruel and heartless figure. He uses his authority over poor and orphan children without compassion for their well-being.

Mr. Bumble can be seen as a representation of the larger picture of the society who mistreated low class people.

(v) **What does the tone of the extract reveal about Oliver's situation at the workhouse? (4)**

Ans. The tone of the extract is dark and cruel, highlighting the harsh treatment. Words like 'dark room', 'prisoner', and 'beat him with a stick' convey punishment, cruelty, and neglect, reflecting the dehumanising conditions of the workhouse and the harshness of society towards orphan children.

Extract 6

"Mr. Sowerberry was a tall, thin man who wore black clothes and made coffins. Many of his coffins were for the poor people who died in the workhouse. "I have prepared the coffins for the two women who died last night," he said to Mr. Bumble. "Good, said Mr Bumble. You will be rich one day, Mr. Sowerberry! Do you know anybody who wants a boy? And five pounds?" He raised his stick and pointed to the notice on the gate."

(i) What was Mr. Sowerberry's job? What does the mention of the coffins for poor people suggest about the society in the story? **(3)**

Ans. Mr. Sowerberry was a coffin maker, who often made coffins for poor people who died in the workhouse. The mention of coffins for poor people suggests that the society in the story is harsh and uncaring, especially towards the poor. Even in death, the poor are not given respect or dignity.

(ii) Why do you think Mr. Bumble tells Mr. Sowerberry, "You will be rich one day"? **(3)**

Ans. Mr. Bumble says this because he sees Mr. Sowerberry's work as a profitable business. He likely thinks that the more people die, especially poor people in the workhouse. Additionally, he is indirectly suggesting that Mr. Sowerberry takes Oliver away and collects the five pounds offered for him, indicating that taking Oliver would be a way to make money.

(iii) Analyse the theme shown in Mr. Bumble and Mr. Sowerberry's conversation about Oliver? **(3)**

Ans. The theme of treating poor people badly is shown in their conversation. Mr. Bumble and Mr. Sowerberry see Oliver not as a person, but as something they can use to make money. This shows how poor people were often treated unfairly in Victorian society.

(iv) What does the notice on the gate offer? Why is it important? **(3)**

Ans. The notice on the gate offers five pounds for anyone who will take Oliver Twist.

This is important because it shows how little value society places on Oliver's life, like a simple transaction. Dickens attempts to critique 19th century society where people considered poor as an object.

(v) Explain how Mr. Bumble and Mr. Sowerberry seem to view Oliver? What does the conversation reveal about their characters? **(4)**

Ans. Mr. Bumble and Mr. Sowerberry view Oliver as a commodity, something to be traded. They talk about him as if he has no value. This reflects how society, particularly in the context of the workhouse, often regarded the poor as a commodity. The conversation shows that both Mr. Bumble and Mr. Sowerberry are unsympathetic to the well-being of others. They seem focused on money and their own gain rather than showing any care or kindness towards Oliver or the poor people.

03

THE MODEL MILLIONAIRE

Oscar Wilde

Introduction

The Model Millionaire is a witty and ironic tale written by Oscar Wilde, known for his sharp wit and love of beauty. The story is about generosity and unexpected fortune. Wilde also critiques the superficiality of high society, where status and wealth determine one's worth. The story highlights ideas of kindness, appearances versus reality and the unexpected rewards of good deeds. With its simple yet impactful storytelling, *The Model Millionaire* remains an engaging tale with a timeless moral lesson.

About the Story

The story is about Hughie Erskine who was a kind but poor young man in love with Laura. Her father demanded £10,000 for their marriage. One day, Hughie met an old beggar posing for his artist friend's painting and gave him a sovereign out of kindness. The beggar was actually a wealthy man, Baron Hausberg. Impressed by Hughie's generosity, Baron gifted him £10,000, allowing Hughie to marry Laura.

Character Introduction

- **Hughie Erskine** A charming but poor young man, in love with Laura Merton.
- **Laura Merton** Hughie's love interest, daughter of a retired Colonel.
- **Alan Trevor** Hughie's close friend, a talented painter with a unique perspective on art.
- **Baron Hausberg** A wealthy millionaire who pretends to be a beggar for an art project.

Story at a Glance

Hughie Erskine is a young man who is good-looking but poor. He loves Laura Merton but her father, a wealthy man, says Hughie must have £10,000 before he can marry her. Hughie worries about how he can get the money.

One day, while heading to see Laura, Hughie stops by to visit his good friend Alan Trevor, a talented artist. In Trevor's studio, there is a beggar who is posing for a painting. The beggar looks very poor and Hughie feels sorry for him. He offers the beggar some old clothes, thinking he might need them. Trevor, on the other hand, finds the beggar's rags to be ideal for the painting, and he calls them 'romance'.

Trevor is focused on capturing the 'picturesqueness' of the beggar, as he sees it as an essential part of the art. Trevor explains that as an artist, his job is to show the world as it is, not try to change it. He believes artists should focus on their art, not worry about fixing the world's problems.

When Hughie finds out that the beggar model is actually the wealthy Baron Hausberg, he is embarrassed by his earlier generosity. Baron was so impressed by Hughie's kindness and generosity that he decided to reward him. He gave an envelope which contained a cheque for £10,000, a wedding present for Hughie and Laura.

In the final part of the story, Hughie and Laura get married, with Alan Trevor as the best man. At the wedding, Alan jokes about how rare it is to find a rich person who is also a model for art. The story ends with humour and shows how Hughie's kindness leads to unexpected rewards.

Vocab Vault

Bequeathed Left by will

Pekoe A light quality black tea

Freckled Covered with small pale spots on the face.

Buoyant Cheerful and happy; able to float.

Wizened Wrinkled with age

Forlorn Sorrowful

Sovereign A British gold coin or a term for a ruler or monarch.

Hansoms A horse-drawn carriage

Extravagance Lavish spending

Wretch A person who is in a very poor or unhappy condition.

Picturesqueness The quality of being visually attractive or charming, often in an unusual way.

Relentless Cruel

Commissioned To formally order or request the creation of something.

Theme

The story 'The Model Millionaire' highlights themes of kindness, generosity and appearance. The story shows how true wealth lies in being kind and helping others, even when you have little to give. It also teaches that appearances can be misleading, as the beggar turns out to be a wealthy baron. Oscar Wilde uses humour and irony to show that good deeds can lead to unexpected rewards.

Message conveyed by the story

The message of the story is that true kindness and generosity come from unexpected places. It reminds us that wealth and status do not define a person's character. Real wealth is not just about money but being generous.

Style Tone and Mood

- **Style** The story uses simple and clear language with some humour.
- **Tone** The tone is cheerful with a touch of kindness.
- **Mood** The mood is happy and positive.

Title

'The Model Millionaire' is an appropriate title for the story as it highlights the generosity of a rich man. Baron is both a model for Trevor's painting and a great example of a kind and generous person. The title shows that real richness is not just about money but about helping others and having a good heart.

Figures of Speech

- **Irony** "Poor Hughie! Intellectually, we must admit, he was not of much importance." "Millionaire models are rare enough; but, by Jove, model millionaires are rarer still!" "The Baron made a speech at the wedding breakfast."
- **Hyperbole** "He could buy all London to-morrow without overdrawing his account." "Men who are dandies and women who are darlings rule the world, at least they should do so." "The best thing I can do is to go to bed."
- **Metaphor** "His face is his fortune." "The only people a painter should know are people who are bete and beautiful." "An artist's heart is his head."
- **Satire** "Unless one is wealthy there is no use in being a charming fellow." "It is better to have a permanent income than to be fascinating." "Few people escape that nowadays."
- **Personification** "The old model was quite interested in her." "The sovereign seemed to burn in Hughie's pocket." "His face told a thousand stories."
- **Simile** "A wizened old man, with a face like wrinkled parchment." "He was as popular with men as he was with women." "His beard was like a red ragged curtain."
- **Paradox** "An artist's heart is his head." "Men who are dandies and women who are darlings rule the world, at least they should do so." "Art almost attains to the dignity of manual labour."
- **Epigram** "It is better to have a permanent income than to be fascinating." "Romance is the privilege of the rich, not the profession of the unemployed." "Few people escape that nowadays."

EXAM ORIENTED QUESTIONS

TYPE - 1 Multiple Choice Questions

01 Mark

Q.1 Hughie feels sorry for the beggar at the beginning of the story because ....
(a) the beggar is too old and frail.
(b) the beggar's clothes are in very poor condition.
(c) the beggar is asking for money.
(d) the beggar is causing trouble on the street.

Q.2 What does Trevor's response about the beggar's clothes reveal about his perspective on poverty?
(a) He believes poverty is a tragic and unfortunate situation.
(b) He sees poverty as a source of inspiration and beauty for art.
(c) He thinks the beggar should wear nicer clothes.
(d) He believes poverty is a sign of laziness.

Q.3 Hughie offers .... to the beggar?
(a) money (b) food
(c) old clothes (d) a place to stay

Q.4 "What you call rags I call romance." Who says this line, and to whom?
(a) Hughie to the beggar
(b) Baron Hausberg to Hughie
(c) Trevor to Hughie
(d) The beggar to Trevor

Q.5 Who was the beggar in reality?
(a) An actual beggar
(b) Alan Trevor's assistant
(c) A model for Alan's painting
(d) A millionaire named Baron Hausberg

Q.6 What does Trevor say about the artist's heart?
(a) It is filled with kindness.
(b) It is the same as his emotions.
(c) An artist's heart is his head.
(d) An artist has no heart.

Q.7 How does Hughie's reaction to the beggar's clothes differ from Trevor's?
(a) Hughie wants to give the beggar clothes, while Trevor appreciates the beggar's appearance as it is.
(b) Hughie criticises the beggar's rags, while Trevor criticises Hughie.
(c) Hughie wants to help the beggar by offering money, while Trevor offers advice.
(d) Hughie is indifferent, while Trevor is excited.

Q.8 Why does Trevor say, "What you call rags I call romance"?
(a) To explain why he likes the beggar's clothes.
(b) To criticise Hughie for his views on poverty.
(c) To suggest that the beggar should wear better clothes.
(d) To express that poverty is beautiful for artists.

Q.9 What lesson does Hughie learn after the beggar's true identity is revealed?
(a) Appearances can be deceiving.
(b) Rich people do not need help.
(c) Poverty is always heartbreaking.
(d) Artists always tell the truth.

Q.10 Alan Trevor's view of art influenced his actions in the story as ....
(a) he is motivated by wealth and status in his art.
(b) he believes that artists should only paint what they see, without trying to change reality.
(c) he feels obligated to help the beggar financially.
(d) he dislikes the idea of using real people as models for his paintings.

Q.11 Which of the following is not performed by Hughie in the story?
(a) One morning, as he was on his way to Holland Park, he dropped in to see Alan Trevor.
(b) He walked across the studio and slipped the sovereign into the beggar's hand.
(c) He walked across the studio and stole a sovereign from the beggar's hand.
(d) He had gone on the Stock Exchange for six months.

Q.12 .... was written on the envelope given to Hughie by the Baron.
(a) "Thank you for your kindness, Hugh Erskine and Laura Merton"
(b) "A wedding present to Hugh Erskine and Laura Merton, from an old beggar"
(c) "Your painting payment, Hugh Erskine and Laura Merton"
(d) "From Alan Trevor"

Q.13 What motivates the Baron to give Hughie a wedding present?
(a) Hughie was kind to him.
(b) Baron wants to show off his wealth.

(c) He wants to be friends with Alan.
(d) He feels sorry for Hughie's poverty.

Q.14 Alan Trevor refers to the Baron as a 'model millionaire' ....
(a) because the Baron is both a millionaire and a model
(b) because the Baron agreed to pose for Trevor's painting
(c) because the Baron is a rare example of a millionaire who poses as a beggar
(d) because the Baron is very generous with his wealth

Q.15 What does the Baron's decision to give Hughie a gift suggest about his character?
(a) He is self-centered and only cares about his own interests.
(b) He is deeply moved by Hughie's kindness and wants to repay him.
(c) He wants to impress Alan Trevor with his wealth.
(d) He does not value wealth and gives it away freely.

Q.16 How effective is the story's twist at conveying the message about judging others based on appearances?
(a) It is very effective, as it highlights the unpredictability of people's true circumstances.
(b) It is ineffective, as it feels too unrealistic for the reader to believe.
(c) It is somewhat effective, but the reveal does not significantly impact the characters.
(d) It is unnecessary because the story would have worked without the twist.

Q.17 'Millionaire models', remarked Alan, 'are rare enough'. This indicates that ....
(a) millionaire models are rare and hence modelling does not pay well
(b) models who are always available, are poor
(c) it is hard to find models who are millionaires
(d) a model is a millionaire as models are costly

Q.18 The main message highlighted by the story is ....
(a) kindness and charity have their own rewards
(b) people change with money and fame
(c) people should not be judged by their appearance
(d) beauty, in whatever form you find, should be appreciated

Q.19 Select the option that shows the correct relationship between statements (1) and (2).
Statement 1 Hughie offers to help the beggar by giving him some old clothes.
Statement 2 Trevor mocks Hughie for his offer and praises the beggar's rags as 'picturesque'.
(a) Both statements are true.
(b) Both statements are false.
(c) Statement 1 is true, and Statement 2 is false.
(d) Statement 1 is false, and Statement 2 is true.

Q.20 What is the correct sequence of events when Hughie learns about the beggar's true identity?
1. The old man reveals he is from Baron Hausberg.
2. Hughie opens the letter and finds a cheque for £10,000.
3. Hughie apologises to the old man for his earlier comments.
4. The old man gives Hughie a letter from the Baron.

(a) 2, 1, 3, 4
(b) 1, 4, 3, 2
(c) 3, 4, 1, 2
(d) 4, 3, 1, 2

Answers

1. (b)	2. (b)	3. (c)	4. (c)	5. (d)	6. (c)	7. (a)	8. (d)	9. (a)	10. (b)
11. (b)	12. (b)	13. (a)	14. (c)	15. (b)	16. (a)	17. (c)	18. (c)	19. (a)	20. (b)

TYPE - 2 Extract Based Questions

16 Marks

Extract 1

"Unless one is wealthy there is no use in being a charming fellow. Romance is the privilege of the rich, not the profession of the unemployed. The poor should be practical and prosaic. It is better to have a permanent income than to be fascinating. These are the great truths of modern life which Hughie Erskine never realised."

(i) What are the 'great truths of modern life' that Hughie Erskine never realised, as mentioned in the passage? **(3)**

Ans. The great truths mentioned in the passage explain that having wealth is very important because it gives charm and attractiveness real value.

Romance, too, is seen as something that only rich people can truly enjoy since they have the time for it.

On the other hand, people who are poor need to focus on being practical and realistic in life. The poor should focus on earning a stable income for survival instead of worrying about being charming.

(ii) **Why does the author emphasise that the poor should be practical instead of charming or romantic?** **(3)**

Ans. The author believes that charm and romance are luxuries that require financial stability. The poor cannot afford these as they need to focus on securing a livelihood. The poor should be realistic about life's demands and not focus on being charming.

(iii) **If Hughie Erskine had understood the importance of having a permanent income, how might his life situation and relationships have been different?** **(3)**

Ans. In this case, Hughie might have focused on building a stable career and increasing his income which could have made him more financially secure. This might have also helped him get the approval of Laura's father for their relationship.

(iv) **How does the passage reflect societal attitudes towards wealth, charm and romance during the time it was written?** **(3)**

Ans. The passage shows that society considered wealth necessary to enjoy special things like charm and romance. It highlights the class divide, where the rich have the freedom to enjoy beauty, love, and other luxuries because they have money.

On the other hand, poor people have to focus on being practical and meeting their basic needs for survival. This shows a clear difference between the lives of the rich and the poor.

(v) **Why do you think Hughie failed to understand the importance of the 'great truths'? Do you believe his personality played a role in shaping his perspective?** **(4)**

Ans. Hughie Erskine failed to understand the 'great truths' about wealth and practicality because of his carefree and cheerful personality. He was charming and good-looking, which made him focus more on living in the moment rather than thinking about long-term financial stability.

He inherited little money and had no serious profession but his charm often allowed him to get by without facing the harsh realities of life. He focused on love rather than material success.

Extract 2

An amazing model?' shouted Trevor at the top of his voice; 'I should think so! Such beggars as he are not to be met with every day. A trouvaille, mon cher; a living Velasquez! My stars! what an etching Rembrandt would have made of him!'

'Poor old chap!' said Hughie, 'how miserable he looks! But I suppose, to you painters, his face is his fortune?'

'Certainly,' replied Trevor, 'you don't want a beggar to look happy, do you?'

'How much does a model get for sitting?' asked Hughie, as he found himself a comfortable seat on a divan.

(i) **Where is the scene set? Who are the characters? How much did Trevor say the model earned for sitting?** **(3)**

Ans. The scene is set in Alan Trevor's studio, a painter.

The characters involved in this particular moment are Hughie Erskine, a charming but poor young man and Alan Trevor, the artist. Hughie is curious about the modeling process and asks how much the model earns for sitting, to which Trevor responds that the model gets a shilling an hour.

(ii) **Why did Trevor describe the beggar as 'an amazing model'?** **(3)**

Ans. Trevor called the beggar 'an amazing model' because he thought the beggar's appearance was unique and interesting. He believed that the beggar's sad, worn-out look made him a perfect subject for a painting. It would create a realistic image. Trevor saw the beggar's rough appearance as something valuable for his artwork.

(iii) **Justify Trevor's claim that painting can be as demanding as manual labour?** **(3)**

Ans. Trevor justifies his claim by mentioning the physical effort involved in painting, especially in the process of applying paint and standing for long hours. He claims that artists require physical strength, similar to manual labour. Art is not just about creativity but also involves hard work. This gives an idea that art is a serious profession.

(iv) **Compare Hughie's perspective on the model's earnings with Trevor's view on the effort involved in painting.** **(3)**

Ans. Hughie's perspective on the model's earnings shows his generous nature and one who values fairness. He feels that the model, who works hard by sitting for long hours deserves a higher share of the money. On the other hand, Trevor, as an artist, views the effort of the painter as prestigious. Trevor focuses on the physical labour and artistic skill involved in painting, which reflects his pride in his work and his belief in the higher value of the artist's role.

(v) **Trevor mentions that "painters, poets and physicians always get guineas." What does this statement reveal about his view on the value of art and artists?** **(4)**

Ans. Trevor mentioned that painters, poets and physicians always get guineas to emphasise that these professions are well-paid and respected.

By using 'guineas', a term that refers to a larger amount of money than pounds, he attempts to emphasise that artists earn more money because their work is seen as valuable and important. This shows that Trevor believes his job as an artist is prestigious and deserving of a good income.

Extract 3

"Poor old wretch! I wish I could do something for him. I think it is dreadful that any one should be so miserable. I have got heaps of old clothes at home - do you think he would care for any of them? Why, his rags were falling to bits.'

(i) What is Hughie's reaction to the beggar's condition, and what does he offer him? (3)

Ans. Hughie feels sorry for the beggar when he sees how poor and miserable the man looks. He finds it heartbreaking that anyone could be in such a bad condition. Hughie wants to help in any way he can, so he decides to offer the beggar some of his old clothes. Hughie believes that the beggar would be grateful for even the smallest gesture of kindness, thinking he might care for them since the beggar's rags are falling apart.

(ii) What does Trevor mean by "What you call rags I call romance"? How does this statement reflect his attitude towards poverty and art? (3)

Ans. Trevor views the beggar's ragged clothes not as a symbol of poverty but as something that adds to the artistic appearance of the beggar. For him, poverty enhances the beggar's beauty and makes him a more interesting subject for his art. Trevor sees poverty from the lens of an artist, something of value and importance.

(iii) Why does Hughie call painters like Trevor 'heartless'? What does this reveal about Hughie's values? (3)

Ans. Hughie calls Trevor 'heartless' because he feels that artists, like Trevor, are detached from the human suffering around them. They view poverty as something beautiful for art instead of caring for the poor. Hughie values empathy over the perspective of seeing others' suffering as simply an artistic opportunity.

(iv) Trevor believes that an artist should only depict the world as they see it and not try to change it. Justify. (3)

Ans. Trevor feels that the role of an artist is to reflect reality without altering it. According to Trevor, the purpose of art is not to reform society but to capture and represent the world as it is. He believes that artists should simply present what they observe without adding their personal values. He sees the beggar's torn clothes as beautiful and artistic.

(v) Hughie and Trevor's views on poverty reflect the theme of compassion versus artistic detachment in the story? Explain. (4)

Ans. The contrast between Hughie and Trevor's views on poverty reflects the theme of compassion versus artistic detachment. Hughie shows compassion for the beggar and wants to help by offering him old clothes. On the other hand, Trevor, as an artist, takes a more detached approach, viewing the beggar's ragged clothes as 'romance' and 'picturesqueness' that adds to the art he is creating. He sees poverty as not something to fix but something that enhances his work. This contrast highlights the society's different approaches to human suffering.

Extract 4

'The old man you saw to-day in the studio was Baron Hausberg. He is a great friend of mine, buys all my pictures and that sort of thing, and gave me a commission a month ago to paint him as a beggar. Que voulez-vous? La fantaisie d'un millionnaire! And I must say he made a magnificent figure in his rags, or perhaps I should say in my rags; they are an old suit I got in Spain.'

(i) Who was the old man in the studio, and what was his connection to Trevor? (3)

Ans. The old man in the studio was Baron Hausberg. He was a great friend of Trevor, who bought all his pictures and had commissioned Trevor to paint him as a beggar.

(ii) Why does Trevor find it amusing that Hughie gave the beggar a sovereign. How does this reveal Trevor's character? (3)

Ans. Trevor finds it amusing because he knows that Baron Hausberg is extremely wealthy, and Hughie's gesture of giving him a sovereign was unnecessary. This shows Trevor's detached attitude and his tendency to find humour in situations where others might feel embarrassed.

(iii) What does Trevor mean by "Son affaire c'est l'argent des autres"? How does this phrase reflect his view on money? (3)

Ans. The phrase "Son affaire c'est l'argent des autres" translates to "His business is other people's money." Trevor is saying that Baron Hausberg uses other people's money for his own purposes.

This reflects Trevor's view that the rich have no concern for where money comes from. They see money as a tool to be used, often without ethical consideration.

(iv) **Do you think Trevor should have informed Hughie about the beggar's true identity beforehand? (3)**

Ans. Trevor should have informed Hughie about the beggar's true identity because Hughie's gesture of giving the sovereign was made out of compassion, and he would have felt embarrassed to know that the beggar was actually a wealthy man. By not telling Hughie, Trevor took advantage of Hughie's innocence and good nature.

(v) **How does the tone of Trevor's response to Hughie's act of giving the sovereign reflect his attitude towards money and people? What mood does this create for the reader? (4)**

Ans. The tone of Trevor's response is sarcastic and mocking as he laughs at Hughie's act of kindness. This reflects Trevor's negative attitude towards money and people, showing his detachment from emotions. The mood created is ironic and sarcastic.

Extract 5

'I have come from Baron Hausberg,' he continued.

'The Baron -' 'I beg, sir, that you will offer him my sincerest apologies,' stammered Hughie.

'The Baron,' said the old gentleman with a smile, 'has commissioned me to bring you this letter'; and he extended a sealed envelope. On the outside was written, 'A wedding present to Hugh Erskine and Laura Merton, from an old beggar,' and inside was a cheque for £10,000.

(i) **Where did the old gentleman come from, and what did he bring for Hughie? (3)**

Ans. The old gentleman came from Baron Hausberg and brought a letter for Hughie, which contained a cheque for £10,000 as a wedding present for Hughie and Laura Merton.

(ii) **What is the significance of the letter's message "A wedding present to Hugh Erskine and Laura Merton, from an old beggar"? How does it change Hughie's life? (3)**

Ans. The message "A wedding present to Hugh Erskine and Laura Merton, from an old beggar" shows a dramatic change in Hughie's life. He went from being poor to unexpectedly receiving a large sum of money. This changes the situation of his relationship with Laura and ultimately helps them to get married.

(iii) **Why does Alan Trevor refer to the Baron as a 'model millionaire' at the wedding breakfast? (3)**

Ans. Alan Trevor calls the Baron a 'model millionaire' because, even though the Baron was very rich, he pretended to be a beggar for the purpose of art.

Trevor makes a joke by comparing the idea of a 'millionaire model' to the rare idea of a 'model millionaire'. This suggests that Baron, despite being wealthy, chose to humble himself and take part in the artist's work.

(iv) **Do you think Hughie deserved the £10,000 from Baron Hausberg? What does this gift reveal about the nature of generosity and reward in the story? (3)**

Ans. Hughie did deserve the £10,000 as even when he did not know the true identity of the beggar, he decided to help him.

The reward came not because Hughie expected anything but because of his selfless and compassionate act of helping someone in need. The story asserts that genuine kindness exists.

(v) **How does the story explore the themes of generosity, humility, and the true value of wealth? (4)**

Ans. The story shows themes of kindness, humility, and the real meaning of wealth. Hughie Erskine, even though he is not rich, shows kindness by wanting to help a beggar. Later, it is revealed that the beggar is actually Baron Hausberg, a very rich man who humbly poses as a model for art.

This surprises everyone because rich people are usually seen as distant from simple life. In the end, the Baron's generous gift for Hughie's wedding shows that real wealth is about being kind, humble, and helping others, not just having a lot of money.

04

THE HOME-COMING

Rabindranath Tagore

Introduction

The Homecoming is a short story written by Rabindranath Tagore, a famous Indian writer, poet, and Nobel laureate. It is a touching story about a young boy, Phatik, who feels unwanted and longs for love. The story belongs to the genre of realistic fiction and explores themes of childhood, family, and loneliness. Its unique aspect is how it shows the deep emotions of a child who is misunderstood. The story leaves a lasting impact by highlighting the pain of separation and neglect.

About the Story

The Home-Coming by Rabindranath Tagore is about Phatik, a playful village boy sent to live with his uncle in the city. He feels lonely and misses his mother and village life. His aunt doesn't treat him well and he struggles to fit in. Phatik becomes very sick. In his final moments, he dreams of going back home. The story shows a child's love for his home and family.

Character Introduction

- **Phatik** A playful and mischievous village boy.
- **Makhan** Phatik's younger brother, quiet and favoured by their mother.
- **Phatik's Mother** A strict woman who often scolds Phatik and favours Makhan.
- **Bishamber** Phatik's kind uncle who takes him to Calcutta to educate him.
- **Phatik's Aunt** A cold and unwelcoming woman who dislikes having Phatik in her home.

Story at a Glance

'The Home-Coming' by Rabindranath Tagore tells the story of Phatik Chakravorti a 14 years old, a mischievous and rebellious boy from a village. He leads his younger brother Makhan and other boys in a prank involving a log, which causes Phatik to get into trouble.

Phatik's relationship with his mother is strained as his behaviour and mischief cause constant friction between them. Phatik's uncle, Bishamber, who lives in Calcutta, offers to take Phatik with him to educate him. Phatik's mother agrees to send him away, hoping for a better future for him. Phatik is eager to leave, seeing it as an escape from his mother's harsh treatment and the routine of village life. However, once in Calcutta, he feels neglected by his aunt, who is unwelcoming.

At school, Phatik struggles academically and is further alienated by his classmates and aunt. One day, he loses his lesson book, and his aunt criticises him harshly. He gets a fever and runs away. He is found later, brought back to his uncle's home and is taken care of by his uncle and the doctor. During his illness, Phatik repeatedly calls for his mother, expressing his longing for her.

By the time she arrives, Phatik is near death. He passes away in his uncle's house. However, in his final moments, he thinks of his mother and the home that he longs for. His last words, 'Mother, the holidays have come,' reflect his deep emotional connection to his village and his mother, even when he is on his death bed.

Vocab Vault

Mast Uphight support for the sails

Sauntered Walked in a slow, relaxed manner.

Manoeuvre A clever or skillful action or strategy.

Discomfit To make someone feel uneasy or embarrassed.

Hoarse Rough and harsh

Indignantly Despite, dislike hate

Prejudice A preconceived opinion or bias, often negative.

Despised Strongly disliked or looked down upon.

Cramped Lacking space; confined.

Abjectly In a hopeless or miserable way.

Clumsy Awkward

Futile Worthless, useless

Delirious In a disturbed or confused state due to illness.

Theme

The story explores themes of childhood loneliness, the longing for love and belonging and the pain of neglect and misunderstanding. The story highlights the emotional struggles of a boy craving acceptance and affection, contrasting the warmth of familial bonds with the isolation of being unwelcome. It also portrays the deep yearning for home and the innocence of childhood amidst life's harsh realities.

Message Conveyed by the Story

The story conveys the message that every child needs love, understanding and a sense of belonging to thrive. Neglect and lack of empathy can deeply affect a child's emotional well-being, leading to feelings of isolation and despair.

Style Tone and Mood

- **Style** The story is written in a simple and descriptive style
- **Tone** The tone is empathetic and reflective, highlighting the struggles of a neglected child.
- **Mood** The mood is melancholic.

Title

The title 'The Home-Coming' reflects the emotional and physical journey of Phatik, the protagonist, as he longs to return to his home and his mother. Though he is sent to Calcutta for his education, Phatik feels alienated and out of place in his aunt's house.

Ultimately, the title symbolises Phatik's deep yearning for a sense of belonging. In his final moments, he calls out for his mother, marking a metaphorical homecoming. The title highlights the themes of family, love and the desire for emotional comfort.

Figures of Speech

- **Simile** 'Makhan rose from Mother Earth blind as Fate and screaming like the Furies.' 'A silent cry of the inmost heart for the mother, like the lowing of a calf in the twilight.'
- **Metaphor** 'For a boy of fourteen his own home is the only Paradise.' 'He became very much like a stray dog that has lost his master.'
- **Personification** 'The cramped atmosphere of neglect in his aunt's house oppressed Phatik so much that he felt that he could hardly breathe.' 'His fertile brain rapidly seized upon a new manoeuvre.'
- **Hyperbole** 'There is no worse nuisance than a boy at the age of fourteen.' 'He was on pins and needles all day long with excitement.'
- **Symbolism** 'By the mark! - three fathoms. By the mark - four fathoms.'
- **Irony** Phatik eagerly wants to leave his home, but once in Calcutta, he desperately longs to return. His mother, who was relieved to send him away, is heartbroken when he is dying.
- **Alliteration** 'Phatik's patience was already exhausted.' 'The fever rose very high, and all that night the boy was delirious.'

REVISION NOTES

EXAM ORIENTED QUESTIONS

TYPE - 1 Multiple Choice Questions

01 Mark

Q.1 The initial mischief Phatik planned with his friends was ....

(a) to steal a boat (b) to roll a heavy log

(c) to swim across the river (d) to climb a tree

Q.2 What does the incident with the log and Makhan reveal about Phatik's character?

(a) Phatik is impulsive and seeks amusement at the expense of others.

(b) Phatik is responsible and tries to prevent the boys from causing trouble.

(c) Phatik is timid and afraid of conflict.

(d) Phatik is obedient and follows his mother's instructions.

Q.3 What did Makhan do when the boys tried to roll the log?

(a) He joined them enthusiastically

(b) He ran away to tell their mother

(c) He sat on the log and refused to move

(d) He started crying loudly

Q.4 The grey-haired stranger who came to Phatik's house was ....

(a) a police officer

(b) Phatik's school teacher

(c) Phatik's uncle, Bishamber

(d) Makhan's friend's father

Q.5 How does Phatik's relationship with his mother influence his eagerness to go to Calcutta?

(a) He feels unloved and rejected by her, so he seeks approval elsewhere.

(b) He wants to escape the strict rules of village life.

(c) He desires to prove his academic worth to his mother.

(d) He believes Calcutta will offer him more freedom and joy.

Q.6 What was Phatik's reaction when his uncle asked him if he wanted to go to Calcutta?

(a) He refused outright

(b) He expressed hesitation

(c) He was overjoyed and eager

(d) He remained silent

Q.7 The mood that dominates the story as Phatik struggles in Calcutta is ....

(a) joyful and uplifting

(b) nostalgic and reflective

(c) oppressive and melancholic

(d) hopeful and optimistic

Q.8 Why does Phatik feel like an outcast in his aunt's home in Calcutta?

(a) He is scolded constantly for his behaviour and academic failure.

(b) He is not given any responsibility to prove his worth.

(c) His village manners and awkwardness make him feel alienated.

(d) He longs for his mother's love and familiar surroundings.

Q.9 Phatik's mother hesitated to let him go to Calcutta with his uncle because ....

(a) she feared losing her elder son's help at home

(b) she doubted his uncle's intentions

(c) she wanted him to stay and take care of her

(d) she believed city life would be bad for him

Q.10 How does the depiction of Phatik's struggles in Calcutta critique societal attitudes towards adolescents?

(a) It highlights the neglect and misunderstanding young boys often face during a vulnerable stage.

(b) It emphasises the importance of strict discipline in shaping adolescents.

(c) It praises urban environments for teaching resilience to rural boys.

(d) It supports the idea that boys should remain in their native villages for better upbringing.

Q.11 Identify the primary reason Phatik felt out of place in his uncle's home.

(a) He missed his friends and the freedom of his village life.

(b) He struggled with the school curriculum in the city.

(c) He did not receive enough food or clothing.

(d) His cousins were unkind to him.

Q.12 The scene where Phatik falls ill signifies in the story.

(a) The indifference of his aunt and uncle towards him.

(b) The emotional toll of homesickness and neglect.

(c) The harsh consequences of disobedience.

(d) Childhood illnesses in a new environment.

Q.13 What happened to Phatik the night he lost his lesson-book?

(a) He stayed up all night studying

(b) He ran away from home in the rain

(c) He got a fever and was found by the police

(d) He was praised for his courage

Q.14 'Mother, the holidays have come'

What does the line symbolise in the context of Phatik's life and death?

(a) His longing for freedom and reunion with his mother is finally fulfilled.

(b) His realisation that he will never return to Calcutta.

(c) His neglect of death as a permanent holiday.

(d) His belief that he has completed his academic duties.

Q.15 How does the setting of the village contrast with that of the city in the story?

(a) The village is peaceful and free, while the city feels restricting and lonely.

(b) The village is chaotic and unpleasant, while the city is disciplined and orderly.

(c) Both the village and city are depicted as equally harsh for Phatik.

(d) The village is filled with natural beauty, while the city is depicted as a dreamland.

Q.16 Analyse the significance of the title 'The Home-Coming'?

(a) It reflects Phatik's longing for his mother and his home in the village.

(b) It highlights the joy of returning home after a long journey.

(c) It signifies the physical journey from Calcutta back to the village.

(d) It refers to Phatik's ultimate realisation about the value of education.

Q.17 Which theme is central to 'The Home-Coming' by Rabindranath Tagore?

(a) The conflict between rural and urban life.

(b) The struggles of adolescence and family relationships.

(c) The impact of poverty on education.

(d) The importance of ambition and hard work.

Q.18 Select the option that shows the correct relationship between statements (1) and (2).

Statement 1 Phatik dislikes staying in Calcutta as he feels isolated and misunderstood.

Statement 2 Phatik's uncle is compassionate and tries to make him feel at home.

(a) Both statements are true.

(b) Both statements are false.

(c) Statement 1 is true, and Statement 2 is false.

(d) Statement 1 is false, and Statement 2 is true.

Q.19 What is the correct sequence of events in 'The Home-coming'?

1. Phatik's uncle offers to take him to Calcutta for better education.
2. Phatik's aunt expresses displeasure at his presence in the house.
3. Phatik loses his lesson book and is punished at school.
4. Phatik runs away due to his miserable condition and falls ill.

(a) 1, 3, 4, 2 (b) 2, 4, 3, 1

(c) 1, 2, 3, 4 (d) 3, 1, 4, 2

Q.20 Identify the chronological order the events as they happen in the story.

1. Phatik becomes excited about going to Calcutta.
2. Phatik's mother recognises her brother, Bishamber, when he arrives.
3. Phatik feels neglected and longs for his village home.
4. Phatik's uncle brings him to Calcutta for better education.

(a) 1, 3, 4, 2 (b) 4, 1, 2, 3

(c) 2, 1, 4, 3 (d) 3, 4, 1, 2

Answers

1. (b)	2. (a)	3. (c)	4. (c)	5. (a)	6. (c)	7. (c)	8. (c)	9. (a)	10. (a)
11. (a)	12. (b)	13. (c)	14. (a)	15. (a)	16. (a)	17. (b)	18. (c)	19. (c)	20. (c)

TYPE - 2 Extract Based Questions 16 Marks

Extract 1

"But he overlooked the fact, like those who attempt earthly fame in other matters, that there was peril in it. The boys began to heave at the log with all their might, calling out, 'One, two, three, go,' At the word 'go' the log went; and with it went Makhan's philosophy, glory and all. All the other boys shouted themselves hoarse with delight. But Phatik was a little frightened. He knew what was coming."

(i) Who was Makhan? What were the boys trying to do with the log? **(3)**

Ans. Makhan was Phatik's younger brother, who was sitting on the log and refused to move. He seems to have a peaceful nature compared to his older brother, who is eager for action and leadership.

The boys were trying hard to push and roll the log to move it.

(ii) Why did Phatik give the command to roll the log with Makhan on it? (3)

Ans. Phatik gave the command to roll the log with Makhan on it because he wanted to embarrass his younger brother and teach him a lesson for not getting up from the log.

Phatik likely saw it as a way to show his authority in front of the other boys. He overlooked the harm it could cause.

(iii) How did the fun turn into a serious situation? (3)

Ans. Makhan fell to the ground when the boys heaved the log. While the other boys were amused by the idea, the situation quickly turned serious.

Makhan's angry reaction-scratching and beating Phatik-changed the mood from playful mischief to a more intense situation. When the others laughed, Phatik ended up being beaten by his brother.

(iv) Was it fair for Phatik to take such action against his brother? (3)

Ans. No, it was not fair for Phatik to do that to his brother. Phatik wanted to have fun by rolling the log with Makhan on it, but he didn't think about how it might hurt his brother.

Even though he was angry, doing such an action was not correct. It hurt Makhan and caused trouble. Phatik should have acted more kindly.

(v) The two brothers have different characteristics. Explain in reference to the extract. (4)

Ans. The two brothers are very different in their nature. Phatik is bold and takes risks. He decides to roll the log even though Makhan is sitting on it. He enjoys leading the group of boys.

On the other hand, Makhan is stubborn and doesn't like to be told what to do as he refuses to get off the log. When he is hurt, he becomes very angry and reacts aggressively by scratching, kicking and crying. This shows that Makhan is more sensitive than Phatik.

Extract 2

"It was just at this critical juncture that the grey-haired stranger arrived. He asked what the matter was. Phatik looked sheepish and ashamed. But when his mother stepped back and looked at the stranger, her anger was changed to surprise. For she recognised her brother and cried: "Why, Dada! Where have you come from? "As she said these words, she bowed to the ground and touched his feet."

(i) Who was the grey-haired stranger and how did Phatik's mother react when she recognised him? (3)

Ans. The grey-haired stranger was Phatik's maternal uncle. Phatik's mother recognised him and her anger turned into surprise. She respectfully bowed to the ground and touched his feet.

(ii) Why did Phatik feel sheepish and ashamed when the stranger arrived? (3)

Ans. Phatik felt sheepish and ashamed because the stranger arrived at a moment when he was likely being scolded by his mother for causing trouble and hurting his brother.

(iii) Analyse your inference about Phatik's relationship with his mother from her initial reaction to the situation and her later behaviour towards the stranger? (3)

Ans. Phatik's relationship with his mother seems tense, as she first reacts with anger and frustration towards him. However, when her brother arrives, her change in behaviour shows that her anger might have been a reaction of stress.

(iv) Do you think the mother's sudden change in tone upon recognising her brother was justified? (3)

Ans. Yes, the mother's change in tone was justified because it was a significant and emotional moment which made her forget her frustration. However, it shows a sudden shift in priorities that may seem unfair to Phatik.

(v) Compare and contrast the mother's descriptions of Phatik and Makhan. What does this reveal about her perspective on the two boys? (4)

Ans. Phatik's mother sees him as a troublemaker. She thinks he is wild, lazy and always causing problems. In contrast, she describes Makhan as good, obedient, and studious. She trusts Makhan but fears Phatik will harm him. This shows that she favours Makhan and has little patience for Phatik. She does not understand Phatik's need for love and attention. Her biased view makes Phatik feel unwanted. Only when he is dying does she realise her love for him. This reveals that her perspective is based on misunderstanding rather than true affection for both her sons.

Extract 3

"She was in daily fear that he would either drown Makhan some day in the river or break his head in a fight or run him into some danger or other. At the same time she was somewhat distressed to see Phatik's extreme eagerness to get away. Phatik, as soon as all was settled, kept asking his uncle every minute when they were to start. He was on pins and needles all day long with excitement and lay awake most of 3 the night. He bequeathed to Makhan, in perpetuity, his fishing-rod, his big kite and his marbles. Indeed, at this time of departure his generosity towards Makhan was unbounded. When they reached Calcutta, Phatik made the acquaintance of his aunt for the first time. She

was by no means pleased with this unnecessary addition to her family. She found her own three boys quite enough to manage without taking any one else. And to bring a village lad of fourteen into their midst was terribly upsetting."

(i) **What items did Phatik leave to Makhan before his departure? Why did he do so?** **(3)**

Ans. Phatik gave Makhan his fishing rod, big kite and marbles before leaving. He did this because he was happy and excited about going away.

Even though they often fought, Phatik wanted to be kind to Makhan and leave him something special before starting his new life.

(ii) **Why do you think Phatik's mother distressed despite being relieved that he was leaving?** **(3)**

Ans. Phatik's mother was relieved because she thought his mischief would no longer trouble her or Makhan. However, she felt distressed because Phatik was extremely eager to leave, which made her realise he was unhappy at home and wanted to get away. This made her feel a bit guilty and sad.

(iii) **Analyse Phatik's action of generosity towards Makhan before his departure. What does this reveal about his character?** **(3)**

Ans. Phatik's generosity towards Makhan, as seen when he gave him his fishing rod, kite, and marbles, shows his kind and selfless nature. Despite their usual fights and disagreements, Phatik wanted to leave Makhan with things he valued, indicating that he cared for his younger brother.

This act of giving reflects his affectionate side. It reveals that Phatik is a thoughtful and considerate person beneath his mischievous behaviour.

(iv) **Give a reason why Phatik's aunt was displeased with his arrival? Do you think the reaction was justified?** **(3)**

Ans. Phatik's aunt was displeased with his arrival because she found it difficult to manage an additional child, especially one from the village.

She already had her own three boys to look after and bringing a fourteen-year-old boy into their household disrupted her routine.

From a practical standpoint, she may have been stressed by the extra responsibility and the challenges of caring for a new child, especially in a busy household.

(v) **Explain the tone of Phatik's aunt. How does it contribute to the story?** **(4)**

Ans. Phatik's aunt speaks in a harsh and unkind tone. She does not welcome him and treats him as a burden. Her words are filled with irritation and scorn, making Phatik feel unwanted. She calls him names and constantly reminds him that he is not part of her family. This adds to Phatik's loneliness and makes his suffering worse. Her cold attitude highlights the theme of neglect. It also contrasts with Phatik's innocent desire for love, making his struggles more painful. Her tone plays a key role in showing how deeply Phatik longs for kindness and acceptance.

Extract 4

"If he talks with a childish lisp he is called a baby, and if he answers in a grown-up way he is called impertinent. In fact any talk at all from him is resented. Then he is at the unattractive, growing age. He grows out of his clothes with indecent haste; his voice grows hoarse and breaks and quavers; his face grows suddenly angular and unsightly. It is easy to excuse the shortcomings of early childhood, but it is hard to tolerate even unavoidable lapses in a boy of fourteen. The lad himself becomes painfully self-conscious. When he talks with elderly people he is either unduly forward or else so unduly shy that he appears ashamed of his very existence.

(i) **What happens to the boy if he talks with a childish lisp, according to the passage? What is his description like?** **(3)**

Ans. If the boy talks with a childish lisp, he is called a baby. His description mentions the challenges he faces at this stage of life.

He is at the 'unattractive, growing age', growing out of his clothes quickly, with his voice breaking and his face becoming angular and unsightly.

These physical and behavioural changes make him self-conscious.

(ii) **Why does the passage describe a boy of fourteen as being at an 'unattractive, growing age'?** **(3)**

Ans. The passage calls a boy of fourteen 'unattractive' because he goes through many awkward changes. He quickly outgrows his clothes, his voice becomes hoarse and his face looks uneven.

These changes make him feel embarrassed and people are less patient with his mistakes compared to when he was younger.

(iii) **Analyse how the passage highlights the difference between societal expectations and the emotional needs of a fourteen-year-old boy?** **(3)**

Ans. The passage shows that society often criticises a fourteen-year-old boy for how he talks or behaves, whether he speaks like a child or an adult. At the same time, this boy deeply needs kindness and recognition during this awkward phase.

While people find his changes hard to tolerate, he secretly longs for love and understanding, which creates a conflict between what he needs and how he is treated.

(iv) **How does the passage reflect the challenges of adolescence in balancing identity? (3)**

Ans. The passage shows that adolescence is a difficult phase where a boy struggles to balance his sense of self with societal judgement. His physical changes and uncertain behaviour make him painfully self-conscious. Society's lack of tolerance for his mistakes and its expectations create a sense of rejection.

(v) **What mood and tone does the poet creates while describing the struggles of a fourteen-year-old boy? (4)**

Ans. The story creates a sad and emotional mood while describing Phatik's struggles. The tone is sympathetic, showing how lonely and misunderstood he feels. The narrator describes his longing for home, his pain from neglect, and his silent suffering. His aunt's harsh words and his mother's indifference make the reader feel sorry for him. The story also captures the awkwardness of growing up, where a boy is too old for affection but too young for independence. The mood becomes even more tragic when Phatik falls sick and dies, making his suffering seem even more unfair and heartbreaking.

Extract 5

At last his voice became excited: "Mother," he cried, "don't beat me like that! Mother! I am telling the truth!" The next day Phatik became conscious for a short time. He turned his eyes about the room, as if expecting some one to come. At last, with an air of disappointment, his head sank back on the pillow. He turned his face to the wall with a deep sigh. Bishamber knew his thoughts and bending down his head, whispered: "Phatik, I have sent for your mother." The day went by. The doctor said in a troubled voice that the boy's condition was very critical.

(i) **What does Phatik cry out when he becomes restless? Who is sent for when Phatik's condition becomes critical? (3)**

Ans. Phatik cries out: 'By the mark! --three fathoms. By the mark-- four fathoms. By the mark--.' He recalls hearing this during his river-steamer journey, associating it with an unfamiliar and vast world. This cry reflects Phatik's own journey towards the unknown-his nearing death.

Phatik's mother is sent for when his condition becomes critical.

(ii) **What does Phatik mean when he says, 'Mother, the holidays have come'? (3)**

Ans. When Phatik says, 'Mother, the holidays have come', he is expressing his longing for comfort, peace and relief from the struggles and hardships he has faced.

This statement reflects his desire to be reunited with his mother and return to the sense of security and love. The 'holidays' could also signify his acceptance of death, as he sees it as an escape from the suffering of life.

(iii) **Why does Phatik turn his face to the wall with a sigh when he becomes conscious? (3)**

Ans. Phatik turns his face to the wall with a sigh when he becomes conscious because he is disappointed and heartbroken. He looks around the room, hoping to see his mother, but when she is not there, he feels abandoned.

His sigh reflects his deep sadness and emotional pain. He craves the comfort and recognition that only his mother's presence can provide.

(iv) **The description of Phatik's restlessness and his mother's arrival show the emotional bond between them. How does it do so? (3)**

Ans. The description of Phatik's restlessness and his mother's arrival highlights their emotional bond by showing the deep longing and love that exists between them, despite their earlier conflicts. Phatik's restlessness, marked by his cries, reflects his fragile emotional and physical state.

He subconsciously yearns for his mother's presence. The mother's entrance filled with grief reveal her regret and the depth of her attachment. This interaction reveals the unspoken bond between a mother and her child.

(v) **How does the passage explore the themes of longing, regret and maternal love? (4)**

Ans. The story explores longing through Phatik's deep desire to return home. He dreams of his village, his friends and even his strict mother, showing his need for love. Regret is shown in his mother's realisation of her love too late. She wanted him to leave but mourns when she sees him dying. Maternal love is portrayed as complicated. Phatik's mother prefers Makhan and does not show much love for Phatik. However, when Phatik is on his deathbed, she finally cries for him. This shows that sometimes love is understood only when it is almost lost forever.

05

THE BOY WHO BROKE THE BANK

Ruskin Bond

Introduction

The Boy Who Broke the Bank is a short story written by Ruskin Bond, India's most beloved writer. It is a humorous yet thought-provoking tale about how rumours spread and create unintended consequences. Set in a small Indian town, the story revolves around a sweeper boy named Nathu, who casually complains about his delayed salary. Through this story, Bond highlights the ideas of miscommunication, gossip and the unpredictability of human behaviour in a light-hearted yet satirical manner. The story's brilliance lies in its simplicity-how a casual remark transforms into a major financial crisis due to hearsay.

About the Story

The Boy Who Broke the Bank by Ruskin Bond is a funny and insightful story about how a small complaint turns into a big problem. Nathu, a sweeper, is upset because the bank hasn't paid him on time. When his friend Sitaram mentions this to someone, the news spreads like wildfire and people start believing the bank is going bankrupt.

This leads to chaos in the town, with everyone rushing to withdraw their money. The story shows how quickly rumours can grow and how they affect people. Ruskin Bond uses humour and simple language to teach a lesson about the dangers of spreading gossip.

Character Introduction

- **Nathu** A young sweeper at the Pipalnagar Bank, frustrated about not receiving his salary on time.
- **Sitaram** The washerman's son who unknowingly starts the rumour.
- **Mrs. Srivastava** A customer who hears about Nathu's complaint.
- **Mrs. Bhushan** A friend of Mrs. Srivastava who exaggerates the rumour, adding to the panic.
- **The Bank Manager** An official struggling to calm the angry crowd demanding their money.
- **Ganpat** A beggar

Story at a Glance

'The Boy Who Broke the Bank' by Ruskin Bond is a humorous story dealing with destructive power. It is about how a small complaint can escalate into chaos due to rumours. Nathu, a sweeper at the local Pipalnagar Bank, is upset because he hasn't been paid his salary on time. His frustration grows and when he complains loudly, Sitaram, the washerman's son, casually mentions it to a customer, Mrs. Srivastava. The news spreads quickly through the town, with people speculating that the bank is about to collapse on the basis of the rumours start gathering around the bank.

As the rumour circulates, panic sets in and people rush to the bank to withdraw their money. The situation intensifies when a crowd gathers, demanding their savings and the bank manager struggles to control the chaos.

The news about the bank's collapse spreads across the bazaar, with many people joining in, each adding their own version of the story. Even a beggar, Ganpat, who has saved money in the bank, rushes to withdraw his funds.

The panic leads to violence when a brick is thrown through the bank's window. The next day, Nathu returns to sweep the bank steps. He reflects on how his small complaint unintentionally led to such a crisis, highlighting the power of rumours and misinformation.

Vocab Vault

Grumbled Complained in a bad-tempered or muttering way.

Plodded Walked slowly and heavily, typically with effort.

Imminent Near at hand

Frenzy A state of wild excitement or uncontrolled activity.

Dilemma A situation where a difficult choice has to be made between two or more alternatives.

Persuade Convince

Aggravated Exasperated

Placate To comfort, pacify

Hurtled Move at high speed

Hooligans Young people who engage in disruptive or violent behaviour.

Theme

The story 'The Boy Who Broke the Bank' explores several important themes. One major theme is the impact of rumours, as the small issue of Nathu not being paid on time quickly spirals into widespread panic about the bank's collapse.

The story also explores human behaviour, showing how people tend to act impulsively and with fear when faced with uncertainty. Another theme is the importance of communication and responsibility. Additionally, there is a reflection on socioeconomic disparities, particularly through Nathu's struggles as a low-paid worker, highlighting the challenges faced by the working class.

Message Conveyed by the Story

The story conveys the message that rumours and misinformation can cause unnecessary panic and chaos. It also highlights the importance of being responsible with communication and understanding the consequences of careless words. Through humour, the story reminds us how human behaviour can be easily influenced by fear and gossip.

Style Tone and Mood

- **Style** The story uses simple language and humour to highlight human behaviour and societal flaws.
- **Tone** Light-hearted and satirical, with a touch of irony.
- **Mood** Amusing at first but shifts to chaotic and tense as the rumour spreads.

Title

The title 'The Boy Who Broke the Bank' is justified because Nathu, though unintentionally, sets off a chain of events that causes a financial panic in the town. His complaint about not being paid on time leads to rumours of the bank's collapse, making the bank seem on the verge of breaking down. Thus, the title reflects how a small action by Nathu indirectly causes a major crisis.

Figures of Speech

- **Metaphor** 'The news spread through the bazaar with the rapidity of a forest fire.'
- **Simile** *(Comparison using 'like' or 'as')* 'You go from one shop to another, like a bee in a flower garden.'
- **Hyperbole** *(Exaggeration for emphasis)* 'The heat is trying enough. I don't know what's happening to Pipalnagar.'
- 'Fetch the Seth, we know he's hiding in a safe deposit locker!'
- **Irony** The entire story revolves around dramatic irony—Nathu's innocent complaint leads to a major crisis that he remains unaware of until the end. 'Who would have thought the bank would collapse?'—Nathu wonders this, not realising that his own words unknowingly started the panic.
- **Personification** *(Giving human qualities to non-human things)* 'The dust, after rising in a cloud above his head, settled down again on the steps.'
- **Onomatopoeia** *(Words that imitate sounds)*'Nathu banged the pan against the dustbin.' 'A brick hurtled through the air and crashed through the plate glass window.'

EXAM ORIENTED QUESTIONS

TYPE - 1 Multiple Choice Questions

01 Mark

Q.1 Why was Nathu upset while sweeping the steps of the Pipalnagar Bank?
(a) He was angry about the dust
(b) He hadn't received his regular pay
(c) The bank was too dirty
(d) He was annoyed by Sitaram

Q.2 Identify the main reason for Nathu's dissatisfaction with his job at the Pipalnagar Bank.
(a) He dislikes the work environment.
(b) He is not being paid on time.
(c) He is not getting along with his colleagues.
(d) He is overworked and underpaid.

Q.3 How does Nathu react to the news of the bank's collapse?
(a) He feels relieved as he was planning to leave anyway.
(b) He complains about the bank's downfall but is eager to continue working.
(c) He immediately leaves his job and moves to another town.
(d) He is surprised and starts questioning how the collapse happened.

Q.4 Who was the first person to inform Mrs. Srivastava about the bank's situation?
(a) Sitaram (b) Kamal Kishore
(c) Mrs. Bhushan (d) Nathu

Q.5 The primary reason for Nathu's frustration at the beginning of the story is ....
(a) He is upset with his friend Sitaram.
(b) He has not received his salary from the bank.
(c) He dislikes working at the bank.
(d) He is angry about the gossip in town.

Q.6 Who did Mrs. Srivastava tell about the bank's financial trouble?
(a) Kamal Kishore (b) Deep Chand
(c) Mrs. Bhushan (d) Sitaram

Q.7 Sitaram suggests Nathu ....
(a) to go to another town
(b) to quit his job and find a new one
(c) to speak to the bank manager
(d) to wait until the bank reopened

Q.8 How did the towns people react when they heard about the bank's crisis?
(a) They ignored it
(b) They rushed to the bank to withdraw their money
(c) They celebrated the news
(d) They contacted the bank manager for clarification

Q.9 Identify the main rumour about Pipalnagar Bank.
(a) It was expanding its business
(b) It was opening new branches
(c) It was running out of money and going bankrupt
(d) It was planning to hire more staff

Q.10 Analyse the mood of the story as it progresses with the bank's crisis.
(a) Hopeful and calm (b) Tense and anxious
(c) Joyful and celebratory (d) Indifferent and detached

Q.11 Which setting detail contributes most to the feeling of chaos in the story?
(a) The sunny streets of Pipalnagar
(b) The bustling market filled with vendors
(c) The panic outside the Pipalnagar Bank
(d) The calm and peaceful atmosphere of the tamarind tree

Q.12 The tone that the author adopts when describing the behaviour of the crowd is ....
(a) critical and mocking (b) neutral and objective
(c) humorous and light-hearted
(d) urgent and frantic

Q.13 The central theme of the story, as seen through the events surrounding the bank's collapses ....
(a) the power of community unity
(b) the unpredictability of financial crises
(c) the struggle for power and control
(d) the value of trust and loyalty

Q.14 How does the spreading rumours about the bank's collapse affect the people of Pipalnagar?
(a) They remain unaffected and continue with their daily lives.
(b) They panic and start withdrawing their money.
(c) They plan to start a protest against the bank's management.
(d) They ignore the rumour and continue banking as usual.

Q.15 Identify your inference about the town's perception of Seth Govind Ram and the Pipalnagar Bank by the end of the story.
(a) People trust the bank and are confident about its future.
(b) The people believe Seth Govind Ram is hiding after the crisis.
(c) The town believes that the bank will soon recover and continue business.
(d) People are indifferent to the collapse of the bank.

Q.16 Why does the crowd outside the bank become increasingly aggressive?
(a) They believe they can get their money if they force the bank.
(b) They are angry at the bank's employees for not helping them.
(c) They are upset with Seth Govind Ram's decision to leave town.
(d) They want to get even with the bank for paying late salaries.

Q.17 What does the reaction of the people in the town reveal about their perception?
(a) They are indifferent and unconcerned.
(b) They are skeptical about the bank's future.
(c) They believe the bank is financially stable.
(d) They are panic-stricken and distrustful.

Q.18 Highlight what the spread of rumours about the bank's collapse indicates about the community in Pipalnagar.
(a) They are usually calm and do not react to crises.
(b) They like gossiping and jumping to conclusions.
(c) They rely on official sources for news.
(d) They are uninterested in the bank's affairs.

Q.19 How does the bank manager's response to the crowd reflect the bank's situation?
(a) He is calm and reassures the crowd about the bank's stability.
(b) He is unsure and unable to provide a clear solution.
(c) He is confident and ready to resolve the issue.
(d) He ignores the crowd and avoids confrontation.

Q.20 The significance of Nathu's reaction to the broken glass and stones the next day is ....
(a) it shows his concern for the bank's future
(b) it highlights his frustration with his increased workload
(c) it reflects his anger towards the bank's management
(d) it demonstrates his indifference to the bank's collapse

Q.21 What does the reaction of the elderly gentleman who rushed to withdraw his money suggest about the community's financial fears?
(a) He is indifferent to the rumours and stays calm.
(b) He feels a sense of urgency and fear of losing his savings.
(c) He trusts the bank and ignores the rumours.
(d) He believes the bank will recover from the crisis.

Q.22 Select the option that shows the correct relationship between statements (1) and (2).
Statement 1 Nathu is frustrated because he hasn't received his salary and plans to leave his job.
Statement 2 The manager of the Pipalnagar Bank effectively calms the crowd by promising immediate payments.
(a) Both statements are true.
(b) Both statements are false.
(c) Statement 1 is true and Statement 2 is false.
(d) Statement 1 is false and Statement 2 is true.

Q.23 Identify is the correct sequence of events in the story about Nathu and the Pipalnagar Bank.
1. **Sitaram tells Mrs. Srivastava about Nathu's job search.**
2. **Nathu complains about not receiving his salary on time.**
3. **A crowd gathers outside the bank, demanding their money.**
4. **Rumours about the bank's collapse spread across the bazaar.**

(a) 2, 1, 4, 3 (b) 1, 2, 4, 3
(c) 2, 4, 1, 3 (d) 1, 4, 3, 2

Q.24 What does this story suggest about human behaviour in times of crisis?
(a) People remain rational and seek facts before acting
(b) Small incidents can lead to mass hysteria and panic
(c) People trust banks unconditionally
(d) Rumours rarely affect people's decisions

Answers

1. (b)	2. (b)	3. (d)	4. (c)	5. (b)	6. (c)	7. (b)	8. (b)	9. (c)	10. (b)
11. (c)	12. (d)	13. (b)	14. (b)	15. (b)	16. (a)	17. (d)	18. (d)	19. (b)	20. (b)
21. (b)	22. (c)	23. (a)	24. (b)						

TYPE - 2 Extract Based Questions

16 Marks

Extract 1

'Are you annoyed because they are still refusing to pay you an extra two rupees a month?' 'I don't wish to talk about it,' complained the sweeper-boy. 'I haven't even received my regular pay. And this is the twentieth of the month. Who would think a bank would hold up a poor man's salary? As soon as I get my money, I'm off! Not another week I work in this place.' And Nathu banged the pan against the dustbin several times, just to emphasise his point and giving himself confidence.

(i) Identify the second speaker in this conversation. Why was Nathu upset while sweeping the steps of the bank? (3)

Ans. The second speaker in the conversation is Sitaram, the washerman's son. He speaks to Nathu, asking if he is annoyed about not being paid the extra two rupees and later offers to help Nathu find a new job.

Nathu was upset because it was the twentieth of the month and he had not yet received his regular pay.

(ii) What did Nathu mean when he said, "Not another week I work in this place"? What emotion does it create? (3)

Ans. When Nathu said, 'Not another week I work in this place,' he meant that he was fed up with the situation at the bank and would not tolerate working there any longer once he received his pay.

This statement conveys feelings of frustration, anger and a sense of being disrespected. It highlights his desire to leave the job due to the mistreatment of not being paid on time.

(iii) How does Nathu's action of banging the pan against the dustbin emphasise his feelings about his unpaid salary? (3)

Ans. Nathu's action of banging the pan against the dustbin highlights his frustration and anger. It serves as an expression of his distress and a way to release some of his pent-up emotions while making his point stronger.

(iv) Do you think Nathu's decision to leave the bank after receiving his pay was a reasonable response to his situation? Why or why not? (3)

Ans. Nathu's decision to leave the bank after receiving his pay seems reasonable as he feels disrespected by the delay in his salary. However, it could also be seen as an impulsive decision, depending on the availability of another job and the urgency of his financial situation.

(v) What does Sitaram's offer to look for other jobs for Nathu suggest about their relationship? (4)

Ans. Sitaram's offer suggests that he cares for Nathu and wants to help him find better work opportunities. It reflects a sense of friendship and concern for Nathu's well-being beyond just a casual acquaintance.

Additionally, it highlights a sense of community and mutual support, as Sitaram is looking out for someone in his community, even though they may not be closely related.

Extract 2

Mrs. Bhushan was fanning herself with a large handkerchief. She complained of the summer, which she affirmed, was definitely the hottest in the history of Pipalnagar. She then showed Mrs. Srivastava a sample of the cloth she was going to buy, and for five minutes they discussed its shade, texture and design. Having exhausted this topic, Mrs. Srivastava said, 'Do you know, my dear, that Seth Govind Ram's bank can't even pay its employees?

(i) What was Mrs. Bhushan doing when Mrs. Srivastava met her? What was her reaction? (3)

Ans. When Mrs. Srivastava met Mrs. Bhushan, she was fanning herself with a large handkerchief. This suggests that Mrs. Bhushan was likely feeling hot and uncomfortable due to the intense summer heat.

Additionally, Mrs. Bhushan was showing Mrs. Srivastava a sample of the cloth she was going to buy. She was focused on her shopping and the fabric's shade, texture and design.

As someone who could afford to buy and discuss fine cloth, Mrs. Bhushan's concern about the weather and shopping reflects a lifestyle that is likely more privileged compared to others in the community.

(ii) Analyse why Mrs. Bhushan complained about the summer in Pipalnagar? What does it tell us about her lifestyle as compared to the characters mentioned before? (3)

Ans. Mrs. Bhushan complained about the summer in Pipalnagar because she found it to be the hottest in the history of the town. Her complaint reveals that she was feeling uncomfortable due to the extreme heat, which indicates that she was sensitive to the weather conditions.

This reaction gives us an idea about her lifestyle, especially in comparison to the other characters, such as Nathu, the sweeper boy. While Mrs. Bhushan's concern is centered around the discomfort of the heat during her shopping trip, characters like Nathu are struggling with issues like delayed wages, job insecurity and financial hardship. The author attempts to indicate class divide.

(iii) **How did the conversation between Mrs. Bhushan and Mrs. Srivastava shifts from discussing clothes to discussing the bank's situation? How might the news about the bank affect the residents of Pipalnagar? (3)**

Ans. The conversation between Mrs. Bhushan and Mrs. Srivastava shifted from discussing the cloth to discussing the bank's situation after Mrs. Srivastava mentioned hearing a complaint from the bank's sweeper about not receiving wages.

The news about the bank could lead to panic or concern among the residents of Pipalnagar, affecting their trust in the bank and financial decisions.

(iv) **Do you think Mrs. Srivastava's sharing of the bank's financial issue with Mrs. Bhushan was appropriate? Why or why not? (3)**

Ans. Mrs. Srivastava's sharing of the bank's financial issue was appropriate if she intended to inform and protect Mrs. Bhushan but it could also have been seen as spreading panic. It could also be seen as a mere act of gossiping.

(v) **What does the complaint from the sweeper reveal about the bank's financial situation? What does it tell us about the condition of the people? (4)**

Ans. The complaint from the sweeper reveals that the bank was struggling financially, as it couldn't even pay its employees on time. This suggests that the bank was likely facing a severe cash flow problem, unable to maintain regular operations such as paying employees.

This situation reflects the vulnerability of people like the sweeper, who rely heavily on timely payments to meet their basic needs. It highlights the sad condition of the working class in Pipalnagar, where even minor disruptions in income can cause significant distress. The sweeper's frustration and desire to leave his job also highlight the lack of security and support for low-income workers, emphasising the unequal distribution.

Extract 3

The Pipalnagar Bank is about to collapse. You'd better get your money out as soon as you can!' Deep Chand who was cutting the hair of an elderly gentleman, was so startled that his hand shook and he nicked his customer's right ear. The customer yelped with pain and distress: pain, because of the cut and distress because of the awful news he had just heard.

(i) **Who was Deep Chand? What caused Deep Chand to accidentally nick his customer's ear? (3)**

Ans. Deep Chand was a barber who was cutting the hair of an elderly gentleman in his shop. Deep Chand was startled by the news that the Pipalnagar Bank was about to collapse, which caused his hand to shake and accidentally nick the customer's ear.

(ii) **Why did the elderly gentleman feel both pain and distress after hearing the news? (3)**

Ans. The elderly gentleman felt pain because of the cut on his ear and distress because of the shocking news about the bank's possible collapse, which likely affected his finances.

(iii) **What does the phrase 'the bird has flown' suggest about Seth Govind Ram's actions? (3)**

Ans. The phrase 'the bird has flown' suggests that Seth Govind Ram has left town, possibly to escape the consequences of the bank's financial troubles.

It implies that he may have abandoned his responsibilities. It further made the people sure that the bank had collapsed.

(iv) **Do you think the elderly gentleman's reaction to the news was justified? Why or why not? How does the reaction of people differ based on their class difference? (3)**

Ans. Yes, the elderly gentleman's reaction to the news was justified because the potential collapse of a bank where he likely had savings would naturally cause panic and urgency.

The reactions to the news differed based on class differences. For lower-class individuals like Nathu, the crisis was a personal issue tied to delayed wages, directly affecting their livelihood. Middle-class individuals, like the elderly gentleman, panicked. In contrast, the upper class, represented by Seth Govind Ram, appeared to avoid the crisis entirely by leaving town.

(v) **Why did the elderly gentleman doubt that Seth Govind Ram was in Kashmir? What does it reflect about Seth? (4)**

Ans. The elderly gentleman doubted that Seth Govind Ram was in Kashmir because it seemed suspicious for the owner of a bank to be on holiday during a financial crisis. This raised concerns that Seth might have deliberately left town.

This reflects that Seth Govind Ram may have been irresponsible, avoiding accountability when his presence was most needed.

Extract 4

... they gathered outside, on the steps of the bank shouting 'Give us our money or we'll break in!' and 'Fetch the Seth, we know he's hiding in a safe deposit locker!' Mischief makers who didn't have a paisa in the bank, joined the crowd and aggravated their mood. The manager stood at the door and tried to placate them. He declared that the bank had plenty of money but no immediate means of collecting it; he urged them to go home and come back the next day.

(i) **What did the crowd shout while gathering outside the bank? Who joined the crowd to aggravate the situation, even though they had no money in the bank? (3)**

Ans. The crowd shouted, 'Give us our money or we'll break in!' and 'Fetch the Seth, we know he's hiding in a safe deposit locker!'

Mischief makers who didn't have any money in the bank joined the crowd and aggravated their mood.

(ii) **Why did the manager ask the crowd to return the next day? (3)**

Ans. The manager asked the crowd to return the next day because he explained that while the bank had plenty of money, it did not have the immediate means to collect or distribute it.

(iii) **How did the crowd's behaviour escalate the tension outside the bank? (3)**

Ans. The crowd's chanting and aggressive demands, along with the actions of mischief makers created chaos. The situation escalated when a brick was thrown and shattered the window of the bank, adding violence to the unrest.

(iv) **Do you think the crowd's reaction to the bank's situation was justified? Why or why not? (3)**

Ans. The crowd's reaction was understandable due to their fear and frustration over not receiving their money. However, their violent actions, like breaking the window, were not justified.

While the bank's situation was difficult, violence is not an appropriate response to resolve such issues.

(v) **What does the crowd's reaction to the bank's financial crisis reveal about the themes of trust and fear in a community? (4)**

Ans. The crowd's reaction highlights the theme of trust and fear in a community. It shows how quickly trust in an institution can collapse when financial stability is questioned. The panic and aggressive demands develop from fear of losing their savings, which reflects the community's deep reliance on the bank. The situation also highlights how rumours and misinformation can amplify fear, leading to chaos and irrational behaviour.

Extract 5

You'll have to, I suppose, now that the bank is going out of business.' 'How's that?' said Nathu. 'Haven't you heard? Well you'd better wait here until half the population of Pipalnagar arrives to claim their money.' And he waved cheerfully he did not have a bank account and sped away on his cycle. Nathu went back to sweeping the steps, muttering to himself. When he had finished his work, he sat down on the highest step, to await the arrival of the manager.

(i) **Where did Nathu sit while waiting for the manager? What did Nathu decide to do after finishing his work at the bank? (3)**

Ans. Nathu sat on the highest step of the bank while waiting for the manager.

Nathu decided to wait for the manager to demand his unpaid salary.

(ii) **The conversation between Nathu and the washerman's boy reflect the growing tension in Pipalnagar. How does it do so? Explain. (3)**

Ans. The conversation between Nathu and the washerman's boy reflects the growing tension in Pipalnagar by highlighting the spread of rumours and the uncertainty surrounding the bank's collapse. The washerman's boy mentions that the bank is going out of business and warns Nathu to expect a crowd demanding their money. The conversation highlights how the crisis has become a topic of widespread discussion and panic.

(iii) **What can Nathu's determination to wait for the manager tell us about his character and condition? (3)**

Ans. Nathu's decision to wait for the manager shows that he is determined and doesn't give up easily. It also shows that he is in a tough situation, as he hasn't been paid and needs the money badly.

This tells us that Nathu is strong-willed but also struggling because of his job and the bank's problems. His situation shows the challenges faced by individuals like Nathu in uncertain circumstances.

(iv) **How does the theme of financial insecurity affect the characters in the story, especially Nathu and the people of Pipalnagar? (3)**

Ans. The theme of financial insecurity deeply affects both Nathu and the people of Pipalnagar. For Nathu, the inability to receive his wages highlights his struggle with poverty. His determination to get paid reflects the anxiety and frustration caused by financial instability.

The townspeople are also impacted as they panic about the bank's collapse, fearing they will lose their savings. This creates a sense of unrest and chaos.

(v) **What role does gossip and rumour play in shaping the reactions of the people in Pipalnagar to the bank's situation? (4)**

Ans. In 'The Boy Who Broke the Bank,' gossip and rumour play a crucial role in creating panic among the people of Pipalnagar. The story begins with Bankey complaining about his unpaid salary, which Nathu, the gardener, casually mentions. This small talk spreads through different people, each adding their own assumptions. As the rumour spreads, people begin to believe the bank is failing. Fear and uncertainty lead to mass panic, with depositors rushing to withdraw their money. The story humorously shows how misinformation can turn a minor issue into a crisis, affecting the entire town's behaviour and decisions.

TREASURE CHEST: POETRY

1. A Work of Artifice
2. Skimbleshanks: The Railway Cat
3. I Remember, I Remember
4. A Doctor's Journal Entry for August 6, 1945
5. The Night Mail

01

A WORK OF ARTIFICE

Marge Piercy

Introduction

A Work of Artifice is a poem by Marge Piercy, an American poet known for her feminist and social justice themes. It explores themes of oppression and control. The poem, written in free verse, compares cultural conditioning to shaping a tree. It highlights how women's potential is deliberately limited. The poem's strength lies in its subtle yet striking critique of gender roles.

About the Poem

The poem **A Work of Artifice** criticises the restrictions society places on women, using the metaphor of a bonsai tree to illustrate their stunted potential. It compares women to a tree that could grow large and strong on its own. It is pruned lovingly to keep it small in height. It is purposefully kept small and decorative so that it does not grow big.

The gardener, therefore, becomes a symbol of patriarchal influences. Such forces shape a woman's role to conform to social norms while preventing her from reaching her full potential.

Exploring the Stanzas

The bonsai .... inches high.

In the above lines, the poet uses the image of a bonsai tree to symbolise the stunted growth of individuals, particularly women, due to societal constraints. The tree could have naturally grown tall and strong symbolising potential, freedom and growth. The phrase 'could have grown eighty feet tall' creates the image of a flourishing life, full of possibilities. However, the gardener's intervention, symbolising societal forces, carefully clips the tree, preventing it from reaching its natural height. This 'pruning' represents the deliberate restrictions placed on women by societal expectations.

The tree is 'nine inches high' as a result of this control, symbolising how women are often confined to limited roles, preventing them from reaching their full potential. The image of the tree 'split by lightning' suggests that if left to grow freely, it could have faced challenges but also reached greatness, implying untapped possibilities.

Every day .... grow in.

In the above lines, the gardener's actions and words represent the societal forces that justify and reinforce the restrictions imposed on the bonsai tree, symbolising women. When the gardener 'whittles back the branches', it symbolises the painstaking job of controlling development to keep the tree small and under control. 'It is your nature to be small and cozy, domestic and weak', the gardener croons, symbolising the concept that women should continue to play passive, submissive roles because of social norms.

The tree is made to believe that its smallness and confinement are natural. This emphasises the idea of women being confined to domestic, weak and dependent roles in society. The phrase "How lucky, little tree, to have a pot to grow in" is ironic. It implies that being limited and controlled is a blessing. In fact, it is an oppressive force preventing freedom and growth.

With living .... love to touch.

In the above lines, the poet emphasises that society's control and limitations on women begin at a very young age. The lines suggest that women are conditioned to conform to societal expectations from childhood. This restricts their personal development and potential. The imagery of 'bound feet' and 'crippled brain' symbolises the physical and intellectual limitations imposed on women by society's standards.

'The hair in curlers' symbolises the pressure to conform to beauty standards. Further, the line "the hands you love to touch" reflects how these controls even extend to personal expressions of affection and human connection. Overall, the lines critique the early and general societal conditioning that stunts growth, independence and freedom.

Vocab Vault

Artifice Clever or skillful trickery, deception or artificial behaviour.

Bonsai tree A small tree or plant that is cultivated and shaped to remain small, often grown in a pot.

Split To be divided.

Pruned To cut branches or parts of branches off a tree or bush in order to make it a better shape.

Croon To sing or hum in a soft, soothing or gentle voice.

Cozy Comfortable

Whittle Carve (wood) into an object by repeatedly cutting small slices from it.

Dwarf To stunt or hinder the growth of something, making it smaller than it would naturally be.

Crippled To damage or impair, often used to describe something that is weakened or handicapped.

Theme of the Poem

The poem uses the bonsai tree as a metaphor to explore themes of feminism, gender roles and societal control. It critiques how women are expected to remain small, decorative and confined to household duties, limiting their intellectual and personal growth. Societal pressures, symbolised by the gardener, like an ornamental piece to enforce conformity to restrictive norms, making women believe that being diminished is their natural state.

The line, 'It is your nature to be small and cozy', highlights the constructed and false nature of these expectations, which suppress individuality and potential.

Message Conveyed by the Poem

Marge Piercy's A Work of Artifice criticises how society limits women's growth and potential. Using the metaphor of a bonsai tree, the poem shows how women, like the tree, are shaped to fit narrow roles. These restrictions, imposed from a young age, confine women to domesticity and dependence. Piercy urges readers to challenge these unnatural and unfair societal expectations.

Style, Tone and Mood

- **Style** The style of the poem is simple yet deeply symbolic, using vivid imagery and metaphor to critique societal norms.
- **Tone** The tone is critical and ironic as the poet exposes the subtle oppression of women disguised as care and artistry.
- **Mood** The mood is reflective and sombre. It evokes a sense of injustice and loss as readers consider the denied potential of individuals forced into restrictive roles. The poem's style amplifies its feminist message.

Title

The title 'A Work of Artifice' captures the poem's central theme of artificial societal constraints. The term 'artifice' describes something that has been created or altered, often in a dishonest or unnatural manner. The poem portrays society's constraints and expectations as artificial, purposefully reshaping women into limited, predeterminedpositions. The title suggests that the societal forces controlling and limiting growth are not inherent or natural; rather, they are deliberately constructed, much like a work of art that is carefully crafted.

Literary Devices

- **Metaphor** "The bonsai tree in the attractive pot..." ***[Stanza 1]***
- **Personification** "The gardener croons, It is your nature to be small and cozy." ***[Stanza 2]***
  [The gardener represents societal forces that shape and limit individuals, giving a human-like role to abstract societal norms.]
- **Irony** "How lucky, little tree, to have a pot to grow in." ***[Stanza 2]***
- **Symbolism** "The bound feet, the crippled brain." ***[Stanza 3]***
- **Imagery** "Every day as he whittles back the branches." ***[Stanza 2]***

EXAM ORIENTED QUESTIONS

TYPE - 1 Multiple Choice Questions

01 Mark

Q.1 What, according to Marge Piercy in 'A Work of Artifice', should begin very early with living creatures?
(ICSE Specimen 2024)
(a) Trimming their branches
(b) Teaching them life lessons
(c) Assigning gender roles
(d) Preparing them for life's struggles

Q.2 What does the bonsai tree symbolise in the poem?
(a) Nature
(b) Women confined by societal norms
(c) Strength and resilience
(d) Artistic beauty

Q.3 What is the role of the gardener in the poem?
(a) A symbol of nature's beauty
(b) A caretaker of the bonsai tree
(c) A representation of societal control
(d) A metaphor for personal growth

Q.4 Identify the literary device used in the following line "The bonsai tree in the attractive pot".
(a) Metaphor
(b) Simile
(c) Personification
(d) Irony

Q.5 What is the significance of the phrase 'Could have grown eighty feet tall'?
(a) It highlights the tree's beauty.
(b) It represents untapped potential.
(c) It critiques natural limitations.
(d) It praises the gardener's skills.

Q.6 "The bound feet,
the crippled brain,
the hair in curlers"
In the above lines, the phrase 'bound feet' symbolise ....
(a) cultural heritage
(b) physical restrictions imposed on women
(c) feminine beauty
(d) religious customs

Q.7 "It is your nature to be small and cozy"
The above line signifies ....
(a) true care for the bonsai tree
(b) societal justification of oppression
(c) natural limitations of the tree
(d) encouragement of growth

Q.8 Which of the following options contains the figure of speech that appears in the following line
'The hair in curlers'.
(a) The bound feet, the crippled brain
(b) could have grown eighty feet tall
(c) With living creatures/ one must begin very early
(d) Whittles back the branches

Q.9 What is the significance of the phrase "How lucky, little tree, to have a pot to grow in"?
(a) Genuine care for the tree
(b) Irony highlighting confinement
(c) Celebration of growth
(d) Symbol of freedom

Q.10 What is the central message of the poem?
(a) Art is a reflection of nature.
(b) Society restricts women's potential.
(c) Gardening is an act of love.
(d) Freedom leads to chaos.

Q.11 What does the repetition of 'dwarf their growth' emphasise?
(a) The inevitability of limitations
(b) The deliberate act of stunting potential
(c) Natural growth patterns
(d) Care for the tree's health

Q.12 What mood does the poem create?
1. Joyful
2. Uplifting
3. Reflective
4. Sombre
5. Romantic
6. Suspenseful
(a) 1 and 2
(b) 2 and 4
(c) 3 and 4
(d) 5 and 6

Q.13 What does the gardener's crooning represent?
(a) Genuine affection
(b) Manipulative reassurance
(c) Encouragement of freedom
(d) Celebration of beauty

Q.14 What does the line "One must begin very early to dwarf their growth" suggest?
(a) Natural growth takes time.
(b) Suppression starts from a young age.
(c) Growth is unpredictable.
(d) Early care ensures strength.

Q.15 Select the option that shows the correct relationship between statements (1) and (2).

Statement 1 The bonsai tree couldn't grow to its natural height of eighty feet.

Statement 2 The bonsai tree was deliberately pruned and confined by the gardener.

(a) Statement 1 is true and Statement 2 is false
(b) Statement 2 is true and Statement 1 is false.
(c) Statement 2 is the cause for Statement 1.
(d) Statement 1 and Statement 2 are independent of each other.

Q.16 'With living creatures
one must begin very early
to dwarf their growth'

These lines tell us that the poet is feeling ....

(a) content (b) disappointed
(c) anxious (d) withdrawn

Q.17 What is the significance of the phrase 'nine inches high' in the poem?

(a) It refers to the ideal size of a bonsai tree.
(b) It highlights the stunted growth due to external control.
(c) It symbolises the strength of women.
(d) It shows the beauty of small things.

Q.18 Which of the following best critiques the societal implications of the poem?

(a) It portrays women as helpless victims of societal norms.
(b) It suggests that societal control is necessary for discipline.
(c) It exposes how restrictive norms disguise themselves as nurturing care.
(d) It argues that people should not interfere with nature.

Answers

1. (a)	2. (b)	3. (c)	4. (a)	5. (b)	6. (b)	7. (b)	8. (a)	9. (b)	10. (b)
11. (b)	12. (c)	13. (b)	14. (b)	15. (c)	16. (b)	17. (b)	18. (c)		

Explanations

8. The line 'the hair in curlers' metaphorically represents societal restrictions on women, similar to 'the bound feet, the crippled brain', which symbolise imposed limitations on physical and intellectual growth. Both use imagery to convey the theme of restriction and conformity.

12. The poem creates a reflective and sombre mood as it critiques the societal restrictions placed on women, symbolised by the stunted bonsai tree. The tone invites contemplation on oppression and the loss of individuality, evoking serious and thoughtful emotions.

TYPE - 2 Extract Based Questions 16 Marks

Extract 1

The bonsai tree
in the attractive pot
could have grown eighty feet tall
on the side of a mountain
till split by lightning.
But a gardener
carefully pruned it.
It is nine inches high.

(i) What does the bonsai tree symbolise in the stanza? **(3)**

Ans. The bonsai tree symbolises women whose natural growth and potential are stunted by societal constraints.

The tree, confined to a small pot and pruned by the gardener, reflects how society limits individuals to fit restrictive roles. This further denies them the freedom to grow fully.

(ii) How does the 'attractive pot' contribute to the poem's theme? **(3)**

Ans. The 'attractive pot' represents societal structures or norms that appear appealing but are, in fact, confining. It suggests that the limitations imposed on individuals are often masked as care or beauty, hiding their restrictive nature.

(iii) What is the significance of the phrase 'Could have grown eighty feet tall'? How does it stand in contrast with the tree being 'nine inches high'? **(3)**

Ans. This phrase emphasises the bonsai tree's potential for greatness and freedom. It signifies the natural ability to thrive and grow which is stifled by external control. This symbolises the loss of individuality due to societal oppression.

This potential contrasts sharply with the reality of the tree being 'nine inches high' which highlights its artificially stunted state. The contrast emphasises the limitation imposed by external forces, such as societal norms, which limit individuality and freedom under the guise of care or nurture.

(iv) **What role does the gardener play in the stanza?** **(3)**

Ans. The gardener symbolises societal forces that impose restrictions and shape individuals to adhere to specific expectations. Through pruning the tree, the gardener limits its growth, reflecting how society stifles personal freedom and potential.

(v) **Identify and elaborate on the literary devices used in the above lines.** **(4)**

Ans. Marge Piercy employs the following literary devices to enhance the poem's meaning

(a) **Metaphor** The bonsai tree represents women whose growth and potential are stunted by societal constraints. The gardener symbolises the forces or institutions that impose these restrictions.

(b) **Imagery** Phrases like 'eighty feet tall' and 'on the side of a mountain' evoke vivid pictures of the tree's natural potential. Meanwhile, the phrase 'nine inches high' highlights its diminished state.

(c) **Contrast** The juxtaposition between the tree's potential height of 'eighty feet' and its actual height of 'nine inches' underscores the extent of its suppression.

(d) **Symbolism** The 'attractive pot' symbolises societal norms that appear appealing but restrict freedom. The 'lightning' represents natural challenges the tree might face if allowed to grow freely.

Extract 2

Every day as he
whittles back the branches
the gardener croons,
It is your nature
to be small and cozy,
domestic and weak;
how lucky, little tree,
to have a pot to grow in.

(i) **Who is crooning to the tree? What is the significance of this act?** **(3)**

Ans. The gardener is crooning to the tree.

The act of crooning, which is typically soothing and gentle, holds significant irony in the poem. It represents societal forces gently enforcing limitations under the guise of care and affection. It highlights how manipulation and control can be subtly imposed, making restrictions seem natural or beneficial.

(ii) **How does the phrase 'It is your nature to be small and cozy' reflect societal expectations?** **(3)**

Ans. The given phrase reflects societal expectations by implying that women are naturally suited for limited, domestic roles. It suggests that their natural state is to be confined, submissive and content within a restricted space.

This assertion serves to justify the societal imposition of constraints and diminishes their potential for growth and independence. It critiques how society justifies limiting personal growth by framing it as inherent or desirable.

(iii) **How does the stanza critique societal roles for women?** **(3)**

Ans. The stanza critiques societal roles by illustrating how women are conditioned to accept limited, domestic roles as their natural state. It highlights the deceptive and manipulative nature of this conditioning which limits their true potential.

(iv) **What does the act of 'whittling back the branches' symbolise?** **(3)**

Ans. The act of 'whittling back the branches' symbolises the deliberate and continuous restriction of an individual's potential and freedom by societal forces. It reflects how society systematically prunes away personal growth and aspirations to fit predetermined roles for women. This act represents the ongoing control and manipulation that limits women's natural development. It forces them to conform to confined, traditional expectations rather than realising their full potential.

(v) **What does the line 'How lucky, little tree, to have a pot to grow in' suggest about societal control?** **(4)**

Ans. The given line suggests that societal control is often presented as a benevolent or protective measure even though it is restrictive. The 'pot' symbolises the societal norms and roles that confine women under the disguise of providing security and care.

The use of irony in the word 'lucky' highlights how the tree (and by extension, individuals) is made to believe that its limited, controlled existence is fortunate. This masks the reality of its stunted growth and lost potential. It critiques the deceptive nature of societal constraints disguised as nurturing.

Extract 3

But a gardener
carefully pruned it.
It is nine inches high.
Every day as he
whittles back the branches
the gardener croons,
It is your nature
to be small and cozy,
domestic and weak;

(i) Identify the title of the poem from which the above extract has been taken. What is the significance of the title? (3)

Ans. The extract is from the poem 'A Work of Artifice' by Marge Piercy.

The title 'A Work of Artifice' highlights the deliberate and unnatural manipulation of something natural. 'Artifice' refers to a skilled craft or deception, implying that the gardener's actions are an intentional act of control and distortion.

The title underscores the themes of the poem – the artificial restrictions placed on women, to conform to societal expectations, limiting their true potential and growth.

(ii) What is the significance of the bonsai tree being 'nine inches high' in the context of the poem? (3)

Ans. The specific measurement of 'nine inches high' emphasises the extent to which the tree's growth has been artificially stunted. It highlights the loss of potential and serves as a metaphor for how women are kept small and diminished by societal constraints.

(iii) Why does the gardener's 'crooning' add a sinister tone to the poem? (3)

Ans. The gardener's 'crooning', is typically associated with comfort and care but here it, adds a sinister tone.

It contrasts the nurturing implication with the oppressive act of stunting the tree's growth. This suggests that the control is disguised as benevolence, making the act of suppression seem acceptable or even loving.

(iv) Analyse the literary device used in the lines 'Every day as he whittles back the branches'. (3)

Ans. In the line 'Every day as he whittles back the branches', the imagery of 'whittling' suggests a repetitive, deliberate act of suppression. The branches symbolise potential growth which is continuously limited. This daily action highlights the relentless control and manipulation exerted by societal forces.

The imagery effectively conveys how women are systematically restrained and shaped to conform to restrictive societal expectations.

(v) Identify the themes of the poem based on the above extract. Elaborate. (4)

Ans. The poem 'A Work of Artifice' explores the following themes in the above lines

(a) **Control and Manipulation** The gardener's act of 'carefully pruned it' and 'whittles back the branches' symbolises the deliberate control exerted over the bonsai tree. This represents how society manipulates and restricts women to fit into narrowly defined roles.

(b) **Suppression of Potential** The bonsai tree being 'nine inches high' despite its potential to grow much larger reflects the theme of suppressed potential. It symbolises how women's abilities and aspirations are limited by societal expectations.

(c) **Gender Roles and Expectations** The lines 'It is your nature to be small and cozy, domestic and weak' illustrate the reinforcement of traditional gender roles. This theme highlights how women are often conditioned to accept roles that confine them to domesticity and submissiveness, under the guise of it being their natural place.

(d) **Deceptive Nurturing** The gardener 'croons' as he prunes the tree, which adds a layer of deception, presenting control and limitation as care and nurturing. This theme critiques how oppressive societal structures often disguise their restrictive nature as benevolent or for the individual's own good.

Extract 4

With living creatures
one must begin very early
to dwarf their growth:
the bound feet,
the crippled brain,
the hair in curlers,
the hands you
love to touch.

(i) What does the phrase 'One must begin very early to dwarf their growth' imply? (3)

Ans. The phrase suggests that societal conditioning and limitations on women begin at a very young age. It emphasises the deliberate and systematic effort to restrict their natural growth, potential and independence from early life.

(ii) **The phrase 'the bound feet' is symbolic in the poem A Work of Artifice. Explain its significance.** **(3)**

Ans. 'The bound feet' symbolises physical constraints imposed by societal norms, referencing practices like foot binding that limited women's freedom and movement. It serves as a metaphor for the ways society controls and restricts women.

(iii) **How does the poet use 'the crippled brain' to convey societal oppression?** **(3)**

Ans. 'The crippled brain' represents the intellectual stifling caused by societal norms. It suggests that women's potential for intellectual growth and creativity is suppressed through restrictions on education and freedom of thought.

(iv) **What does 'the hair in curlers' symbolise in the context of the stanza?** **(3)**

Ans. 'The hair in curlers' symbolises societal beauty standards and the pressure on women to conform to prescribed appearances. It reflects how women are often judged based on their looks rather than their abilities.

(v) **How does the line 'the hands you love to touch' create a contrasting image in the stanza?** **(4)**

Ans. The line 'the hands you love to touch' creates a contrasting image by juxtaposing the tenderness of love and affection with the oppressive act of societal control.

While the phrase suggests intimacy and warmth, it is ironically paired with the earlier lines about physical and intellectual restrictions, such as 'bound feet' and 'crippled brain'.

This contrast highlights the subtle manipulation of society where even the most cherished aspects of a person are shaped and confined. The line exposes the tension between love and control, reflecting the poem's critique of oppressive societal norms.

02

SKIMBLESHANKS: THE RAILWAY CAT

T.S. Eliot

Introduction

Skimbleshanks: The Railway Cat is a poem by T.S. Eliot, a famous poet known for his works on modern life and whimsical themes. This poem belongs to the genre of narrative poetry with a touch of humour. The poem highlights Skimbleshanks' discipline and responsibility in running the Night Mail smoothly. Its unique charm comes from its playful rhythm and the idea of a cat being in charge of a train.

About the Poem

Skimbleshanks: The Railway Cat is a delightful poem from T.S. Eliot's 'Old Possum's Book of Practical Cats'. The poem celebrates Skimbleshanks, a meticulous and punctual cat who plays a crucial role in the railway. He ensures that everything on the train runs smoothly, from passenger comfort to the crew's responsibilities. The poem reflects Eliot's ability to infuse everyday subjects with humour and personality.

Exploring the Stanzas

There's a whisper .... luggage van!

In these lines, there is a sense of urgency and anticipation as the Night Mail train is about to depart at 11:39 pm. However, the departure is delayed because Skimbleshanks, the essential Railway Cat, is missing. The train staff, including guards, porters and even the stationmaster's daughters, are frantically searching for him.

The train cannot start without Skimbleshanks emphasising his importance. Just before the signal at 11:42 pm, as passengers grow anxious, Skimbleshanks casually appears having been busy in the luggage van. His calm demeanour contrasts with the frantic search showcasing his pivotal role in ensuring the train runs smoothly.

He gives .... the move.

In these lines, Skimbleshanks is portrayed as a vigilant and authoritative figure aboard the Sleeping Car Express. With a flash of his glass-green eyes, he signals the train's readiness, setting it in motion for its journey in the Northern part of Northern Hemisphere. Skimbleshanks assumes a supervisory role, overseeing everyone from the driver and guards to passengers and card-playing bagmen. His regular patrol through the train ensures order and discipline.

His piercing gaze and intuitive nature allow him to sense any mischief, discouraging any unruly behaviour. His presence brings calm and quiet, as passengers remain well-behaved under his watchful eyes. Skimbleshanks ensures that everything runs smoothly, emphasising his critical role in maintaining order and efficiency on the train.

You can play .... Railway Train!

In these lines, Skimbleshanks is depicted as an indispensable figure aboard the Northern Mail train. Known for his strict and vigilant nature, no mischief or pranks can escape his notice. His presence ensures that everything runs smoothly making the journey pleasant for passengers. The poem describes the comfortable accommodations, highlighting the cleanliness and the thoughtful amenities such as adjustable lights, a small basin and a crank to control the window.

The guard checks on passengers politely and asks you very brightly if you like your morning tea weak or strong. However, it's Skimbleshanks who truly ensures nothing goes wrong. His watchful presence even keeps mice at bay offering passengers peace of mind. The poem celebrates Skimbleshanks as a reliable and essential guardian of the train, ensuring a safe and orderly journey for all.

In the watches .... Railway Train."

In these lines, Skimbleshanks is portrayed as a tireless guardian of the train staying alert throughout the night. He enjoys a cup of tea, sometimes with a bit of scotch while on duty, only pausing briefly for minor distractions like catching a flea. As passengers sleep through stops like Crewe and Carlisle, Skimbleshanks remains active, patrolling and interacting cheerfully with the stationmaster.

At Dumfries, he even communicates with the police, ensuring all is in order. His efficiency ensures passengers won't face delays at Gallowgate. Skimbleshanks, with his wave of the tail, assures passengers they'll see him again. This symbolises his unwavering presence and dedication.

Vocab Vault

Thimble A small cover, usually made of metal or plastic, worn to protect the finger.

Porter A person whose job is to carry suitcases, etc. at a railway station, airport, etc.

Nimble Quick

Frantic Quite restlessness

Saunter Walk in a slow, relaxed manner

Rear Backside or behind

By and large Generally

Patrol Taking rounds in a particular place to keep at encroachment

Hilarity Amusement

Riot Disturbance of peace by group of people

Pranks Tricks

Speck Particle

To reflect To think deeply

Flea Bug

Elation To be over excited over something

Counterpane A bedspread or blanket

Anthromorphism Giving human traits to animals or objects

Theme of the Poem

The poem **Skimbleshanks: The Railway Cat** highlights themes of duty, order and cooperation. Skimbleshanks diligently ensures the smooth running of the train, working alongside guards, porters and passengers, symbolising the value of teamwork. His meticulous nature reflects the importance of organisation, while his essential role shows how even small contributions matter. Eliot's use of anthropomorphism adds humour and charm by blending human and animal behaviours.

Message Conveyed by the Poem

The poem conveys the importance of responsibility, order and diligence in everyday tasks. Skimbleshanks embodies these qualities as he ensures the smooth running of the Night Mail train overseeing every detail from cleanliness to passenger comfort. Through this charming portrayal of a cat's dedication, T.S. Eliot highlights how even the smallest, often overlooked contributions are essential to the functioning of a larger system emphasising the value of reliability and attention to duty.

Style, Tone and Mood

- **Style** The poem features a playful and rhythmic style, capturing the lively and organised nature of Skimbleshanks.
- **Tone** The tone is light-hearted and humorous, highlighting the cat's importance on the train.
- **Mood** The mood is cheerful and comforting, as the poem creates a whimsical yet orderly atmosphere aboard the Night Mail.

Title

The title 'Skimbleshanks' refers to the central character of the poem, a meticulous and responsible railway cat. It sets the tone for a whimsical narrative highlighting the cat's importance on the Night Mail train. The unique name 'Skimbleshanks' reflects the playful and imaginative nature of T.S. Eliot's poetry, drawing readers into the charming world of this industrious feline. The title encapsulates the essence of the poem focusing on Skimbleshanks' vital role in ensuring the smooth operation of the train journey.

Literary Devices

- **Alliteration** "Skimble, where is Skimble?" ***(Stanza 1)*** (repetition of 's' sound)
- **Imagery** "He gives one flash of his glass-green eyes." ***(Line 13)***
- **Repetition** "Skimbleshanks is aboard."
- **Hyperbole** "Nothing goes wrong on the Northern Mail / When Skimbleshanks is aboard." ***(Line 31)***
- **Rhythm and Meter** The poem uses a regular meter, contributing to its lively pace. The rhythm matches the train's journey, creating a sense of movement and energy.
- **Onomatopoeia** "He gives one flash of his glass-green eyes." ***(Line 13)***

EXAM ORIENTED QUESTIONS

TYPE - 1 Multiple Choice Questions — 01 Mark

Q.1 Which of the following tasks is not performed by Skimbleshanks in the poem? **(ICSE Specimen 2024)**
(a) Supervision of the driver
(b) Supervision of the guards
(c) Supervision of the bagmen
(d) Supervision of the police

Q.2 What is Skimbleshanks' role in the poem?
(a) A passenger
(b) A railway cat responsible for maintaining order
(c) A train conductor
(d) A ticket collector

Q.3 What does Skimbleshanks do in the poem?
(a) Sleep in the luggage van
(b) Ensure the smooth operation of the train
(c) Clean the station
(d) Entertain the passengers

Q.4 Which of the following qualities best describe Skimbleshanks?
(a) Lazy and indifferent
(b) Efficient and hardworking
(c) Friendly and playful
(d) Shy and reserved

Q.5 What time of day does Skimbleshanks perform his duties?
(a) During the day (b) During the night
(c) Early morning (d) In the afternoon

Q.6 What is the mood of the poem?
I. Serious II. Humorous
III. Lighthearted IV. Mournful
V. Angry
(a) I and II (b) II and III (c) III and IV (d) IV and V

Q.7 What is Skimbleshanks' attitude towards his work?
(a) Disinterested (b) Enthusiastic and dedicated
(c) Reluctant (d) Careless

Q.8 Where does Skimbleshanks walk while performing his duties?
(a) The passenger compartments
(b) The station
(c) The luggage van and the train
(d) The engine room

Q.9 How does Skimbleshanks interact with the passengers?
(a) He avoids them
(b) He supervises and ensures they are safe
(c) He plays games with them
(d) He sleeps next to them

Q.10 What is one of Skimbleshanks' physical traits?
(a) Large and muscular
(b) Small and fragile
(c) Long brown tail
(d) White fur

Q.11 What does Skimbleshanks do when the train is about to depart?
(a) He hides
(b) He supervises the train's departure
(c) He plays with the passengers
(d) He waits for the conductor

Q.12 What is Skimbleshanks' reaction to the sleeping passengers?
(a) He wakes them up
(b) He ignores them
(c) He continues with his work unnoticed
(d) He talks to them

Q.13 How does Skimbleshanks make sure that no mistakes happen?
(a) By asking for help from others
(b) By being vigilant and checking everything
(c) By taking naps
(d) By avoiding difficult tasks

Q.14 What type of train is Skimbleshanks aboard?
(a) A freight train (b) The Sleeping Car Express
(c) A passenger train (d) A local train

Q.15 What does Skimbleshanks do when passengers need assistance?
(a) He sleeps (b) He ignores them
(c) He helps them without hesitation
(d) He waits for the conductor

Q.16 Which city does Skimbleshanks visit during the train's journey?
(a) Glasgow (b) London (c) Edinburgh (d) Paris

Q.17 What kind of atmosphere does Skimbleshanks maintain on the train?
(a) Chaotic (b) Peaceful and orderly
(c) Loud and busy (d) Quiet and gloomy

Q.18 What is the primary function of Skimbleshanks on the train?
(a) To entertain the passengers
(b) To maintain order and safety
(c) To manage the luggage
(d) To ensure the train runs on time

Q.19 What is one of Skimbleshanks' methods of checking on the passengers?
(a) He watches them while they sleep
(b) He speaks to them directly
(c) He checks their belongings
(d) He walks up and down the train

Q.20 What makes Skimbleshanks different from the other cats?
(a) He is very lazy
(b) He is a hardworking and vigilant cat
(c) He enjoys playing with passengers
(d) He sleeps all day

Q.21 What does Skimbleshanks do at the stations?
(a) He rests
(b) He greets the stationmaster and checks the passengers
(c) He eats food
(d) He plays games with the children

Q.22 What does Skimbleshanks' tail represent at the end of the journey?
(a) His happiness (b) His farewell
(c) His exhaustion (d) His triumph

Q.23 How does the poem describe Skimbleshanks' behaviour towards the train and its operations?
(a) Careless and inattentive (b) Playful and mischievous
(c) Responsible and watchful (d) Indifferent and lazy

Q.24 Arrange the following events in the correct sequence as described in the poem.
1. Skimbleshanks inspects the faces of passengers.
2. Skimbleshanks helps passengers to get out of the train.
3. Skimbleshanks has a cup of tea with a drop of Scotch.
4. Skimbleshanks supervises the driver and the guards.
5. Skimbleshanks makes sure that no pranks are played.

(a) 1, 4, 5, 3, 2 (b) 5, 1, 3, 4, 2
(c) 4, 1, 3, 5, 2 (d) 1, 5, 4, 3, 2

Q.25 Arrange the following events in the correct sequence as described in the poem.
1. Skimbleshanks appears on the scene, causing the train to depart.
2. Skimbleshanks is described as checking the faces of passengers.
3. Skimbleshanks supervises the sleeping car, ensuring everything is in order.
4. Skimbleshanks helps passengers get out of the train at the station.
5. Skimbleshanks is seen keeping watch at different stations like Crewe and Carlisle.

(a) 1, 2, 3, 5, 4 (b) 2, 1, 4, 3, 5
(c) 5, 1, 4, 2, 3 (d) 1, 3, 2, 4, 5

Q.26 Select the option that shows the correct relationship between statements (1) and (2).
Statement 1 Skimbleshanks is not mentioned as interacting with any station staff during the journey.
Statement 2 Skimbleshanks's duties include checking the sleeping carriages and ensuring no mischief takes place during the train ride.
(a) Statement 1 is true and Statement 2 is false
(b) Statement 2 is true and Statement 1 is false.
(c) Statement 2 is the reason for Statement 1.
(d) Statement 1 and Statement 2 are independent of each other.

Q.27 Select the option that shows the correct relationship between statements (1) and (2).
Statement 1 The passengers on the train enjoy their journey without any disruption.
Statement 2 Skimbleshanks supervises the train's operation, making sure the journey proceeds without any problems or disturbances.
(a) Statement 1 is true and Statement 2 is false
(b) Statement 2 is true and Statement 1 is false.
(c) Statement 2 is the reason for Statement 1.
(d) Statement 1 and Statement 2 are independent of each other.

Answers

1. (d)	2. (b)	3. (b)	4. (b)	5. (b)	6. (b)	7. (b)	8. (c)	9. (b)	10. (c)
11. (b)	12. (c)	13. (b)	14. (b)	15. (c)	16. (a)	17. (b)	18. (b)	19. (d)	20. (b)
21. (b)	22. (b)	23. (c)	24. (a)	25. (a)	26. (b)	27. (c)			

Explanations

6. The mood of is both humorous and lighthearted, as T.S. Eliot playfully describes the cat's important role on the train. The lively tone and charming depiction of Skimbleshanks' meticulous duties create an enjoyable and whimsical atmosphere.

23. The poem portrays Skimbleshanks as a diligent and responsible cat who ensures the smooth operation of the train. He is attentive to details, works alongside the train staff and maintains order, symbolising discipline and efficiency.

TYPE - 2 Extract Based Questions — 16 Marks

Extract 1

We must find him or the train can't start".
All the guards and all the porters and the stationmaster's daughters
They are searching high and low, Saying
"Skimble where is Skimble for unless he's very nimble

(i) **What is the significance of Skimbleshanks' role in the departure of the Night Mail? (3)**

Ans. Skimbleshanks plays a crucial role in ensuring the train's timely departure.

The lines suggest that his absence creates chaos and worry among the train staff and passengers. They search for him because the train cannot start without his presence.

This highlights Skimbleshanks' importance as the one who keeps everything in order, even in the small details like checking the luggage van.

(ii) **How does the poet create suspense in the lines describing Skimbleshanks' search? (3)**

Ans. The poet builds suspense by describing the frantic search for Skimbleshanks just before the train's departure. The whispering, the anxious search of the guards, porters and stationmaster's daughters and the repeated concern about the train not starting without Skimbleshanks heighten the tension.

The suspense is only relieved when Skimbleshanks appears, having been busy in the luggage van.

(iii) **Explain the meaning of the phrase "Skimble where is Skimble has he gone to hunt the thimble"? (3)**

Ans. The phrase 'hunt the thimble' is likely a playful reference to Skimbleshanks' behaviour, suggesting he is busy with something small or insignificant, like searching for a thimble.

This phrase conveys both Skimbleshanks' elusive nature and the light-hearted tone of the poem where even the train's operation is under the humorous watch of the cat.

(iv) **How does the poet describe the urgency of the situation when Skimbleshanks is missing? (3)**

Ans. The poet conveys the urgency of the situation by showing the frantic behaviour of the train staff and passengers. The phrase 'passengers are frantic to a man' suggests a sense of panic.

The line 'unless he's very nimble / Then the Night Mail just can't go' underscores the importance of Skimbleshanks' timely appearance for the train's departure adding to the sense of urgency.

(v) **Why is Skimbleshanks' appearance at the last moment significant in the poem? (4)**

Ans. Skimbleshanks' appearance at the last moment is important because it shows his reliability and the order he brings to the train. His absence causes worry among the staff and passengers, as the train cannot start without him. When he finally arrives, he calmly walks to his place, reassuring everyone that everything is under control. This moment highlights his importance in maintaining discipline and ensuring a smooth journey. His timely arrival turns chaos into order, proving that he is the real authority on the train despite being just a cat. His presence brings peace and security to all travellers.

Extract 2

You may say that by and large
it is Skimble who's in charge
Of the Sleeping Car Express.
From the driver and the guards
to the bagmen playing cards

(i) **What is the significance of Skimbleshanks' 'glass-green eyes' in the poem? (3)**

Ans. Skimbleshanks' 'glass-green eyes' symbolise his keen observation and authority. The flash of his eyes signals readiness and control initiating the train's departure with the 'All Clear' signal. This emphasises his role as the overseer of the train's smooth operation.

(ii) **How does Skimbleshanks' supervision extend throughout the train? (3)**

Ans. Skimbleshanks supervises the entire train staff – from the driver and guards to the bagmen playing cards. His vigilance extends to both the first and third-class travellers as he patrols the corridors, maintaining order and ensuring everything is under control. This highlights his comprehensive oversight.

(iii) **What does the poet imply by stating, 'It is Skimble who's in charge of the Sleeping Car Express'? (3)**

Ans. The poet implies that Skimbleshanks holds a significant position of responsibility and control on the train. Despite being a cat, he is portrayed as the central figure ensuring the train's smooth operation, suggesting his indispensable role in maintaining order and efficiency.

(iv) **Why is Skimbleshanks' ability to 'know at once if anything occurred' important for the narrative? (3)**

Ans. Skimbleshanks' immediate awareness of any occurrences underscores his attentiveness and reliability. This trait ensures the safety and smooth running of the train, reinforcing his role as an efficient overseer who can quickly address any issues that arise.

(v) **What does the poet convey through Skimbleshanks' 'regular patrol' down the corridor? (4)**

Ans. The poet conveys that Skimbleshanks' 'regular patrol' shows his dedication to keeping the train in perfect order. He walks through the corridors, carefully checking on passengers, staff and the train's condition. His constant vigilance ensures that everything runs smoothly and safely. By keeping a close watch on every detail, he creates a sense of security and comfort for the travelers. His presence and discipline make sure that nothing goes wrong. This also highlights his responsibility and authority over the train, even though he is just a cat. His patrol ensures a peaceful, organised and efficient journey.

Extract 3

He will watch you without winking and he sees what you are thinking
And it's certain that he doesn't approve
Of hilarity and riot, so the folk are very quiet
When Skimble is about and on the move.

(i) **What does the poet suggest about Skimbleshanks' ability to maintain order on the train? (3)**

Ans. The poet suggests that Skimbleshanks has a strong presence and authority which ensures that everything on the train runs smoothly. His mere presence prevents any mischief or chaos, as he disapproves of 'hilarity and riot', making the passengers behave quietly and orderly.

(ii) **How does Skimbleshanks contribute to the comfort of the passengers on the Northern Mail? (3)**

Ans. Skimbleshanks ensures that the passengers' berths are neat and comfortable. The poet describes how the berths are tidy, with freshly folded sheets and no dust, creating a pleasant and orderly environment for the travellers.

(iii) **'He will watch you without winking and he sees what you are thinking' what does this line imply about Skimbleshanks' character? (3)**

Ans. This line implies that Skimbleshanks is highly observant and attentive. He is vigilant and perceptive, capable of understanding and anticipating the needs or actions of the passengers which contributes to his effective supervision of the train.

(iv) **The poet emphasises that 'Nothing goes wrong on the Northern Mail when Skimbleshanks is aboard'. Why does he do so? Give a reason. (3)**

Ans. The poet emphasises this to highlight Skimbleshanks' crucial role in ensuring the smooth operation of the train. His presence instils a sense of order and reliability, suggesting that his vigilance and authority are key to preventing any issues during the journey.

(v) **How does the description of the berths reflect the overall mood created by Skimbleshanks' presence? (4)**

Ans. The neat and dust-free berths reflect the order and discipline Skimbleshanks brings to the train. His presence ensures cleanliness and comfort, making passengers feel safe and relaxed. The freshly folded sheets and tidy atmosphere show his attention to detail and dedication to maintaining a well-organised journey. The passengers trust him to keep everything in order, which creates a calm and peaceful mood. His meticulous care ensures that there is no mess or discomfort, making the train journey pleasant and smooth. This highlights his efficiency and reliability in making sure everything runs perfectly.

Extract 4

There is every sort of light-you can make it dark or bright;
There's a handle that you turn to make a breeze.
There's a funny little basin you're supposed to wash your face in
And a crank to shut the window if you sneeze.

(i) **What amenities are described in the poem to ensure passenger comfort on the train? (3)**

Ans. The poem describes several amenities, such as adjustable lighting to make the compartment dark or bright, a handle to control the breeze, a small basin for washing, and a crank to shut the window. These features highlight the attention to passenger comfort and convenience.

(ii) **How does Skimbleshanks ensure that nothing goes wrong on the train?** **(3)**

Ans. Skimbleshanks stays vigilant and supervises everything, even standing behind the guard to ensure that all tasks are performed correctly. His watchful presence and readiness to intervene guarantee that any potential issues are swiftly addressed, maintaining smooth operations.

(iii) **Explain the role of guard in the passengers' experience, and how is Skimbleshanks involved?** **(3)**

Ans. The guard plays a role in personalising the passenger experience by asking about preferences for morning tea. Skimbleshanks supports the guard by being present to ensure that everything is done properly, adding an extra layer of assurance that all is well on the train.

(iv) **Analyse the significance of mentioning that passengers won't be bothered by mice.** **(3)**

Ans. The mention that passengers won't be bothered by mice emphasises Skimbleshanks' role in maintaining not only order but also a hygienic and comfortable environment. It underscores his thoroughness in ensuring the train is a pleasant space for everyone.

(v) **How does the poet create a sense of coziness and security in the passengers' experience?** **(4)**

Ans. The poet creates a sense of coziness and security by describing how Skimbleshanks ensures everything on the train is clean, organised, and well-maintained. The berths are neat, with freshly folded sheets and no dust, making passengers feel comfortable. Skimbleshanks' constant patrol and watchful eyes reassure everyone that nothing will go wrong. His strict discipline keeps mischief and chaos away, allowing travellers to feel safe. Even the smallest details, like checking the luggage van, add to the feeling of care and reliability. His presence guarantees a smooth journey, making passengers feel at home and at ease.

Extract 5

In the watches of the night he is always fresh and bright;
Every now and then he has a cup of tea
With perhaps a drop of Scotch while he's keeping on the watch,
Only stopping here and there to catch a flea.

(i) **How does Skimbleshanks maintain his vigilance during the night?** **(3)**

Ans. Skimbleshanks stays vigilant by keeping himself fresh and bright through regular activities like having a cup of tea, sometimes with a drop of Scotch. He also moves around, stopping occasionally to catch a flea, indicating his constant alertness and activity throughout the night.

(ii) **What does the poem reveal about Skimbleshanks' interactions at different stations?** **(3)**

Ans. The poem shows that while passengers are asleep, Skimbleshanks is actively patrolling stations like Crewe and Carlisle, where he even greets the stationmaster with enthusiasm.

At Dumfries, he communicates with the police to ensure everything is in order, demonstrating his role in maintaining security and coordination.

(iii) **Elaborate how the poet emphasises the unnoticed work of Skimbleshanks during the journey?** **(3)**

Ans. The poet emphasises Skimbleshanks' unnoticed work by contrasting the passengers' sleep with his tireless activities.

While they sleep at stations like Crewe and Carlisle, Skimbleshanks is busy patrolling and interacting with station staff, showing his behind-the-scenes efforts to ensure the train runs smoothly.

(iv) **What does the gesture of Skimbleshanks waving his tail symbolise at the end of the journey?** **(3)**

Ans. Skimbleshanks' gesture of waving his long brown tail symbolises a friendly farewell and assurance.

It indicates his continuous presence and dedication, as he promises to meet the passengers again on the Midnight Mail. It reinforces his role as the dependable Railway Cat.

(v) **How does Skimbleshanks contribute to the passengers' ease of travel at Gallowgate? How does it make Skimbleshanks relevant to the journey?** **(4)**

Ans. Skimbleshanks contributes to the passengers' ease of travel at Gallowgate by ensuring that everything runs smoothly and efficiently. His presence guarantees there are no delays and he assists passengers in disembarking promptly.

This role highlights his relevance to the journey as more than just a mascot; he is a vital part of the train's operation, providing comfort, security and seamless coordination.

His diligent oversight and interaction with station staff ensure that every aspect of the journey is handled with care making him indispensable to the smooth functioning of the Northern Mail.

I REMEMBER, I REMEMBER

Thomas Hood

Introduction

I Remember, I Remember is written by Thomas Hood, a 19th-century English poet known for his humorous and sentimental poetry. This poem talks about childhood memories and the loss of innocence. It belongs to the genre of reflective and lyrical poetry. It contrasts the happiness of youth with the sadness of adulthood. Its unique appeal lies in its simple language and deep emotions, making it relatable to many readers.

About the Poem

I Remember, I Remember is a nostalgic poem reflecting on the poet's childhood and the passage of time. The speaker recalls the innocence and joy of youth contrasting it with the realities of adulthood. He fondly describes the natural beauty and carefree moments of his early years but also expresses a sense of loss and melancholy.

The poem captures the bittersweet nature of memories, emphasising the fleeting nature of happiness and the inevitability of change.

Exploring the Stanzas

I remember .... my breath away!

In these lines, the poet reflects on his childhood home and the simple joy of sunlight streaming through the window each morning. The sun's timing seemed perfect back then bringing neither too much nor too little light.

However, in his present life, he feels a sense of despair and longs for escape, even wishing for death to take him during the night.

This contrast highlights the loss of innocence and the burdens of adulthood.

I remember .... living yet!

In these lines, the poet fondly recalls the vibrant flowers and trees from his childhood. He describes the red and white roses, violets and lilies as almost magical and glowing with light.

He remembers the lilac bushes where a robin nested and the laburnum tree planted by his brother on his birthday. The fact that the tree is still living symbolises the lasting impact of those happy memories even though the poet's life has since changed.

I remember .... on my brow!

In these lines, the poet reminisces about the carefree days of his youth when he would swing and feel the fresh air. He imagined it as refreshing as the wind beneath a bird's wings. Back then, his spirit felt light and joyful but, as an adult, he feels burdened and weighed down by life's challenges.

Even the coolness of summer pools can no longer provide relief from the emotional or mental strain he now experiences.

I remember .... I was a boy.

In these lines, the poet recalls his childhood belief that the tall fir trees touched the sky. This symbolises his innocent and simplistic view of the world. He reflects on how this 'childish ignorance' once brought him joy.

Now, as an adult, he finds little comfort in the knowledge that heaven is not physically closer. Furthermore, he feels emotionally and spiritually distant from the happiness and wonder he experienced as a child.

Vocab Vault

Peeping To look at something quickly and secretly, especially through a small opening.

Borne Carried by the thing mentioned.

Violets A type of flower blooms in the spring season

Laburnum A small European tree, with hanging groups of yellow flowers

Spirit Soul or essence

Slender Slim or lean

'tis It is

Theme of the Poem

The poem 'I Remember, I Remember' reflects on childhood memories with fondness, contrasting the innocence of youth with the burdens of adult life. It highlights the beauty of nature and explores how time brings inevitable changes, shaping perspectives and emotions. The poet's longing for the simplicity and joy of lost youth is central to the poem's themes.

Message Conveyed by the Poem

The poem revolves around the bittersweet nature of memory. The poem reflects the poet's longing for the innocence and joy of childhood, contrasting it with the emotional burden and disillusionment of adulthood. Through vivid recollections of nature and simple pleasures, the poem explores how time changes one's perspective.

It emphasises that the passage of years distances one from the carefree happiness of youth, leaving behind a sense of loss and yearning.

Style, Tone and Mood

- **Style** The poem is written in a lyrical and reflective style, using vivid imagery and simple language to evoke the poet's childhood memories.
- **Tone** The tone is nostalgic. It blends fond recollection with a subtle undercurrent of melancholy as the poet contrasts his joyful past with the disillusionment of adulthood.
- **Mood** The mood shifts from light and whimsical when describing youthful experiences to sombre and contemplative. It highlights the emotional weight of lost innocence and the passage of time.

Title

The title 'I Remember, I Remember' reflects the poem's central theme of nostalgia and recollection. It emphasises the act of reminiscing about the poet's childhood and the contrast between past joys and present disillusionment.

The repetition in the title underscores the significance of memory and the emotional impact of revisiting those formative experiences. The simple, repetitive phrasing suggests a personal and reflective tone drawing readers into the poet's introspective journey through his memories.

Literary Devices

- **Imagery** "Roses, red and white." ***(Stanza 2)***
- "Fir trees dark and high." ***(Stanza 4)***
- **Contrast** Hood contrasts the innocence of childhood with the disillusionment of adulthood, highlighting the emotional shift over time.
- **Personification** "The Sun came peeping in at morn." ***(Stanza 1)***
- **Repetition** "I remember, I remember." ***(Stanza 1, 2, 3, 4) Title***
- **Metaphor** My spirit flew in feathers then, that is so heavy now ***(Stanza 3)***

EXAM ORIENTED QUESTIONS

TYPE - 1 Multiple Choice Questions

01 Mark

Q.1 Which of the following options contains the figure of speech that appears in the following line?
'...where the Sun came peeping in at morn...'
(ICSE Specimen 2024)
(a) A dozen eyeballs on the floor
(b) Tossing their heads in sprightly dance
(c) The tangled bine-stems scored the sky
(d) I remember I remember

Q.2 What is the primary theme of the poem?
(a) Nature's beauty
(b) Nostalgia and the passage of time
(c) Love and friendship
(d) Political change

Q.3 What did the poet remember about his childhood home?
(a) The garden
(b) The house where he was born
(c) The road to school
(d) The school playground

Q.4 What is the tone of the poem?
I. Joyful II. Sarcastic
III. Nostalgic IV. Melancholic
V. Angry
(a) I and II (b) II and III (c) III and IV (d) IV and V

Q.5 What does the poet compare the flowers to?
(a) Bright colours (b) Stars in the sky
(c) Flowers made of light (d) The Sun

Q.6 What childhood activity does the poet recall in the poem?
(a) Swinging (b) Running
(c) Reading books (d) Swimming

Q.7 What did the poet believe about the fir trees in his childhood?
(a) They were very tall and beautiful
(b) Their tops touched the sky
(c) They were always green
(d) They smelled sweet

Q.8 'My spirit flew in feathers then'
The significance of the above line is ....
(a) the poet felt free and light-hearted as a child
(b) the poet wanted to be a bird
(c) the poet was sick
(d) the poet liked birds

Q.9 What is the mood of the poem as the poet reflects on his childhood?
(a) Happy and carefree (b) Melancholic and longing
(c) Angry and frustrated (d) Indifferent

Q.10 What does the poet wish for in the lines 'And summer pools could hardly cool / The fever on my brow'?
(a) He wishes for cold water to cool his fever
(b) He wishes for more sunny days
(c) He wishes to go swimming
(d) He wishes for more excitement in life

Q.11 What does the poet mean by 'a childish ignorance'?
(a) He didn't understand things as a child
(b) He was too wise for his age
(c) He always made mistakes
(d) He was always curious

Q.12 Why does the poet feel that he is 'farther off from heav'n' as an adult?
(a) He has grown old and feels distant from his youthful happiness.
(b) He has lost his religious faith.
(c) He feels disconnected from nature.
(d) He is physically far from the sky.

Q.13 What does the poet long for as he reflects on his childhood?
(a) To relive his youth
(b) To become a famous poet
(c) To move to a new place
(d) To forget his past

Q.14 Which of these flowers does the poet mention in his memories?
(a) Tulips (b) Roses (c) Orchids (d) Daisies

Q.15 How does the poet describe the trees he remembers from his childhood?
(a) Large and green (b) Tall and slender
(c) Shady and dark (d) Covered in flowers

Q.16 What did the poet believe about the air while swinging?
(a) It was cold
(b) It rushed as fresh as to the swallows

(c) It smelled like flowers
(d) It made him feel dizzy

Q.17 What does the poet suggest has changed in adulthood?
(a) His memories are clearer
(b) His spirit has become heavy
(c) His feelings have become more joyful
(d) His love for nature has faded

Q.18 How does the poet feel about the passage of time in the poem?
(a) He accepts it cheerfully
(b) He is indifferent to it
(c) He regrets it and wishes for his childhood
(d) He feels excited about the future

Q.19 What is the effect of the line 'I remember, I remember' being repeated?
(a) It emphasises the poet's deep nostalgia
(b) It shows that the poet is forgetful
(c) It makes the poem sound like a song
(d) It shows the poet's excitement

Q.20 What does the poet mean by 'the tree is living yet'?
(a) The tree is still growing
(b) The tree is a symbol of his childhood memories
(c) The tree has changed
(d) The tree has been cut down

Q.21 Why does the poet feel the 'night' should have taken him away?
(a) He feels the weight of adulthood and the loss of his youthful joy
(b) He is tired of remembering the past
(c) He wants to escape his responsibilities
(d) He wants to live forever

Q.22 Select the option that shows the correct relationship between statements (1) and (2).
Statement 1 The poet expresses a desire to return to his childhood.
Statement 2 The poet's childhood was a time of innocence and joy, which he now misses.
(a) Statement 1 is true and Statement 2 is false.
(b) Statement 2 is true and Statement 1 is false.
(c) Statement 2 is the reason for Statement 1.
(d) Statement 1 and Statement 2 are independent of each other.

Q.23 Select the option that shows the correct relationship between statements (1) and (2).
Statement 1 The poet believes that childhood intelligence brought him happiness.
Statement 2 The poet thinks that as a child, he didn't understand the complexities of life, which allowed him to experience more joy.
(a) Statement 1 is true and Statement 2 is false
(b) Statement 2 is true and Statement 1 is false.
(c) Statement 2 is the reason for Statement 1.
(d) Statement 1 and Statement 2 are independent of each other.

Answers

1. (b)	2. (b)	3. (c)	4. (c)	5. (c)	6. (a)	7. (b)	8. (a)	9. (b)	10. (a)
11. (a)	12. (a)	13. (a)	14. (b)	15. (b)	16. (b)	17. (b)	18. (c)	19. (a)	20. (b)
21. (a)	22. (c)	23. (b)							

TYPE - 2 Extract Based Questions
16 Marks

Extract 1

I remember, I remember,
The house where I was born,
The little window where the sun
Came peeping in at morn;

(i) How does the poet use the metaphor of the sun's arrival to reflect on the nature of childhood? **(3)**

Ans. The poet uses the metaphor of the Sun coming in at dawn 'neither too soon nor too late' to suggest the perfect unhurried rhythm of childhood. The sun's arrival signifies a time of innocence and simplicity when everything was in harmony and at the right pace. It contrasts with the poet's current feelings of unease or discomfort in adulthood marked by the desire for escape.

(ii) In what way does the poet's reference to the Sun highlight the passage of time and its impact on the poet's emotions? **(3)**

Ans. The poet's reference to the Sun arriving 'just at the right time' during childhood suggesting that, in the past, everything fell into place naturally with no hurry or delay.

As an adult, however, this natural rhythm is lost. The poet feels that time has become more burdensome. The desire for the night to take him away reflects a deeper feeling of discontent with the passage of time.

(iii) **Why does the poet juxtapose childhood memories with his present sorrow in these lines? How does it reflect on his emotional state? (3)**

Ans. The poet juxtaposes childhood memories of innocence and peacefulness with his current sorrow and sense of loss. The contrast emphasises his emotional state—longing for the carefree days of youth and wishing to escape the burdens of adulthood.

This emotional state reveals the poet's despair and sense of alienation from the simpler joys of life.

(iv) **Explain the significance of the phrase 'Had borne my breath away' in the final line. What does it reveal about the poet's current state of mind? (3)**

Ans. The phrase 'Had borne my breath away' is significant as it suggests a longing for death or an escape from the harshness of life. The poet's wish that night would take him away indicates a sense of weariness and deep disillusionment.

It reflects his emotional exhaustion, implying that life has become so difficult that death seems like a preferable alternative to enduring the struggles of adulthood.

(v) **Highlight the thematic connection between the poet's memories of his childhood home and his present-day desire for escape. (4)**

Ans. The memories of the childhood home, with the Sun shining 'just at the right time' and the simplicity of the past, are in stark contrast to the poet's present feelings of disillusionment. The childhood home represents a time of peace, innocence and perfect timing.

On the contrary, the present is filled with longing for release from life's hardships. The thematic connection lies in the tension between nostalgia for an idealised past and the painful reality of the present where escape seems to be the only solution.

Extract 2

The roses, red and white,
The vi'lets, and the lily-cups,
Those flowers made of light!
The lilacs where the robin built,
And where my brother set

(i) **How does the poet use imagery to evoke a sense of nostalgia and idealise his childhood garden? (3)**

Ans. The poet employs vivid imagery such as 'roses, red and white', 'violets', 'lily-cups' and 'flowers made of light' to create a serene and almost magical picture of the garden. The reference to 'flowers made of light' adds an ethereal quality, elevating the garden to a place of beauty and purity.

This imagery not only evokes nostalgia but also highlights the poet's yearning for the innocence and joy of his childhood – a stark contrast to his current sorrow.

(ii) **What is the significance of the poet mentioning the robin and his brother in the second stanza? (3)**

Ans. The robin building its nest in the lilacs and the mention of the poet's brother planting the laburnum tree both evoke the themes of growth, life and familial bonds. The robin's nest represents the natural cycle of life and the innocence of childhood.

Meanwhile, the brother planting the tree symbolises familial love and the passing of time.

(iii) **Elaborate the role that the laburnum tree plays in the poet's recollections of childhood. How does it contribute to the poem's overall tone? (3)**

Ans. The laburnum tree, planted by the poet's brother, plays a significant role in the poet's childhood memories. The mention of the tree 'living yet' suggests continuity and survival, contrasting the poet's own sense of loss and disillusionment. The tree symbolises endurance, growth and the passage of time.

This enduring image of the tree contributes to the tone of longing and melancholy as the poet reflects on the innocence of childhood and the impermanence of life.

(iv) **How does the contrast between the 'flowers made of light' and the present reality contribute to the emotional depth of the poem? (3)**

Ans. The phrase 'flowers made of light' contrasts with the poet's current emotional state as these radiant and pure memories of childhood stand in stark opposition to his adult sorrow and sense of loss. The idealisation of the past, where everything seemed bright and perfect, deepens the sense of longing for the simplicity of youth.

This contrast creates an emotional depth emphasising the poet's discontent with the present and his desire to return to a time of innocence and peace.

(v) **What is the deeper significance of the line 'The tree is living yet!' in the context of the poem's exploration of time and memory? (4)**

Ans. The line 'The tree is living yet!' holds deeper significance as it symbolises endurance and survival. While the poet reflects on his childhood with a sense of nostalgia and loss, the fact that the tree remains alive highlights the continuity of life despite the passage of time.

The tree's survival contrasts with the poet's emotional disillusionment emphasising the inevitability of change. It suggests that while memories may fade, some aspects of the past, such as nature and life itself, endure through time.

Extract 3

And thought the air must rush as fresh
To swallows on the wing;
My spirit flew in feathers then,
That is so heavy now.

(i) **How does the poet use the imagery of 'swallows on the wing' to convey the sense of freedom and innocence in childhood?** **(3)**

Ans. The poet compares the rush of air while swinging to the freedom of swallows flying. This image symbolises the boundless energy and joy of childhood where everything felt light and effortless.

The comparison emphasises the contrast between the weightless, carefree nature of youth and the heavy burdens of adulthood. The swallows represent an idealised state of freedom and grace, further deepening the poet's longing for the simplicity of his past.

(ii) **What is the significance of the poet describing his spirit as having 'flown in feathers' during his childhood? How does this contrast with his present state?** **(3)**

Ans. The phrase 'my spirit flew in feathers then' is significant as it evokes a sense of lightness, freedom and vitality that the poet associates with his childhood. It contrasts sharply with the 'heavy' spirit he experiences in adulthood, suggesting a loss of innocence and joy. The imagery of feathers emphasises the ease with which he navigated life as a child.

It contrasts with his present state as the heaviness of his current state symbolises the emotional burdens and disillusionment that come with age and experience.

(iii) **Why does the poet mention that "Summer pools could hardly cool the fever on my brow"? How does this contribute to the theme of lost youth?** **(3)**

Ans. The phrase 'Summer pools could hardly cool the fever on my brow' metaphorically expresses the intensity of the poet's present emotional turmoil. Despite the cooling effect of the summer pools, the fever represents an inner heat, possibly symbolic of stress, anxiety or dissatisfaction.

This image contrasts the cool, carefree days of childhood with the intensity and emotional suffering of adulthood. It further underscores the theme of lost youth where the ease of childhood has given way to the burdens of growing up.

(iv) **How does the poet's nostalgic recollection of swinging and the rush of air relate to his current perception of the world?** **(3)**

Ans. The poet's recollection of swinging and the fresh rush of air reflects the feeling of freedom, vitality and boundless potential he once had. In childhood, he believed the air felt as fresh as it did for the swallows. However, his current perception is vastly different.

The contrast between the light, carefree experience of swinging and the heaviness he now feels suggests a disillusionment with adulthood.

(v) **Explain how the poet's references to physical sensations—such as the rush of air and the fever on his brow—enhance the emotional depth of the poem?** **(4)**

Ans. The poet uses physical sensations like the rush of air while swinging and the fever on his brow to intensify the emotional themes of the poem. The rush of air evokes a sense of freedom and vitality creating a vivid memory of youth. In contrast, the fever on his brow symbolises the physical manifestation of emotional distress or discontent in adulthood.

By using these sensory details, the poet deepens the emotional resonance of the poem, highlighting the stark contrast between the lightness of childhood and the burdens of growing up.

Extract 4

My spirit flew in feathers then,
That is so heavy now.

(i) **What does the poet recall at the beginning of the poem? What does he wish for at the end of the stanza?** **(3)**

Ans. The poet recalls the house where he was born, the little window where the sun came in and the beautiful morning he experienced as a child.

At the end of the stanza, the poet wishes that the night had taken his life away, indicating a feeling of sadness or despair in the present.

(ii) **What words does the poet use to create a sense of nostalgia? What memories of the garden does he mention in the second stanza?** **(3)**

Ans. Words like 'I remember', 'where I was born', 'the little window', 'Sun', 'roses', and 'violets' evoke nostalgia by recalling pleasant, innocent memories from childhood.

In the second stanza, the poet recalls the roses, red and white, violets, lily-cups, lilacs and a robin building a nest in the lilacs. He also mentions the laburnum tree his brother planted on his birthday.

(iii) **'The tree is living yet!' What is the significance of this line?**
Who had planted this tree and on what occasion? **(3)**

Ans. This line suggests the persistence of nature and the passage of time. Despite the poet's childhood being a long time ago, the tree, which represents the memories, is still alive. This offers a sense of continuity in life and nature.

The poet's brother had planted the laburnum tree on his birthday.

(iv) **The poet uses various kinds of images in the poem. Give one example for each of the following** **(3)**

(a) Sight (b) Sound (c) Touch

Ans. (a) **Sight** 'The roses, red and white'.

(b) **Sound** 'The robin built' (the sound of the robin building a nest).

(c) **Touch** 'My spirit flew in feathers' (suggesting a light, airy feeling or the sensation of flying).

(v) **The poet compares two stages of his life in the poem. What are they? What moods does he associate with each of them?** **(ICSE Specimen 2024, 4)**

Ans. The poet compares his carefree, innocent childhood with his present, adult life which is weighed down by responsibilities and burdens.

The mood associated with childhood is one of innocence, joy and wonder. The poet recalls a time when life felt light, carefree and full of promise. The mood associated with adulthood is one of nostalgia, longing and regret.

The poet feels the weight of the years, with a sense of loss and an awareness that time has taken away some of the vitality and purity of youth.

Extract 5

I remember, I remember,
The fir trees dark and high;
I used to think their slender tops
Were close against the sky:

(i) **How does the poet's perception of the fir trees change from childhood to adulthood? What does this shift signify?** **(3)**

Ans. In childhood, the poet imagines the slender tops of the fir trees to be 'close against the sky' signifying a sense of wonder, innocence and an idealised view of the world.

As an adult, however, he realises this perception was a product of 'childish ignorance', highlighting the loss of innocence and the diminishing of wonder with age.

This shift signifies the poet's growing awareness of the limitations of his world, both physically and spiritually, as he distances himself from the purity of childhood.

(ii) **What does the phrase 'It was a childish ignorance' reveal about the poet's perspective on his youthful thoughts and feelings?** **(3)**

Ans. The phrase 'It was a childish ignorance' reveals the poet's awareness of the limitations of his youthful understanding. As a child, he viewed the world through an innocent, simplistic lens imagining the fir trees' tops to be near the sky.

The use of 'ignorance' suggests that the poet now recognises that such perceptions were naïve as adulthood brings a more realistic and often less hopeful view of the world.

(iii) **Explain the significance of the poet's realisation that he is 'farther off from heav'n than when I was a boy'.** **(3)**

Ans. The poet's realisation that he is 'farther off from heav'n than when I was a boy' expresses a feeling of spiritual or existential distance. As a child, he had a sense of closeness to the divine or the ideal, represented by the image of heaven.

However, with age, he feels that he has moved farther away from this sense of purity, joy or connection. This line reflects a loss of innocence, a diminishing sense of wonder and a disillusionment that often accompanies the passage from childhood to adulthood.

(iv) **Analyse how the poet uses the image of the fir trees to symbolise the contrast between childhood and adulthood?** **(3)**

Ans. The fir trees in the poem serve as a metaphor for the difference between the simplicity of childhood and the complexity of adulthood. As a child, the poet imagines the trees' tops reaching the sky symbolising a boundless, idealised view of the world.

In contrast, as an adult, he recognises the trees' true distance from the sky, symbolising the loss of innocence and the more grounded, realistic view of life that comes with age.

(v) **What does the reference to 'heav'n' in the final line suggest about the poet's spiritual journey or state of mind?** **(4)**

Ans. The reference to 'heav'n' in the final line suggests that the poet's spiritual state has changed as he has grown older. In childhood, he may have felt a closer connection to purity, divinity or idealism, represented by heaven.

However, as an adult, he feels spiritually distanced, reflecting a sense of loss, disillusionment or perhaps a deeper, more complex understanding of the world that comes with age. This contrast highlights the spiritual and emotional challenges that often accompany growing up.

04

A DOCTOR'S JOURNAL ENTRY FOR AUGUST 6, 1945

Vikram Seth

About the Poet

A Doctor's Journal Entry for August 6, 1945 is written by Vikram Seth, an Indian author and poet known for his clear and powerful writing. This poem talks about the horrors of the Hiroshima bombing, seen through the eyes of a survivour. It is a narrative poem that describes pain, loss and shock in a simple yet moving way. The poem's unique quality is its calm and detached tone, which makes the tragedy feel even more real. Through vivid imagery, it shows the suffering of people and the terrible impact of war.

About the Poem

Vikram Seth's **A Doctor's Journal Entry for August 6, 1945** portrays the emotional and physical devastation of Hiroshima after the atomic bomb was dropped. Written from the perspective of a doctor, the poem captures his shock, helplessness and moral distress as he witnesses the horrific injuries of survivours.

The vivid imagery and powerful metaphors express the brutality of the bomb's aftermath. Through the doctor's reflections, Seth critiques the destructive nature of war and its psychological toll on humanity.

Exploring the Stanzas

The morning .... startled me.

These lines describe a peaceful morning where the speaker, a doctor, is relaxing and enjoying the warm, calm atmosphere. While lying down and looking at the shimmering leaves and shadows, the doctor is suddenly shocked by two bright flashes of light. These flashes disrupt the peaceful scene and startle the doctor.

I saw the .... disappeared.

In these lines, the doctor sees an old stone lantern glowing brightly and wonders if it's due to magnesium flares, which are often used in explosions. As the doctor contemplates, the world around them suddenly collapses. The roof and walls crumble and debris fills the air. Dust swirls everywhere, even in the garden.

The doctor notices that his own clothes and personal belongings have vanished, adding to the sense of confusion and destruction caused by the sudden catastrophe.

A splinter .... come to pass.

In these lines, the doctor describes the severe injuries he sustained after the explosion. A piece of debris is sticking out of his injured thigh, his right side is bleeding and his cheek is torn. He casually removes a shard of glass from his body.

However, throughout the pain and shock, he is confused and in disbelief, wondering what exactly has happened to him and why this destruction is taking place. The doctor is detached almost as if in a state of shock.

REVISION NOTES

Where was .... my wife.

In these lines, the doctor becomes alarmed and fearful as he realises that he is badly injured. Blood is flowing from his neck and he is afraid for his life. In a panic, he calls out for his wife, Yecko-san, desperately searching for her. The doctor's fear and worry for her safety grow as he is hurt. He urgently tries to find her amidst the chaos and his own injuries. The situation is terrifying and filled with panic.

Pale, bloodstained .... at our feet.

In these lines, Yecko-san, the doctor's wife, appears looking pale, covered in blood and scared. She is holding her elbow, possibly injured. Despite the fear and pain, the doctor tries to comfort her, telling her that they'll be fine and urging her to leave quickly.

As they move toward the street, they stumble and fall, tripping over something they can't see in the chaos. The scene reflects their struggle to survive and escape the devastation.

I gasped out .... in the dust,

In these lines, the doctor is shocked when he sees a head on the ground, realising that the person is dead. He apologises, feeling disturbed by the sight, as a gate had fallen on the person and killed them. The doctor and his wife stand there, terrified, watching a nearby house begin to lean and collapse.

As the house falls, fire erupts from the debris, adding to the horror and chaos around them. The scene is filled with fear and destruction.

Spread by .... how I could)

In these lines, the doctor realises that the destruction is widespread and he must go to the hospital for help. He also feels the responsibility to assist his staff, even though he himself is badly injured.

At the time, this seemed like the right thing to do but the doctor later questions how he could have even managed it.

My legs gave .... up at length.

In these lines, the doctor becomes weak and collapses to the ground feeling very thirsty but unable to find water. His breathing becomes difficult but he gradually starts to feel a little stronger. Slowly, his energy returns and he manages to get up after struggling with exhaustion.

I was naked .... go on ahead.

In these lines, the doctor notices that he is naked but feels no shame which disturbs him because it seems unnatural. He then sees a soldier who silently offers him a towel which he accepts. The doctor's legs are stiff and painful from dried blood making it difficult to move.

He tells his wife, Yecko-san, to go ahead without him as he is struggling to keep going. The doctor's physical condition and the urgency of the situation make him feel helpless.

She did not .... crept behind.

In these lines, the doctor describes how his wife, though reluctant, had to leave because there was no other option. After she left, the doctor felt a deep sense of loneliness. His mind raced with thoughts but his body was too weak and slow to keep up with his thoughts.

I saw the .... flesh again.

In these lines, the doctor sees people around him, some appearing ghost-like and others like scarecrows, all silent and motionless. Their arms are outstretched. It takes the doctor a while to understand that their bodies are so badly burned that even the slightest touch causes immense pain. The burns are so severe that they fear any movement or friction as it might cause even more suffering. The scene conveys the deep physical trauma these people are experiencing.

Those who .... from the bath?

In these lines, the doctor watches people, some badly injured, slowly making their way toward the hospital. He feels shocked and sad when he sees a woman and a child standing in front of him, both completely naked. He wonders if they had just come from a bath but realises the tragic reality.

I turned .... of our clothes.

In these lines, the doctor feels confused seeing the woman and child naked, not understanding why they are without clothes. As he looks around, he sees a naked man too which makes him realise that something unusual must have happened causing everyone to lose their clothes in the aftermath of the bombing.

The face .... single word.

In these lines, the doctor describes an old woman lying on the ground with a face full of pain but she doesn't make any sound. The scene is eerily silent and the doctor notices that everyone around them is quiet.

There are no cries of pain or words spoken, highlighting the intense suffering and shock caused by the bombing. The silence emphasises the overwhelming nature of the disaster and the emotional numbness it has caused in the survivours.

Vocab Vault

Sprawling To sit or lie with your arms and legs spread out in an untidy way.
Clad Dressed
Debris Wreckage
Swirled Spun
Jutted Stuck out
Mangled Distorted
Gushed Oozed
Stumbling Tripping
Swayed Wavered
Toppled Collapsed
Dawned Occurred
Revive Come around or recover
Rebelled Revolted
Dreadful Terrible
Crept Crawled or tiptoed
Dangling Hanging
Chafe Scrape or scratch
Parade Procession
Dismayed Disheartened or discouraged
Stripped Exposed or uncovered
Marred Disfigured or blemished
Anguish Torment or suffering

Theme of the Poem

The poem highlights the horrors of war, vividly portraying the destruction caused by the Hiroshima bombing and the immense physical and emotional suffering of the survivors. It explores the doctor's moral dilemmas, feelings of helplessness and loneliness as he witnesses the devastation. Themes of human suffering, the dangers of unchecked technological violence, and the profound impact of survival in a shattered world are central to the poem.

Message Conveyed by the Poem

The poem conveys a powerful critique of the destructive nature of war, particularly nuclear warfare. Through the doctor's perspective, the poem emphasises the immense human suffering, moral conflict and helplessness that arise from such violence. It questions the ethics of using atomic bombs and highlights the emotional and physical trauma experienced by both the victims and the witnesses. Thus, urging reflection on the consequences of unchecked technological power.

Style, Tone and Mood

- **Style** The style is reflective and narrative, with the doctor documenting his thoughts and observations in a stream-of-consciousness manner.
- **Tone** The tone is sombre, detached and, at times, conflicted as the doctor grapples with helplessness and the moral implications of the destruction.
- **Mood** The mood is bleak and tragic, capturing the shock, despair and emotional numbness of witnessing the horrors of war.

Title

The title 'A Doctor's Journal Entry for August 6, 1945' is significant as it sets the tone of personal reflection and historical documentation. The date, August 6, 1945, marks the day the atomic bomb was dropped on Hiroshima. By presenting the poem as a journal entry, the poet conveys a sense of immediacy and personal involvement. This allows the readers to experience the emotional and moral turmoil of the doctor witnessing the horrors of war firsthand.

Literary Devices

- **Personification** "The morning stretched calm." ***(Stanza 1)***
- **Imagery** "A strong flash, then another, startled me." ***(Stanza 1)***
- "Magnesium flares." ***(Stanza 2)***
- **Metaphor** "I saw the shadowy forms of people, some were ghosts, some scarecrows, all were wordless dumb." ***(Stanza 11)***
- **Enjambment** "Stumbling to the street." ***(Stanza 5)***
- "We fell, tripped by something at our feet." ***(Stanza 5)***
- **Alliteration** "Of shimmering leaves and shadows." ***(Stanza 1)***
- **Juxtaposition** The poem contrasts the before-and-after effects of the bombing, highlighting the stark differences in Hiroshima's landscape and the suffering of the survivours. This contrast emphasises the devastating impact of the bombing.
- **Rhetorical Questions** The doctor in the poem poses rhetorical questions to express his inner turmoil and confusion. This reflects the moral and existential dilemmas faced in the wake of the attack. These questions highlight his feelings of helplessness. "What is this terrible thing?" is a question that underscores his disbelief and the shock of witnessing such an event.
- **Irony** The doctor, a figure of care and healing, is powerless in the face of such overwhelming destruction, creating a sense of irony about his inability to help.
- **Symbolism** The atomic bomb itself serves as a powerful symbol of both the destructive power of science and the moral conflict of using such weapons. It also symbolises the broader themes of war, suffering and the futility of violence.
- **Stream of Consciousness** The poem captures the doctor's inner turmoil in a way that mirrors the stream of consciousness technique. This allows the reader to experience the doctor's jumbled and confused thoughts as he processes the devastation around him.

EXAM ORIENTED QUESTIONS

TYPE - 1 Multiple Choice Questions

01 Mark

Q.1 The poem, 'A Doctor's Journal Entry for August 6, 1945', describes the devastation caused by the .... **(ICSE Specimen 2024)**
(a) atomic explosion in the lives of ordinary people
(b) earthquake in Japan
(c) tidal waves in Japan
(d) volcanic eruption in Japan

Q.2 What is the setting of the poem, 'A Doctor's Journal Entry for August 6, 1945'?
(a) Hiroshima (b) New York
(c) London (d) Tokyo

Q.3 Which significant event is the poem reflecting on?
(a) World War I
(b) The bombing of Hiroshima
(c) The attack on Pearl Harbour
(d) The fall of the Berlin Wall

Q.4 What was the doctor's role during the bombing of Hiroshima?
(a) A soldier (b) A firefighter
(c) A witness (d) A doctor treating victims

Q.5 Which of the following is a major theme in the poem?
(a) Love (b) War and its impact
(c) Nature (d) Friendship

Q.6 What is described as the cause of the devastation in the poem?
(a) An earthquake
(b) An atomic bomb
(c) A nuclear reactor failure
(d) A fire

Q.7 Which of the following options contains the figure of speech that appears in the following line.

"Shimmering leaves and shadows".
(a) A splinter jutted from my mangled thigh.
(b) Stumbling to the street
(c) A dreadful loneliness
(d) woman with a child stand

Q.8 The poem tells us that the doctor is feeling ....
(a) happiness (b) anger
(c) despair (d) confusion

Q.9 What imagery is frequently used in the poem?
(a) Bright colours
(b) Pain and suffering
(c) Beautiful landscapes
(d) Calmness and serenity

Q.10 Identify the option that lists the tone of the poem.
I. Joyful II. Pensive
III. Sorrowful IV. Angry
V. Sarcastic
(a) I and II (b) II and III (c) III and IV (d) IV and V

Q.11 What kind of medical conditions are most of the patients suffering from in the poem?
(a) Heart disease
(b) Radiation burns and injuries
(c) Malaria
(d) Tuberculosis

Q.12 The poem portrays the effects of war on which of the following?
(a) Soldiers only (b) Civilian population
(c) Only on the enemy (d) Only on animals

Q.13 What does the doctor's journal entry reflect about the human cost of war?
(a) Victory and triumph
(b) Physical and emotional destruction
(c) The importance of strategy
(d) The joy of victory

Q.14 Which of the following best describes the doctor's journal entry?
(a) A letter to a friend (b) A diary entry
(c) A scientific report (d) A newspaper article

Q.15 What does the poem suggest about the use of atomic weapons?
(a) They are justified in war
(b) They have long-lasting consequences
(c) They are always effective
(d) They are humane alternatives

Q.16 Which technique does the poet use to convey the horror of the atomic bombing?
(a) Humour (b) Repetition
(c) Imagery (d) Metaphor

Q.17 What is the doctor's primary concern in the poem?
(a) Treating the injured
(b) His personal safety
(c) Maintaining peace
(d) Winning the war

Q.18 How does the doctor describe the aftermath of the bombing in the poem?
(a) With hope and optimism
(b) With a sense of calm
(c) As chaotic and devastating
(d) As peaceful

Q.19 Which of the following is a key motif in the poem?
(a) Heroism (b) Pain and suffering
(c) Victory (d) Nature

Q.20 The phrase 'atomic bomb' in the poem refers to what aspect?
(a) A weapon of mass destruction
(b) A natural disaster
(c) A political strategy
(d) A medical treatment

Q.21 What does the poet's use of medical imagery suggest about the situation in Hiroshima?
(a) The healing process after war
(b) The destruction and suffering caused by the bomb
(c) A calm, peaceful atmosphere
(d) The importance of medicine in warfare

Q.22 How is the idea of human suffering presented in the poem?
(a) With a sense of joy
(b) As unavoidable and overwhelming
(c) With no emotional response
(d) Through humour

Q.23 The message that Vikram Seth is likely conveying through the doctor's journal entry is ....
(a) war has no real winners
(b) victory is a great achievement
(c) medicine can cure everything
(d) atomic bombs are necessary in war

Q.24 What effect does the use of first-person narration have in the poem?
(a) It makes the events feel impersonal
(b) It adds emotional depth and perspective
(c) It detaches the reader from the events
(d) It makes the poem less serious

Q.25 The phrase, 'a new kind of death' mean .... in the poem.
(a) the death of the enemy soldiers
(b) the slow, painful death caused by the bomb's radiation
(c) the death of a soldier in combat
(d) the death from natural causes

Q.26 How does the poem express the futility of war?
(a) By celebrating the victory
(b) By depicting the devastation caused by the bomb
(c) By showing the joy of soldiers
(d) By focusing on the heroism of the doctor

Q.27 Choose the option that lists the sequence of events in the correct order.
A. The doctor feels the force of the explosion and is unsure of what to do.
B. The doctor writes in his journal, documenting his thoughts and the events of the day.
C. The doctor starts to treat the injured people.
D. There is a sudden, blinding flash and then complete darkness.
(a) ABCD (b) BDCA
(c) CADB (d) DACB

Q.28 Select the option that shows the correct relationship between statements (1) and (2).
Statement 1 The doctor in the poem is deeply affected by the sight of the survivours after the bombing.
Statement 2 He is overwhelmed by the extent of the physical and emotional damage caused by the atomic bomb.
(a) Statement 1 is true and Statement 2 is false
(b) Statement 2 is true and Statement 1 is false.
(c) Statement 2 is the cause for Statement 1.
(d) Statement 1 and Statement 2 are independent of each other.

Q.29 Select the option that shows the correct relationship between statements (1) and (2).
Statement 1 The doctor chooses to write a journal entry on the day of the bombing.
Statement 2 He wishes to document the immediate aftermath of the bombing for historical purposes.
(a) Statement 1 is true and Statement 2 is false
(b) Statement 2 is true and Statement 1 is false.
(c) Statement 2 is the cause for Statement 1.
(d) Statement 1 and Statement 2 are independent of each other.

Answers

1. (a) 2. (a) 3. (b) 4. (d) 5. (b) 6. (b) 7. (b) 8. (c) 9. (b) 10. (b)
11. (b) 12. (b) 13. (b) 14. (b) 15. (b) 16. (c) 17. (a) 18. (c) 19. (b) 20. (a)
21. (b) 22. (b) 23. (a) 24. (b) 25. (b) 26. (b) 27. (d) 28. (c) 29. (a)

Explanations

7. 'Shimmering leaves and shadows' evokes movement and sensory imagery, which aligns with 'stumbling to the street' as both phrases depict dynamic scenes, focusing on action and visual elements.
10. The tone of the poem is both pensive and sorrowful. It reflects deep contemplation about the devastation caused by the Hiroshima bombing and conveys profound grief over the immense human suffering and loss.
16. The poet uses vivid imagery to depict the physical destruction and emotional suffering caused by the atomic bombing. Descriptions of shattered bodies, shimmering leaves, and the desolate aftermath help readers visualise the horror and understand its devastating impact.

TYPE - 2 Extract Based Questions

16 Marks

Extract 1

The morning stretched calm, beautiful, and warm
Sprawling half-clad, I gazed out at the form
Of shimmering leaves and shadows. Suddenly
A strong flash, then another startled me.
I saw the old stone lantern brightly lit.

(i) Who made this journal entry? What is the significance of the date in the title of the poem?

(ICSE Specimen 2024, 3)

Ans. The journal entry is made by a doctor who is recounting his experiences on the day of the Hiroshima atomic bombing.

The date, August 6, 1945, is significant because it marks the day when the atomic bomb was dropped on Hiroshima, Japan, during World War II. This event caused massive destruction and loss of life, making it a pivotal and tragic moment in history.

(ii) Explain how the narrator describes the morning in the opening lines of the poem. **(3)**

Ans. The narrator describes the morning as calm, beautiful and warm. This serene and peaceful depiction contrasts sharply with the sudden disruption caused by the flashes of light that follow. It highlights the shock and chaos brought by the bombing. The tranquil imagery of 'shimmering leaves and shadows' emphasises the normalcy and quiet of the morning before the catastrophe.

(iii) What physical injuries does the narrator suffer? **(3)**

Ans. The narrator suffers several physical injuries due to the bombing. He has a splinter jutting from his mangled thigh, his right side is bleeding, and his cheek is torn. Additionally, he dislodges a piece of glass from his body, reflecting the severity of the wounds inflicted by the explosion and the surrounding debris. These injuries highlight the physical devastation experienced by the survivours.

(iv) Mention any three of the shocking sights he observed as he looked around that morning. **(3)**

Ans. The narrator observed the following shocking sights

(a) **A head crushed by a gate** The narrator sees a head lying on the ground, crushed by a gate, a grim and horrifying sight symbolising the destruction and death caused by the bombing.

(b) **A naked woman and child** He notices a woman and child standing without clothes, which shocks him and makes him question the strange circumstances of their exposure.

(c) **A tilted, swaying house** The narrator witnesses a house tilting, swaying, and eventually collapsing, followed by fire spreading in the dust, illustrating the extensive physical destruction and chaos around him.

(v) What is the tone used by the poet to describe the shocking events happening around the narrator? What is the mood conveyed by the last lines of the poem? **(4)**

'Silence was common to us all. I heard
No cries of anguish, or a single word.'

Ans. The tone used by the poet to describe the shocking events is detached and sombre, reflecting the narrator's shock and disbelief. This detached tone helps convey the overwhelming nature of the devastation and the narrator's struggle to process the traumatic events unfolding around him.

The mood conveyed by the last lines, 'Silence was common to us all. I heard / No cries of anguish, or a single word', is one of eerie calmness and numbness. The silence suggests a collective state of shock and emotional exhaustion among the survivours, emphasising the deep psychological impact of the tragedy.

Extract 2

Magnesium flares? While I debated it,
The roof, the walls and, as it seemed, the world
Collapsed in timber and debris, dust swirled
Around me – in the garden now – and, weird,
My drawers and undershirt disappeared.

(i) How does the narrator's initial reaction to the flashes reflect the confusion and suddenness of the event? (3)

Ans. The narrator's initial reaction, questioning whether the flashes are magnesium flares, reflects his confusion and inability to comprehend the sudden and catastrophic event. This moment of uncertainty highlights the unexpected nature of the bombing and the immediate chaos it caused.

(ii) Analyse the significance of the description 'the roof, the walls and, as it seemed, the world collapsed' in conveying the magnitude of the disaster. How does this imagery enhance the reader's understanding of the event? (3)

Ans. The description 'the roof, the walls and, as it seemed, the world collapsed' is significant as it conveys the overwhelming and all-encompassing nature of the disaster. This imagery portrays not just the physical destruction of the narrator's immediate surroundings but also suggests a symbolic collapse of their entire world.

This enhances the understanding as it helps the reader grasp the enormity of the bombing's impact, both physically and emotionally, reinforcing the sense of helplessness and devastation experienced by the survivours.

(iii) Discuss the emotional and psychological state of the narrator as he dislodges the piece of glass from his body. How does his detachment serve as a coping mechanism in the context of the trauma he is experiencing? (3)

Ans. The narrator's detached demeanour as he dislodges a piece of glass from his body indicates a state of shock and numbness.

This detachment serves as a coping mechanism, allowing him to process the trauma without being overwhelmed by the pain and horror of the situation.

(iv) Examine the significance of the narrator's observation that his drawers and undershirt disappeared. How does this detail contribute to the overall depiction of the bombing's impact on the human body and psyche? (3)

Ans. The narrator's observation that his drawers and undershirt disappeared is significant as it illustrates the sheer force and strange, incomprehensible nature of the explosion. This detail highlights the vulnerability of the human body, stripped bare by the blast, and contributes to the dehumanising effect of the bombing. It emphasises the loss of personal dignity and normalcy, adding to the overall sense of disorientation and helplessness.

(v) Reflect on the narrator's phrase 'wondering what had come to pass' in the context of the poem. How does this line capture the overarching theme of the poem and what does it reveal about the narrator's internal struggle? (4)

Ans. The phrase 'wondering what had come to pass' encapsulates the overarching theme of the poem, which is the sudden and incomprehensible nature of catastrophic events, particularly war. It reveals the narrator's internal struggle to make sense of the unimaginable destruction and loss he is witnessing.

This line highlights the confusion and search for meaning in the face of overwhelming tragedy. It reflects the broader human condition of grappling with unforeseen disasters and the moral and existential questions they raise, reinforcing the poem's themes of loss, devastation and the quest for understanding amidst chaos.

Extract 3

Where was my wife? Alarmed, I gave a shout,
'Where are you, Yecko-san?' My blood gushed out.
The artery in my neck? Scared for my life,
I called out, panic-stricken, to my wife.

(i) How does the narrator's frantic call for his wife 'Where are you, Yecko-san'? reflect his emotional state during the crisis? (3)

Ans. The narrator's frantic call for his wife reflects his overwhelming fear, confusion and desperation in the face of the bombing. The urgency of his shout indicates that he is scared for both his own life and his wife's safety. His emotional state is marked by panic and helplessness as he searches for her in the midst of chaos.

(ii) How does the narrator's physical condition contribute to the urgency of the moment? (3)

Ans. The narrator's physical condition underscores the severity of his injuries and the imminent danger he faces. This emphasises the urgency of the situation, heightening the sense of panic and the race against time to find his wife and escape the catastrophe.

(iii) **What is the significance of Yecko-san emerging 'pale, bloodstained, frightened' in the context of their shared experience?** **(3)**

Ans. Yecko-san's appearance as 'pale, bloodstained, frightened' highlights the extent of the trauma endured by both her and the narrator. Her physical state mirrors the devastation around them and it emphasises their shared suffering.

The imagery of her being bloodstained suggests the intensity of the destruction and the personal impact of the bombing on both individuals.

(iv) **How does the narrator's urging of Yecko-san to 'Let's get out quickly' reflect his mindset in the moment? What does it reveal about his priorities?** **(3)**

Ans. The narrator's urging to 'get out quickly' reveals his heightened sense of urgency and survival instinct. Despite his injuries, his immediate priority is to escape the area of devastation, driven by the need to find safety.

It reflects his focus on survival and the instinctual drive to protect both himself and his wife in the face of extreme danger.

(v) **What is the symbolic significance of the couple stumbling and tripping over something at their feet as they attempt to flee?** **(4)**

Ans. The couple stumbling and tripping over something at their feet symbolises the overwhelming and unpredictable obstacles they face while trying to escape.

This moment reflects the chaotic, disorienting nature of the disaster where even the simplest actions, like walking, become fraught with difficulty. It highlights the struggle for survival amid the devastation and the loss of control over their circumstances.

Extract 4

I gasped out, when I saw it was a head:
'Excuse me, please excuse me' – He was dead:
A gate had crushed him. There we stood, afraid.
A house standing before us tilted, swayed,

(i) **What is the emotional impact on the narrator when he encounters the dead body? How does the discovery of the crushed man affect his perception of the disaster?** **(3)**

Ans. The narrator is shocked and horrified when he discovers the dead body exclaiming, 'Excuse me, please excuse me'.

The image of the crushed man, with a gate on top of him, intensifies his fear and contributes to the realisation of the catastrophic nature of the disaster.

It underscores the indiscriminate violence and chaos of the situation, deepening the narrator's sense of helplessness and dread.

(ii) **Explain the description of the collapsing house and the fire emerging from the dust contribute to the atmosphere of the poem.** **(3)**

Ans. The description of the collapsing house and the fire that springs up in the dust intensifies the sense of destruction and devastation in the poem. The imagery of a house tilting, swaying and then crashing creates an unsettling atmosphere.

Meanwhile, the fire adds a sense of uncontrollable chaos. This contributes to the overall feeling of helplessness and horror emphasising the immediate, catastrophic impact of the bombing.

(iii) **Analyse the shift in the narrator's focus when he realises that he must get to the hospital and help his staff.** **(3)**

Ans. The shift in the narrator's focus from personal survival to the need to help others reveals the complexity of human responses to trauma. Despite his own injuries and the chaos surrounding him, he feels a sense of responsibility toward his staff and the need to provide aid.

(iv) **How does the narrator's reflection on his decision to help his staff illustrate the confusion and emotional conflict caused by the bombing?** **(3)**

Ans. The narrator's reflection on his decision to help his staff demonstrates the emotional conflict and confusion caused by the bombing.

While his desire to assist others seems logical in the moment, his later doubt about how he could have possibly done so reveals the internal struggle between his physical limitations, emotional distress, and the urgency of the situation.

(v) **How does the imagery of 'fire spread by the wind' convey the uncontrollable nature of the destruction in the poem? Answer in reference to the poetic device 'imagery' as used in the poem.** **(4)**

Ans. The imagery of 'fire spread by the wind' conveys the uncontrollable and relentless nature of the destruction. The wind symbolises the unpredictability and widespread effects of the devastation as the fire, once ignited, is no longer confined.

This imagery underscores the chaos and helplessness the narrator feels as forces beyond his control intensify the damage and destruction. Thus, in turn, makes it impossible to escape the calamity.

Extract 5

My legs gave way. I sat down on the ground.
Thirst seized me, but no water could be found.
My breath was short, but bit by bit my strength
Seemed to revive, and I got up at length.

(i) **What does the narrator's physical exhaustion, described in 'My legs gave way' and 'My breath was short', reveal about the severity of the situation he is facing? (3)**

Ans. The narrator's physical exhaustion indicates the extreme toll the disaster has taken on him. His legs giving way and shortness of breath reflect the overwhelming physical strain he is under.

These details highlight the intensity of the crisis and the trauma inflicted by the bombing, revealing how the body's strength falters under such extreme conditions, even as the narrator strives to continue.

(ii) **Explain the narrator's lack of shame about being naked reflect his emotional and psychological state during the disaster. (3)**

Ans. The narrator's lack of shame about being naked reflects a breakdown of normal social constructs and personal identity in the face of catastrophe. In such a traumatic and chaotic moment, survival becomes the priority, and the usual concerns about modesty and self-image fade away.

This lack of shame highlights the psychological shift that occurs during extreme trauma where basic survival instincts take precedence over societal norms.

(iii) **What is the significance of the soldier's gesture of offering the narrator a towel? How does it affect the narrator? (3)**

Ans. The soldier's gesture of offering the towel symbolises a moment of unexpected kindness and humanity amidst the devastation. It represents solidarity and compassion in the face of disaster providing a sense of connection between individuals despite the chaos.

For the narrator, this act offers brief comfort helping him regain some dignity. It marks a fleeting moment of normalcy in an otherwise horrific situation.

(iv) **How does the narrator's statement that his 'legs, stiff with dried blood, rebelled' reflect both physical and emotional conflict? (3)**

Ans. The narrator's statement reflects the intense physical pain he is experiencing, as his body is physically resisting movement due to injury. At the same time, it also conveys the emotional conflict he feels in continuing his journey.

The rebellion of his body indicates the struggle between his determination to survive and the overwhelming toll the trauma has taken on him, both physically and emotionally.

(v) **Explain the reason why narrator asks Yecko-san to go on ahead. What does this decision reveal about his state of mind? (4)**

Ans. The narrator asks Yecko-san to go on ahead because he is physically weakened and struggling to continue. This decision reveals his selflessness and concern for her well-being, even as he faces his own dire condition.

It also shows his acceptance of his own limitations and a recognition that, in order for her to survive, she must keep moving forward even if it means leaving him behind.

Extract 6

She did not wish to, but in our distress
What choice had we? A dreadful loneliness
Came over me when she had gone. My mind
Ran at high speed, my body crept behind.

(i) **How does the narrator feel when Yecko-san leaves him? What does this reveal about his emotional state? (3)**

Ans. The narrator feels a profound sense of loneliness when Yecko-san leaves as described by the 'dreadful loneliness' that overtakes him. This reveals his deep emotional distress and vulnerability. Despite the chaos around him, his sense of isolation becomes prominent.

This highlights the emotional toll of the disaster and the separation from someone he cares about in such a terrifying time.

(ii) **What does the narrator mean when he says, 'My mind ran at high speed, my body crept behind'? How does this reflect his mental and physical condition? (3)**

Ans. The narrator's statement, 'My mind ran at high speed, my body crept behind', reflects a disconnect between his thoughts and his physical capabilities. His mind is racing with thoughts, likely driven by fear and the urgency of the situation, while his body, injured and weakened, is unable to keep up.

This contrast highlights the physical limitations imposed by trauma and the disorienting effects of fear and stress.

(iii) **In what way does the imagery of 'shadowy forms of people, some / Were ghosts, some scarecrows' contribute to the atmosphere of the poem? (3)**

Ans. The imagery of 'shadowy forms of people, some / Were ghosts, some scarecrows' creates an eerie and unsettling atmosphere where the survivours of the bombing appear as mere husks of people, devoid of life or hope.

The comparison to ghosts and scarecrows evokes a sense of death, despair and alienation emphasising the extreme toll the disaster has taken on the human spirit.

(iv) **Analyse the significance of the description of the survivors' arms being 'stretched straight out, shoulder to dangling hand'.** **(3)**

Ans. The description of the survivors' arms being 'stretched straight out, shoulder to dangling hand' symbolises both physical and psychological trauma. Their outstretched arms suggest that they are disoriented, unable to move freely or act and physically scarred.

It also implies that they have become like helpless, lifeless beings, struggling to cope with their injuries. This imagery adds to the sense of hopelessness and the enduring impact of the violence.

(v) **How does the narrator's understanding of the survivors' injuries, 'The friction on their burns caused so much pain', reflect the horror of their situation?** **(4)**

Ans. The narrator's realisation that the friction on the survivors' burns causes them excruciating pain highlights the horrifying physical effects of the bombing. The survivours are depicted as enduring not only the initial trauma but also continuous suffering from their injuries as even the slightest movement causes further agony.

This detail emphasises the brutal, lingering impact of the violence, deepening the sense of human suffering and despair in the aftermath of the disaster.

Extract 7

Those who could, shuffled in a blank parade
Towards the hospital. saw, dismayed,
A woman with a child stand in my path –
Both without clothes. Had they come back from the bath?

(i) **How does the narrator react to seeing the woman and child without clothes? What is his initial interpretation of their appearance?** **(3)**

Ans. The narrator is initially dismayed and confused when he sees the woman and child without clothes. His first thought is that they might have come back from the bath, suggesting a lack of understanding about the horrific circumstances.

His reaction reflects the shock and disorientation he is experiencing in the aftermath of the disaster.

(ii) **Explain the significance of the narrator's realisation that 'some strange thing had stripped us of our clothes'.** **(3)**

Ans. The narrator's realisation that 'some strange thing had stripped us of our clothes' signifies the profound and unsettling effect of the bombing.

The destruction is so intense and dehumanising that the survivors are left naked, stripped of their identities and personal belongings.

This moment highlights the extent of the loss and trauma, both physically and psychologically, in the wake of the catastrophe.

(iii) **The narrator's confusion about the woman and child's state of undress reflect the larger confusion and chaos of the situation. How does it do so?** **(3)**

Ans. The narrator's confusion about the woman and child's undress reflects the disorienting and chaotic nature of the bombing. In the midst of such devastation, normal explanations and understandings collapse.

The narrator's inability to immediately make sense of the situation demonstrates the overwhelming sense of disorder. This confusion mirrors the larger disarray caused by the disaster.

(iv) **How does the imagery of people 'shuffling in a blank parade' contribute to the atmosphere of the poem?** **(3)**

Ans. The imagery of people 'shuffling in a blank parade' evokes a sense of mechanical movement and emotional numbness. The survivors are depicted as moving aimlessly, devoid of purpose or hope, like ghosts or automatons.

This contributes to the poem's atmosphere of despair and helplessness. It further illustrates how the disaster has drained people of their will and humanity.

(v) **Why does the narrator feel at a loss upon seeing the naked man? How does this moment enhance the theme of loss in the poem?** **(4)**

Ans. The narrator feels at a loss upon seeing the naked man because it is a disturbing and surreal image that deepens his sense of helplessness and confusion. The nakedness of the survivors symbolises the complete stripping away of identity and dignity, intensifying the theme of loss in the poem.

This moment reinforces the emotional and physical devastation caused by the bombing highlighting the complete destruction of normal life.

Extract 8

The face of an old woman on the ground
Was marred with suffering, but she made no sound.
Silence was common to us all. I heard
No cries of anguish, or a single word.

(i) **How does the description of the old woman's face reflect the impact of the disaster on the survivors?** **(3)**

Ans. The old woman's face, 'marred with suffering', reflects the profound physical and emotional trauma the survivours have endured. Her silent suffering symbolises how the devastation has robbed people of their ability to express pain or anguish.

It underscores the depth of the disaster's impact where even the most intense suffering is experienced in silence.

(ii) **What is the significance of the phrase 'Silence was common to us all' in the context of the poem?** **(3)**

Ans. The phrase 'Silence was common to us all' emphasises the eerie and unnatural quiet that follows the chaos of the bombing. It suggests that the survivors, overwhelmed by shock, physical pain or fear, are unable to cry out or speak.

The silence reflects a loss of normal human reactions to trauma. It underscores the devastation and helplessness felt by everyone affected.

(iii) **Explain how the absence of cries of anguish contribute to the mood of the poem.** **(3)**

Ans. The absence of cries of anguish heightens the bleak and desolate mood of the poem. It creates an atmosphere of isolation and numbness, where the physical and emotional pain is too great for any expression of grief or sorrow.

This silence contributes to the poem's portrayal of a world turned upside down, where even human suffering seems muted and detached.

(iv) **Why might the poet have chosen not to describe the old woman's physical injuries in detail? Give a reason.** **(3)**

Ans. By not describing the old woman's physical injuries in detail, the poet allows her suffering to be felt more universally and symbolically. Her face being 'marred with suffering' suggests that the pain is not only physical but also emotional and psychological.

The lack of specific details makes her suffering more representative of the collective pain experienced by all survivors emphasising the overwhelming nature of the tragedy.

(v) **What does the narrator's observation of the old woman's silence suggest about the human response to extreme trauma?** **(4)**

Ans. The narrator's observation of the old woman's silence suggests that extreme trauma can lead to a numbing of the emotional and physical self. In the face of overwhelming horror and pain, the usual human responses, such as crying out in anguish, may be suppressed.

This reflects how trauma can shut down normal emotional reactions leaving people in a state of shock and disbelief.

05

THE NIGHT MAIL

W.H. Auden

Introduction

The Night Mail is a poem written by W. H. Auden, a famous English poet known for his unique style and themes of modern life. It is about a mail train delivering letters across the country, highlighting its importance in people's lives. The poem belongs to the narrative and descriptive poetry genre, as it tells a story and paints vivid pictures. Its rhythm matches the train's movement, making it special and engaging. The poem shows how letters bring hope, joy, and connection, making people feel remembered.

About the Poem

The Night Mail was written in 1936 for the documentary film 'Night Mail'. It showcased the journey of the Royal Mail Train travelling from London to Scotland. The poem describes the impact of a night train carrying mail through Scottish countryside. The poem has letters from all over the world on various topics. The poem vividly captures the train's journey, the landscape it passes, and the importance of delivering letters to people from all walks of life.

Exploring the Stanzas

This is the .... wind-bent grasses.

The poem describes the night mail train crossing the Border, delivering important items like cheques and postal orders. It brings letters for people from all walks of life, from the wealthy to the poor and from businesses to neighbours. The train faces a challenge climbing Beattock, but it stays on schedule. As it moves, it passes through natural landscapes like cotton-grass and moorland puffing out steam. The train's snorting sound contrasts with the quiet, windy environment around it, showing its power and determination to complete its journey.

Birds turn .... she descends,

In these lines, the poet describes the quiet and peaceful scene as the Night Mail train passes through the countryside. The birds notice the train as it comes by and they watch with surprise, keenness and pleasure. They see no human faces and find the carriages impression less. The sheepdogs are asleep and unbothered. They are sensitive creatures, quick to rise at the approach of an intruder. The people living along the railway track have grown habitual to the train's arrival and are not disturbed by it. Only the jug shakes in the bedroom due to the train's vibration.

As dawn arrives, the train has finished its climb and begins to descend toward Glasgow. The lines show the stillness and calm of the rural world as the train moves through it.

Towards the steam .... for news.

In these lines, the poet describes the train moving toward busy industrial areas passing steam tugs, cranes and furnaces that look like giant chess pieces on a dark plain. The people of Scotland are eagerly awaiting the train as it carries important news. The mention of glens and lochs shows the contrast between the rural landscape and the anticipation for news in the towns.

Letters of thanks .... spelt all wrong.

The lines describe the wide variety of letters that people receive in their daily lives. They range from formal letters, such as bills or invitations, to personal ones like thank-you notes or declarations of love. The poet mentions that letters can carry news, whether it's gossip or financial updates, and sometimes contain photos from holidays.

There are letters from family members, like uncles, cousins and aunts, and even messages sent from far-off places like the South of France. The letters come in different colours of paper, including pink, violet, white and blue, and the writing varies greatly. Some are well-written and formal while others are messy, informal or full of emotion. The trains carries letters and messages that express a wide range of emotions. Some letters are friendly and chatty while others are boring.

These lines highlight the many different forms of communication that letters represent, each one reflecting the writer's purpose, feelings and intentions. The poem showcases the richness and diversity of human communication through letters.

Thousands are .... himself forgotten?

These lines describe people sleeping in different cities like Glasgow, Edinburgh, and Aberdeen, dreaming of both pleasant and frightening things. As they sleep, they are unaware of the world around them. When they wake up, they eagerly wait for letters. The mention of the postman's knock makes them feel excited as receiving letters brings joy and connection. The poet reflects on how people long for communication and the fear of being forgotten when no letters arrive.

Vocab Vault

Gradient Incline or Slope
Boulder A detached and rounded or much-worn mass of rock.
Shovelling Digging or scooping
Slumber Sleep or rest
Descend Go downhill
Yelping Screeching
Glade Open space
Glens Valleys
Lochs Lakes
Moorland Open, uncultivated land with heather and grass.
Furnaces Large structures used for heating or melting materials.
Condolence An expression of sympathy for someone's loss.

Theme of the Poem

The poem, 'The Night Mail' by W.H. Auden highlights the mail train as a vital link that connects people from all walks of life by delivering personal letters, business messages and news. It symbolises routine and reliability, operating tirelessly to maintain communication despite challenges. The democratic nature of the mail, accessible to both rich and poor, reflects social equality.

Through the varied letters, the poem captures diverse human emotions and experiences. It also portrays industrialisation, showcasing the train as a symbol of modern technology supporting social connections.

Message Conveyed by the Poem

The poem conveys the crucial role of the mail train in connecting distant places, bringing news, letters and communication. The poem emphasises the efficiency of the service as it moves through the night ensuring that people receive letters ranging from personal to official. It portrays the train as a symbol of connection and unity, keeping people informed and emotionally linked despite physical distances.

Style, Tone and Mood

- **Style** The poem The Night Mail is written in a rhythmic, almost musical style, mimicking the steady motion of the train.
- **Tone** The tone is informative yet vivid, focusing on the journey of the mail train and its importance.
- **Mood** The mood is dynamic, evoking a sense of movement and purpose as the train travels through the night, delivering letters.

Title

The title 'The Night Mail' refers to the postal train that travels through the night, delivering letters and parcels across the country. It symbolises the constant, reliable movement of communication connecting people and places. The night setting evokes a sense of quiet, anticipation and mystery. Meanwhile, the mail represents the flow of news, personal messages and societal connections. The title sets the tone for the poem emphasising both the journey and the significance of correspondence.

Literary Devices

- **Imagery** 'Past cotton-grass and moorland boulder' ***(Stanza 1)***
- **Personification** 'She passes' ***(Stanza 1)***; 'she descends' ***(Stanza 2)***
- **Alliteration** 'Shovelling white steam over her shoulder' ***(Stanza 1)***
- **Rhyme and Rhythm** The poem follows a regular rhyme scheme and meter, mimicking the steady movement of the train. This rhythmic flow mirrors the train's predictable, reliable journey.

EXAM ORIENTED QUESTIONS

TYPE - 1 Multiple Choice Questions

01 Mark

Q.1 The poem The Night Mail highlights the importance of .... **[ICSE Specimen 2024]**

(a) a good postal system
(b) the human desire to stay connected
(c) a strong industrial town
(d) travelling by train at night

Q.2 What does the night mail bring?

(a) Letters for the rich and poor
(b) Packages for the wealthy
(c) Food and provisions
(d) Money only

Q.3 The recipients of the mail in the poem are ....

(a) only the wealthy
(b) only the poor
(c) the shop at the corner and the girl next door
(d) only the workers

Q.4 What obstacle does the train face in the poem?

(a) Rain
(b) The wind
(c) The steep climb of Beattock
(d) A broken track

Q.5 What is the significance of the phrase 'the gradient's against her?

(a) The train is moving uphill
(b) The train is facing a storm
(c) The train is delayed
(d) The train is going downhill

Q.6 What does the phrase 'she's on time' refer to?

(a) The train is punctual
(b) The train is late
(c) The train is out of schedule
(d) The train is ahead of schedule

Q.7 "Cotton-grass and moorland boulder"
The above phrase represents ....

(a) the natural landscape the train passes through
(b) the cityscape the train travels across
(c) the industrial zones the train crosses
(d) a nearby village

Q.8 What does the image of 'shovelling white steam' symbolise?

(a) The pollution caused by the train
(b) The labour of the engine and its power
(c) The beauty of the surrounding landscape
(d) The train's speed

Q.9 What does the phrase 'snorting noisily' in the poem suggest about the train?

(a) The train is out of control
(b) The train is struggling to keep pace
(c) The train's noisy and powerful movement
(d) The train is losing steam

Q.10 What does the train's passage through the countryside represent?

(a) The destruction of nature
(b) The harmony between nature and industry
(c) The domination of industry over nature
(d) The stillness of nature

Q.11 Identify the tone of the poem 'The Night Mail'.

I. Melancholic II. Cheerful III. Reflective
IV. Descriptive V. Angry

(a) I and II (b) II and III (c) III and IV (d) IV and V

Q.12 Identify the poetic device used in the line 'Pulling up Beattock, a steady climb'.

(a) Personification (b) Metaphor
(c) Alliteration (d) Imagery

Q.13 What is the significance of 'Beattock' in the poem?

(a) It is the train station where the train stops
(b) It symbolises the train's challenge in its journey
(c) It is the final destination of the train
(d) It represents a quiet village

Q.14 Which literary device is used in the line 'Silent miles of wind-bent grasses'?

(a) Alliteration (b) Personification
(c) Imagery (d) Hyperbole

Q.15 What does the comparison of the furnaces to 'gigantic chessmen' in the poem, 'The Night Mail signify'?

(a) The furnaces are small and insignificant
(b) The furnaces resemble strategic, important structures in the landscape
(c) The furnaces are scattered randomly in the field
(d) The furnaces represent obstacles on the train's path

Q.16 The central theme of the poem, 'The Night Mail' is ....

(a) human struggle against nature
(b) the connection between industry and nature
(c) the need for technological advancement
(d) the slow decline of transportation systems

Q.17 Which of the following lines reflects the routine nature of the night mail?

(a) "Bringing the cheque and the postal order"
(b) "Every day as she passes"
(c) "The gradient's against her, but she's on time"
(d) "This is the night mail crossing the border"

Q.18 What does the 'night mail' symbolise in the poem?

(a) The peaceful night
(b) The efficiency of the postal system
(c) A form of transportation
(d) The stillness of the night

Q.19 How does the poet contrast the train's movement with the landscape?

(a) By describing the train as silent
(b) By using the imagery of noisy movement against a quiet, still landscape
(c) By focusing only on the train's power
(d) By emphasising the train's speed

Q.20 What is the overall mood of the poem?

I. Tense II. Hopeful III. Peaceful
IV. Steady V. Reflective

(a) I and II (b) II and III (c) III and IV (d) IV and V

Q.21 What is the significance of the train's punctuality in the poem?

(a) It emphasises the reliability of the postal system
(b) It shows that the train is always late
(c) It highlights the train's speed
(d) It portrays the train as unreliable

Q.22 What kind of letters are sent to Highlands and Lowlands?

(a) Letters of joy from girl and boy
(b) Letters of condolences
(c) Letters from uncles, cousins and aunts
(d) Letters to Scotland from the South of France

Q.23 Which of the following describes the city of Edinburgh in the poem?

(a) Industrious (b) Refined
(c) Enduring (d) All of these

Q.24 Arrange the following events in the order in which they appear in 'The Night Mail'.

A. The train crosses the border.
B. The train moves through the countryside, delivering letters.
C. The train starts its journey in London.
D. The train arrives at its destination.

(a) C, B, A, D (b) A, C, D, B
(c) C, A, D, B (d) C, B, D, A

Q.25 Arrange the following stages in the train's journey as described in 'The Night Mail'.

A. The train is depicted as crossing rivers and landscapes.
B. The train passes through the dark countryside at night.
C. The train travels through the streets of London.
D. The train carries letters with both good and bad news.

(a) C, D, B, A (b) B, C, D, A
(c) C, B, A, D (d) A, C, B, D

Q.26 Select the option that shows the correct relationship between statements (1) and (2).

Statement 1 The poem The Night Mail presents a sense of urgency in delivering the mail.

Statement 2 The Night Mail is portrayed as a fast, unstoppable force, moving through the night to bring communication to distant places.

(a) Statement 1 is true and Statement 2 is false
(b) Statement 2 is true and Statement 1 is false.
(c) Statement 2 is the correct explanation for Statement 1.
(d) Statement 1 and Statement 2 are independent of each other.

Q.27 Select the option that shows the correct relationship between statements (1) and (2).

Statement 1 The train in 'The Night Mail' is depicted as a natural force that connects people.

Statement 2 The poem conveys a sense of calm and inevitability in the train's journey, emphasising its role in uniting distant regions through communication.

(a) Statement 1 is true and Statement 2 is false.
(b) Statement 2 is true and Statement 1 is false.
(c) Statement 2 is the reason for Statement 1.
(d) Statement 1 and Statement 2 are independent of each other.

Answers

1. (b)	2. (a)	3. (c)	4. (c)	5. (a)	6. (a)	7. (a)	8. (b)	9. (c)	10. (b)
11. (c)	12. (d)	13. (b)	14. (c)	15. (b)	16. (b)	17. (d)	18. (b)	19. (b)	20. (c)
21. (a)	22. (b)	23. (b)	24. (a)	25. (c)	26. (c)	27. (b)			

Explanations

11. The tone of 'The Night Mail' is both reflective and descriptive. Auden thoughtfully reflects on the train's journey, its role in communication, and its connection to diverse human experiences. At the same time, the poem vividly describes the landscape, the movement of the train and its sounds.
12. The line 'Pulling up Beattock, a steady climb' creates a vivid picture of a train ascending a slope, appealing to the reader's sense of sight and motion. This descriptive language evokes imagery, helping the reader visualise the climb and experience the effort involved.
14. The poem creates a peaceful mood through serene imagery of the natural landscape, such as 'silent miles of wind-bent grasses'. At the same time, it evokes a steady mood with the rhythmic and consistent movement of the train, symoblising reliability and routine.

TYPE - 2 Extract Based Questions

16 Marks

Extract 1

This is the night mail crossing the Border,
Bringing the cheque and the postal order,
Letters for the rich, letters for the poor,
The shop at the corner, the girl next door.

(i) What is the role of the night mail? How does the poet describe it in the poem? (3)

Ans. The poet presents the night mail as a vital service that connects people from all walks of life. It brings essential communication like cheques and postal orders, for both the rich and the poor.

The night mail serves a democratic function, delivering letters to a wide range of individuals, from the shop at the corner to the girl next door, emphasising its role in connecting society.

(ii) What does the following line suggest about the train? How is it significant? (3)

'Pulling up Beattock, a steady climb: The gradient's against her, but she's on time'.

Ans. The line illustrates the train's resilience and punctuality. Despite the difficulty posed by the steep incline of Beattock, the train continues its journey without delay.

The phrase 'the gradient's against her' is significant as it highlights the challenge of the uphill climb but 'she's on time' emphasises the train's unwavering reliability and its ability to overcome obstacles.

(iii) Explain how the poet uses imagery to describe the landscape the night mail train passes through? (3)

Ans. The poet uses vivid imagery to depict the natural surroundings, such as 'cotton-grass and moorland boulder', which evoke a peaceful and rugged landscape.

The 'wind-bent grasses' further emphasise the stillness of nature creating a contrast with the train's noisy progress.

The imagery helps to build a tranquil yet industrious atmosphere where the natural world and human labour coexist.

(iv) What does the phrase 'shovelling white steam over her shoulder' symbolise in the poem? (3)

Ans. The given phrase symbolises the hardworking nature of the train. The train's engine is working tirelessly to keep the train moving expelling steam as it climbs the gradient.

The metaphor humanises the train portraying it as a diligent worker, continuously exerting energy to fulfill its task of delivering the night mail on time.

(v) **There is a contrast between the train's noisy movement and the silent countryside. Elaborate on its significance.** **(4)**

Ans. The contrast between the train's noisy movement and the silent countryside highlights its powerful presence. The train snorts, shovels steam and moves steadily, while the countryside remains calm and undisturbed. This contrast shows how the train is full of energy and purpose, carrying important letters, while nature silently watches. The poem also suggests that life moves forward even when the world around it is still. The jug shaking in a bedroom symbolises small effects of a big force. This contrast makes the train seem unstoppable, emphasising the importance of communication in connecting people across distances.

Extract 2

Sheep-dogs cannot turn her course;
They slumber on with paws across.
In the farm she passes no one wakes,
But a jug in a bedroom gently shakes.

(i) **How do the birds respond as the mail train approaches? How is it different from the dogs' response?** **(3)**

Ans. In 'The Night Mail', the birds respond to the approaching train by turning their heads and staring at it from the bushes suggesting curiosity and awareness. They are alert to the train's presence. In contrast, the sheep-dogs remain completely indifferent; they continue to sleep with their paws crossed, unaffected by the train's passing.

This contrast highlights the different ways animals react to the train's movement. The birds are watchful while the dogs are passive and unmoved emphasising the quiet, peaceful nature of the rural landscape despite the train's presence.

(ii) **Analyse how the poet describes the stillness of the farm as the train passes?** **(3)**

Ans. The poet describes the stillness of the farm as the train passes by with vivid calmness. The line 'In the farm she passes no one wakes' highlights the quietness of the farm with no one stirring or reacting.

The only subtle sign of the train's presence is a jug gently shaking in a bedroom emphasising the faint, unnoticed impact the train has on its peaceful surroundings.

(iii) **What is the significance of the jug gently shaking in the bedroom?** **(3)**

Ans. The shaking jug symbolises the subtle impact the train has on its surroundings even in quiet, rural places. It suggests that while life may appear still and undisturbed, the train's passing still causes a faint ripple or movement, connecting the distant world with the peaceful farm.

(iv) **Identify the three literary devices used in the above extract. Elaborate.** **(3)**

Ans. The literary devices used in the given lines are as follows

- **Personification** The train is personified in lines like 'she approaches', 'she descends' and 'her climb is done'. By giving the train human qualities, the poet makes it seem like a living, purposeful being.
- **Imagery** The descriptions 'Birds turn their heads', 'Sheep-dogs...slumber on with paws across' and 'a jug in a bedroom gently shakes' creates vivid pictures in the reader's mind, engaging the senses of sight and sound. It further emphasises the stillness of the rural setting.
- **Alliteration** The repetition of the 's' sound in 'Sheep-dogs slumber' and 'paws across' adds a smooth, rhythmic quality to the lines enhancing the peaceful atmosphere of the scene.

(v) **Explain the tone used by the poet to describe the shocking events happening around the narrator? What is the mood conveyed by the last lines in the above extract?** **(4)**

'Dawn freshens, Her climb is done.
Down towards Glasgow she descends.'

Ans. In these lines from 'The Night Mail', the tone is calm and reflective. The poet describes the end of the train's journey with a sense of quiet completion, focusing on the natural transition from night to dawn. The use of 'Dawn freshens' conveys a gentle and peaceful tone suggesting the beginning of a new day.

The mood of the final lines is serene and tranquil, emphasising the sense of relief and calm as the train descends towards Glasgow. It conveys a feeling of anticipation as the train nears its destination signalling the end of its journey.

Extract 3

Towards the steam tugs yelping down a glade of cranes
Towards the fields of apparatus, the furnaces
Set on the dark plain like gigantic chessmen.
All Scotland waits for her:
In dark glens, beside pale-green lochs
Men long for news.

(i) **How does the poet describe the landscape the train travels through in these lines?** **(3)**

Ans. The poet describes the landscape as industrial and dark, with 'steam tugs yelping' and 'furnaces set on the dark plain like gigantic chessmen'.

These images suggest a contrast between the mechanical, industrial world and the natural environment, emphasising the train's journey through a place filled with machinery and energy.

(ii) Identify the literary device used in the following line. Also, explain its significance.
'Set on the dark plain like gigantic chessmen.' (3)

Ans. The line 'Set on the dark plain like gigantic chessmen' uses a simile as it compares the furnaces to 'gigantic chessmen' using the word 'like'.

The comparison of the furnaces to 'gigantic chessmen' symbolises their strategic importance and immense size. It suggests that the furnaces are carefully placed, powerful and significant within the industrial landscape, much like chess pieces on a board. This emphasises their central role in the industrial process.

(iii) What does the line 'All Scotland waits for her' suggest about the train's importance? (3)

Ans. The line implies that the mail train holds significant value for the people of Scotland. It conveys the idea that the entire country eagerly awaits the train's arrival, highlighting the importance of the mail in delivering news, communication and connection to people in both rural and urban areas.

(iv) How does the poet depict the emotional anticipation of the people in Scotland? Identify the phrases/lines. (3)

Ans. The poet depicts the emotional anticipation of the people in Scotland through phrases like 'All Scotland waits for her' and 'Men long for news'. It is further depicted through the imagery of 'dark glens' and 'pale-green lochs'.

These lines suggest a deep longing and expectation as the people eagerly await the arrival of the train which connects them to the outside world and offers hope, information or comfort.

(v) Two different landscapes are presented in the above extract. Identify them and discuss the juxtaposition between them. (4)

Ans. The lines present two contrasting landscapes – the industrial and the natural. The industrial landscape is depicted through 'steam tugs yelping', 'glade of cranes' and 'fields of apparatus, the furnaces' emphasising human-made machinery and activity.

In contrast, the natural landscape is shown through 'dark glens' and 'pale-green lochs' highlighting Scotland's serene, untouched beauty.

The juxtaposition emphasises the coexistence of progress and tradition. It shows how the industrial world brings communication and news to the tranquil, rural areas of Scotland and thus bridges two very different worlds.

Extract 4

Letters of thanks, letters from banks,
Letters of joy from girl and boy,
Receipted bills and invitations
To inspect new stock or to visit relations,

(i) What types of letters are mentioned in these lines? What do they reveal about the purpose of the mail? (3)

Ans. The lines mention various types of letters, including 'letters of thanks', 'letters from banks', 'invitations', 'applications for situations' and 'timid lovers' declarations'.

These letters reveal the diverse purposes of the mail system. This shows how it facilitates personal, professional and financial communication connecting people across different aspects of life.

(ii) How does the poet use repetition to emphasise the variety of correspondence? (3)

Ans. The poet uses repetition with phrases like 'letters of' and 'gossip, gossip' to emphasise the vast array of correspondence delivered by the mail. This repetition highlights the mail's role in carrying messages of different tones and purposes. They range from joyful news to everyday transactions, underscoring importance of the mail in daily life.

(iii) What do the 'timid lovers' declarations' suggest about personal communication during the time? (3)

Ans. The 'timid lovers' declarations' suggest that personal and emotional communication was a significant part of letter writing. It highlights how people relied on mail to express intimate feelings and maintain personal relationships.

It reflects the importance of the written word in conveying emotions that might be difficult to express in person.

(iv) The poem mentions various human emotions. Identify the phrases that convey the following emotions (3)

(a) Happiness and Excitement
(b) Curiosity and Interest
(c) Nostalgia and Fondness

Ans. The phrases that convey the listed emotions are

(a) **Happiness and Excitement** 'Letters of joy from girl and boy' express joy and excitement.

(b) **Curiosity and Interest** 'Gossip from all the nations' indicates curiosity and a desire for social connection.

(c) **Nostalgia and Fondness** 'Holiday snaps to enlarge in' show the sharing of cherished memories and happiness.

(v) What role do 'holiday snaps to enlarge in' play in the depiction of communication? **(4)**

Ans. 'Holiday snaps to enlarge in' play a role in depicting the personal and intimate aspects of communication. These snapshots represent the sharing of joyful memories and experiences, highlighting how the mail serves as a medium for connecting loved ones through visual and emotional content.

This element adds a sense of warmth and nostalgia, showcasing that communication is not only about serious or practical matters but also about sharing moments of happiness, leisure and personal significance with others. It reflects the human desire to stay connected and share life's special moments.

Extract 5

Letters with faces scrawled on the margin,
Letters from uncles, cousins, and aunts,
Letters to Scotland from the South of France,
Letters of condolence to Highlands and Lowlands

(i) **What do the 'faces scrawled on the margin' symbolise in these lines? (3)**

Ans. The 'faces scrawled on the margin' symbolise the personal and informal nature of some letters. These doodles suggest a sense of intimacy and creativity, indicating that letters are not only about words but also about personal touches that bring warmth and individuality to the communication.

(ii) **What is the significance of mentioning the different colours of paper used in the letters? (3)**

Ans. The mention of different colours of paper—'pink, violet, white and blue'—symbolises the diversity and individuality of the letters. Each colour represents various emotions and purposes from joyful to formal.

This variety highlights the multifaceted nature of human communication, showing how letters can convey a wide range of sentiments, moods and personal touches, making each piece of correspondence unique and significant in its own right.

(iii) **How does the poet contrast different types of letters in these lines? (3)**

Ans. The poet contrasts different types of letters by describing them as 'chatty, catty, boring, adoring' and 'cold and official' versus 'heart's outpouring'. This juxtaposition highlights the wide range of content and emotions expressed through letters, from mundane to deeply emotional, showcasing the multifaceted nature of written communication.

(iv) **What does the mention of 'typed and the printed and the spelt all wrong' suggest about the letters? (3)**

Ans. The mention of the given phrase suggests that letters vary in formality and accuracy reflecting the human imperfections in communication. It indicates that letters come in all shapes and forms, from professionally typed documents to personal, handwritten notes with mistakes, emphasising the authenticity and diversity of human expression.

(v) **Why does the poet include a variety of letter types and tones in these lines? What is the author's tone in the above lines? (4)**

Ans. The poet includes a variety of letter types and tones—such as "chatty, catty, boring, adoring"—to show the diverse nature of human communication. Letters serve many purposes, ranging from formal to personal, trivial to emotional, reflecting the different facets of life. This variety highlights how correspondence serves to express a range of human emotions, thoughts and experiences.

The author's tone in these lines is playful and observant. By describing the letters in a light-hearted, almost whimsical way, the poet captures the essence of how letters reflect the broad spectrum of human interactions and relationships. The tone conveys both the humour and complexity of written communication.

Extract 6

Thousands are still asleep,
Dreaming of terrifying monsters
Or of friendly tea beside the band in Cranston's or Crawford's:

(i) **What is the significance of 'Thousands are still asleep' in these lines? How is this 'sleep' interrupted? (3)**

Ans. The line 'Thousands are still asleep' sets a tranquil, serene tone and introduces the idea of people being unaware of the world around them. It symbolises a sense of stillness where life is paused in the darkness of night.

However, this calm is soon interrupted by the arrival of the mail which carries emotional significance for the people.

(ii) **What do the dreams of 'terrifying monsters' and 'friendly tea' signify in these lines? (3)**

Ans. The 'terrifying monsters' represent the fear and anxiety that people may carry in their subconscious. Meanwhile, the 'friendly tea beside the band' reflects more peaceful, comforting and social dreams.

These contrasting images illustrate the range of emotions people experience in their sleep, from fear to comfort, symbolising the diversity of human experiences.

(iii) **How do the references to the following cities of Glasgow, Edinburgh and Aberdeen contribute to the theme of the poem?** **(3)**

Ans. The references to cities like Glasgow, Edinburgh and Aberdeen emphasise the widespread anticipation felt across Scotland.

These cities represent the unity of the people who, regardless of their location, share the same longing for communication and connection.

It underscores how the mail service impacts people from various walks of life and places.

(iv) **Explain the role that 'postman's knock' plays in these lines.** **(3)**

Ans. The 'postman's knock' symbolises a pivotal moment of connection, marking the arrival of the mail, which is eagerly awaited. The quickening of the heart upon hearing the knock highlights the emotional importance of receiving letters, reinforcing the idea that people long for communication and cannot bear to feel forgotten.

(v) **What is the poet's attitude towards the significance of letters in human life? How does it relate to the theme of communication and connection?** **(4)**

Ans. The poet's attitude towards the significance of letters in human life is one of reverence and sensitivity. The anticipation and emotional response to receiving letters highlight their role as essential carriers of personal connection, joy and hope.

This attitude underscores the theme of communication and its impact on human relationships. By portraying letters as vital links that prevent feelings of isolation and being forgotten, the poet emphasises the universal need for recognition and emotional connection.

This further illustrates how communication bridges distance and sustains the bonds between people, regardless of vast geographical and emotional divides.

SPECIMEN QUESTION PAPER
LITERATURE IN ENGLISH
(ENGLISH PAPER - 2)

General Instructions

Maximum Marks : 80

Time allowed : Two hours

The paper has **four** Sections.

Section A is compulsory – **All** questions in Section **A** must be answered.

You must attempt one question from each of the Section **B, C** and **D** and one other question from any Section of your choice.

The intended marks for questions or parts of questions are given in brackets ().

Section A

*(Attempt **all** questions from this section.)*

Question 1

Read the following questions and choose the most appropriate response from the choices given below.

(Please do not copy the question - simply write out in correct serial order the appropriate word or phrase.) **(16)**

(i) Why does Cassius send notes through Cinna, at the end of Act I?

(a) To warn Caesar about Brutus' betrayal so that he could take necessary action
(b) To assure Brutus that plans for the conspiracy were in place
(c) To remind Caesar to meet at the Capitol at the appointed time
(d) To convince Brutus that the Romans needed him to join the conspiracy

(ii) Why does Brutus oppose the idea of including Cicero in their group?

(a) Brutus dislikes Cicero although the people respect him a lot
(b) he knows Cicero loves Caesar unconditionally
(c) Cicero never follows anything that other people begin
(d) Cicero would not like to be included in a bloody conspiracy

(iii) "I would have had thee there and here again
Ere I can tell thee what thou shouldst do there."

These lines tell us that Portia is feeling ....

(a) angry (b) weak (c) sad (d) anxious

(iv) Which of the following lines reflects Caesar's arrogance?

(a) Danger knows well Caesar is more dangerous.
(b) Go, bid the priest do present sacrifice.
(c) For thy humour, I shall stay at home.
(d) I am ashamed, I did yield to them.

(v) Select the option that shows the correct relationship between Statements (1) and (2).

Statement 1 Flavius tells Marullus that they would have to take all the decorations off Caesar's statues.

Statement 2 Flavius fears that Caesar's growing powers would result in a life of servitude for all Romans.

(a) Statement 1 is true and Statement 2 is false
(b) Statement 2 is true and Statement 1 is false.
(c) Statement 2 is the cause for Statement 1.
(d) Statement 1 and Statement 2 are independent of each other.

(vi) What are the commoners celebrating in Act 1, Scene 1?

(a) Caesar's victory over the sons of Pompey
(b) Caesar's victory over Pompey
(c) The Feast of the Lupercal
(d) The Ides of March

(vii) Choose the option that lists the sequence of events in the correct order.

(i) He noticed a pink glow coming from a giant glass object in the middle of the bamboo grove.

(ii) When he stepped forward to take a closer look, he felt as if an electric shock had passed through his body.

(iii) He grew uneasy as he became aware of an eerie silence that had suddenly descended on the world.

(iv) Although it was a dark, moonless night, Bonku Babu chose to take the shortcut home.

(a) (i), (ii), (iii), (iv) (b) (ii), (iii), (iv), (i) (c) (iv), (iii), (i), (ii) (d) (iv), (ii), (iii), (i)

(viii) "The bowls never needed washing, because the boys cleaned them with their spoons until they shone."

This line means that ....

(a) the boys enjoyed washing their bowls
(b) the boys never got enough to eat
(c) the boys wanted to keep their bowls shiny
(d) the boys did not enjoy washing bowls

(ix) How did the Manager of Pipalnagar Bank try to pacify the crowd?

(a) By declaring that the bank had exhausted all its ready cash
(b) By asking the crowd not to panic
(c) By urging the crowd to come back the next day
(d) By trying to contact the owner, Seth Govind Ram

(x) At the end of the story, 'The Home-coming', Phatik says, "Mother, the holidays have come." What does he mean?

(a) His mother had come to take him home
(b) He would be free of the miseries of life
(c) He was homesick
(d) He missed his brother

(xi) Alan Trevor gave Hughie Erskine permanent entre to his studio because he liked his ....

(a) generous recklessness
(b) careless kindness
(c) kind carelessness
(d) reckless humility

(xii) The poem, 'A Doctor's Journal Entry for August 6, 1945', describes the devastation caused by the ....

(a) atomic explosion in the lives of ordinary people
(b) earthquake in Japan
(c) tidal waves in Japan
(d) volcanic eruption in Japan

(xiii) What according to Marge Piercy in 'A Work of Artifice', should begin very early with living creatures?

(a) Trimming their branches
(b) Teaching them life lessons
(c) Assigning gender roles
(d) Preparing them for life's struggles

(xiv) Which of the following options contains the figure of speech that appears in the following line?

'...where the sun came peeping in at morn...'

(a) A dozen eyeballs on the floor
(b) Tossing their heads in sprightly dance
(c) The tangled bine-stems scored the sky
(d) I remember I remember

(xv) Which of the following tasks is not performed by Skimbleshanks in the poem?

(a) Supervision of the driver
(b) Supervision of the guards
(c) Supervision of the bagmen
(d) Supervision of the police

(xvi) The poem 'The Night Mail' highlights the importance of ....

(a) a good postal system
(b) the human desire to stay connected
(c) a strong industrial town
(d) travelling by train at night

Section (B)

*(Answer **one or more** questions from this section.)*

DRAMA

(Julius Caesar by William Shakespeare)

Question 2

Read the extract given below and answer the questions that follow.

Calphurnia Alas! my Lord. Your wisdom is consum'd in confidence.
Do not go forth today call it my fear
That keeps you in the house, and not your own.
We'll send Mark Antony to the Senate House

(i) Where are the speakers?

Describe the weather outside.

What is Calphurnia trying to prevent Caesar from doing? **(3)**

(ii) State two unusual things Calphurnia had heard of that made her fearful.

What nightmare had she had? **(3)**

(iii) How did Caesar calm his wife's fears?

What does Calphurnia mean by "Your wisdom is consum'd in confidence"? **(3)**

(iv) How does Decius interpret Calphurnia's dream? **(3)**

(v) What does Caesar finally decide to do?

What can you infer about his character from this decision?

Mention two aspects of Calphurnia's character revealed in this scene. **(4)**

Question 3

Read the extract given below and answer the questions that follow.

Brutus What means this shouting? I do fear the people
Choose Caesar for their king.
Cassius Ay, do you fear it?
Then must I think you would not have it so.
Brutus I would not, Cassius; yet I love him well.

(i) Where are Brutus and Cassius?

What does Brutus 'fear' is the reason for 'this shouting'?

Later in the scene, Brutus hears a second shout. What does he think this is about? **(3)**

(ii) Later in the scene, how do Brutus and Cassius come to know of the actual reason for all the shouting? Who gives them the details?

How had they drawn this man's attention? **(3)**

(iii) 'I would not Cassius, yet I love him well.' What does this line reveal about Brutus's mental state?

How did Brutus describe his state of mind earlier in the scene? **(3)**

(iv) What does Cassius say to prove that Caesar was as weak as any other human being?

State any one physical disability of Caesar's that is mentioned in this scene. **(3)**

(v) Important character traits of Cassius are revealed in this scene. Mention any two.

What is your opinion of the man? Give a reason to justify your answer. **(4)**

Section (C)

*(Answer **one or more** questions from this section.)*

Prose - Short Stories

(Treasure Chest — A Collection of Poems and Short Stories)

Question 4

Read the following extract from Satyajit Ray's short story, 'Bonku Babu's Friend' and answer the questions that follow.

"All at once, his ears began ringing. He felt as if someone was humming loudly --- a long, steady noise ---- there was no way he could stop it."

(i) Where was Bonku Babu at this point in the story?

An object came into view as he moved forward. Describe what he saw. **(3)**

(ii) A weird creature soon began talking to Bonku Babu. What did he say to Bonku about having made a mistake? **(3)**

(iii) In what way did the creature prove that he was superior to humans? **(3)**

(iv) How did Bonku Babu's dreams of visiting foreign lands come true? Describe any one such land that he 'saw'. **(3)**

(v) How did the creature's advice affect Bonku Babu?

Comment on his transformation at the end of the story. What do you like about the way the story ends? **(4)**

Question 5

Read the following extract from Charles Dickens' short story, 'Oliver Asks for More' and answer the questions that follow.

Oliver Twist's mother, a young woman, lay ill in bed. A doctor and an old woman stood by her side. She lifted her head from the pillow. 'Let me see the child and die.'

(i) Who is the child referred to in the above extract?

What might have been the young woman's feelings when she said this? **(3)**

(ii) What is a 'workhouse'? How did the young woman who gave birth to the child end up in the workhouse? **(3)**

(iii) Who named the young child? What method did he use to do this? **(3)**

(iv) How did the old woman take care of the child? What does this tell us about her nature? **(3)**

(v) At the end of the story, a notice was posted outside the workhouse gate. What did it say?

Why do you think the reward was mentioned on the notice. **(4)**

Section (D)

(Answer ***one or more*** *questions from this section.)*

Poetry

(Treasure Chest — A Collection of Poems and Short Stories)

Question 6

Read the following extract from Vikram Seth's poem, 'A Doctor's Journal Entry for August 6, 1945' and answer the questions that follow.

The morning stretched calm, beautiful, and warm
Sprawling half-clad, I gazed out at the form
Of shimmering leaves and shadows. Suddenly
A strong flash, then another startled me.
I saw the old stone lantern brightly lit.

(i) Who made this journal entry?
What is the significance of the date in the title of the poem? **(3)**

(ii) How does the narrator describe the morning in the opening lines of the poem? **(3)**

(iii) What physical injuries does the narrator suffer? **(3)**

(iv) Mention any three of the shocking sights he observed as he looked around that morning? **(3)**

(v) What is the tone used by the poet to describe the shocking events happening around the narrator? What is the mood conveyed by the last lines of the poem.

Silence was common to us all. I heard
No cries of anguish, or a single word. **(4)**

Question 7

Read the following extract from Thomas Hood's poem, 'I Remember I Remember' and answer the questions that follow.

My spirit flew in feathers then,
That is so heavy now.

(i) What does the poet recall at the beginning of the poem?
What does he wish for at the end of the stanza? **(3)**

(ii) What words does the poet use to create a sense of nostalgia?
What memories of the garden does he mention in the second stanza? **(3)**

(iii) 'The tree is living yet!' What is the significance of this line?
Who had planted this tree and on what occasion? **(3)**

(iv) The poet uses various kinds of images in the poem. Give one example for each of the following.
(a) Sight (b) Sound (c) Touch **(3)**

(v) The poet compares two stages of his life in the poem. What are they?
What moods does he associate with each of them? **(4)**

Answers

1. (i) (d) To convince Brutus that the Romans needed him to join the conspiracy

   (ii) (c) Cicero never follows anything that other people begin

   (iii) (d) anxious

   (iv) (a) Danger knows well Caesar is more dangerous.

   (v) (c) Statement 2 is the cause for Statement 1.

   (vi) (a) Caesar's victory over the sons of Pompey

   (vii) (c) (iv), (iii), (i), (ii)

   (viii) (b) the boys never got enough to eat

   (ix) (d) By trying to contact the owner, Seth Govind Ram

   (x) (b) He would be free of the miseries of life.

   (xi) (b) careless kindness

   (xii) (a) atomic explosion in the lives of ordinary people

   (xiii) (a) Trimming their branches

   (xiv) (d) I remember I remember

   (xv) (d) Supervision of the police

   (xvi) (b) the human desire to stay connected

2. For answer refer to page no. 34-35 Extract 2.

3. For answer refer to page no. 15-16 Extract 3.

4. For answer refer to page no. 47 Extract 1.

5. For answer refer to page no. 55 Extract 1.

6. For answer refer to page no. 110 Extract 1.

7. For answer refer to page no. 102 Extract 4.

SAMPLE QUESTION PAPER
LITERATURE IN ENGLISH
(ENGLISH PAPER - 2)

General Instructions

Maximum Marks : 80

Time allowed : Two hours

The paper has **four** Sections.

Section A is compulsory – **All** questions in Section **A** must be answered.

You must attempt one question from each of the Section **B, C** and **D** and one other question from any Section of your choice.

The intended marks for questions or parts of questions are given in brackets ().

Section (A)

*(Attempt **all** questions from this section.)*

Question 1

Read the following questions and choose the most appropriate response from the choices given below

(Please do not copy the question - simply write out in correct serial order the appropriate word or phrase.) **(16)**

(i) Why does Calpurnia urge Caesar to stay home on the Ides of March?

(a) She wants him to spend time with her.
(b) She has had a terrible nightmare and fears for his safety.
(c) She believes the Senate will humiliate him.
(d) She wants to test his love for her.

(ii) What does Cassius mean when he says, "The fault, dear Brutus, is not in our stars, but in ourselves, that we are underlings"?

(a) Fate controls everything, and they must accept it.
(b) They are responsible for their own destiny, not fate.
(c) The gods have already determined Caesar's rule.
(d) Brutus and Cassius are powerless against Caesar's rise.

(iii) "Between the acting of a dreadful thing and the first motion, all the interim is like a phantasma or a hideous dream."

What does Brutus express in these lines?

(a) He is struggling with the moral dilemma of killing Caesar.
(b) He is afraid that the conspiracy will fail.
(c) He believes Caesar already knows of their plot.

(d) He is excited about taking power for himself.

(iv) Which line from the play best reflects Cassius' manipulative nature?

(a) 'Men at some time are masters of their fates.' (b) 'Cowards die many times before their deaths.'
(c) 'Friends, Romans, countrymen, lend me your ears.' (d) 'I am constant as the northern star.'

(v) Select the option that shows the correct relationship between statements (1) and (2).

Statement 1 Cassius tells Casca that the storm is a warning sign of Caesar's growing power.

Statement 2 Casca believes the storm is an omen of disaster for Rome.

(a) Statement 1 is true and Statement 2 is false.
(b) Statement 2 is true and Statement 1 is false.
(c) Statement 2 is the cause for Statement 1.
(d) Statement 1 and Statement 2 are independent of each other.

(vi) Why does Brutus refuse to swear an oath with the conspirators?

(a) He believes their cause should be strong enough without an oath.
(b) He does not fully trust the conspirators.
(c) He fears they will be caught.
(d) He is unsure about killing Caesar.

(vii) Why did Bonku Babu feel an electric shock pass through his body?

(a) He was struck by lightning. (b) He touched an alien spacecraft.
(c) He came into contact with an invisible force. (d) He accidentally stepped on an electric wire.

(viii) Why were the workhouse boys always hungry?

(a) They were not allowed to eat. (b) They were given only meagre portions of food.
(c) They had to share their food with the staff. (d) They chose to eat less.

(ix) How did the rumour about the bank's failure start?

(a) The manager announced bankruptcy. (b) Seth Govind Ram left town.
(c) Nathu complained about his unpaid salary. (d) Customers were already suspicious of the bank.

(x) Why did Phatik's mother send him away to Calcutta?

(a) She wanted him to get a better education. (b) She found him difficult to manage.
(c) His uncle insisted on taking him. (d) Phatik wanted to leave the village.

(xi) Why did Baron Hausberg give Hughie a cheque for £10,000?

(a) He wanted to invest in Hughie's business. (b) He was moved by Hughie's generosity.
(c) He wanted to test Hughie's honesty. (d) He was a friend of Alan Trevor.

(xii) What was the immediate reaction of the doctor and his wife after the explosion?

(a) They tried to run toward the hospital.
(b) They were completely unaware of what had happened.
(c) They felt a strong jolt and were thrown to the ground.
(d) They took shelter under a table.

(xiii) What does the gardener symbolise in the poem?

(a) A nurturing teacher (b) Society's control over individuals, especially women
(c) A caring parent (d) A skilled artist

(xiv) What is the tone of the poem?

(a) Joyful and hopeful (b) Nostalgic and regretful
(c) Angry and rebellious (d) Mysterious and eerie

(xv) Why was Skimbleshanks important to the train journey?

(a) He was in charge of cleaning the train.
(b) He made sure everything on the train ran smoothly.
(c) He collected tickets from passengers.
(d) He guarded the cargo hold.

(xvi) How does the poet describe the journey of the Night Mail?

(a) Fast and chaotic
(b) Steady and relentless
(c) Dangerous and unpredictable
(d) Mysterious and eerie

Section (B)

*(Answer **one or more** questions from this section.)*

DRAMA

(Julius Caesar by William Shakespeare)

Question 2

Read the extract given below and answer the questions that follow.

Caesar Yond Cassius has a
lean and hungry look;
He thinks too much: such
men are dangerous.

(i) Where is Caesar at this moment?
What does Caesar mean by 'lean and hungry look'?
What does Antony say in response to this remark? **(3)**

(ii) What are Caesar' s thoughts about Cassius?
Why does Caesar not fear Cassius openly? **(3)**

(iii) What does this remark reveal about Cassius's nature?
How is this remark by Caesar ironic? **(3)**

(iv) Do you think his judgement of Cassius is correct? Why or why not? **(3)**

(v) Mention two qualities of Cassius that make him 'dangerous' according to Caesar.
How does this moment contribute to the rising tension in the play?
What does this scene tell us about Caesar's character? **(4)**

Question 3

Read the extract given below and answer the questions that follow.

Brutus "Between the acting
of a dreadful thing
And the first motion, all the interim is
Like a phantasma or a hideous dream."

(i) Where is Brutus at this moment?
What is the 'dreadful thing' he is referring to?
Why is Brutus feeling disturbed? **(3)**

(ii) What does Brutus mean by "phantasma or a hideous dream"?
How does this statement reflect his internal conflict? **(3)**

(iii) What decision does Brutus make soon after this speech?
How does this moment contribute to his character development? **(3)**

(iv) What does this extract reveal about the theme of fate versus free will?
How does this scene add to the tension in the play? **(3)**

(v) What does this speech reveal about Brutus's nature?
Do you think Brutus is being noble or simply manipulated? Justify your answer. **(4)**

Section (C)

*(Answer **one** or more questions from this section.)*

Prose - Short Stories

(Treasure Chest- A Collection of Poems and Short Stories)

Question 4

Read the following extract from Ruskin Bond's short story, 'The Boy Who Broke the Bank' and answer the questions that follow.

Nathu grumbled to himself as he swept the steps of the Pipalnagar Bank. 'How careless these people are,' he muttered, 'placing the rubbish bins all over the place!' Bending down, he began to sweep the dust away. His mind, however, was on his pending wages.

(i) Who was Nathu? What work was he doing?

Why was he grumbling to himself? **(3)**

(ii) How did Nathu's complaint about his wages lead to a rumour spreading across the town? **(3)**

(iii) What role did Sitaram play in the story?

How did his conversation with Mrs. Srivastava add to the confusion? **(3)**

(iv) How did the news of the bank's failure impact the town?

Describe the reaction of the people to the rumor. **(3)**

(v) What message does the story convey about the nature of rumours?

How does Ruskin Bond use humour to highlight this theme? **(4)**

Question 5

Read the following extract from Rabindranath Tagore' s short story, 'The Home-coming' and answer the questions that follow.

Phatik knew his end had come. With a feeble voice, he said, 'Mother, the holidays have come.' A sudden light came into his eyes, as if the sight of his mother had brought back all his old memories. He wanted to say something but could not. The light in his eyes faded and he sank into his last sleep.

(i) Who was Phatik? Why was he sent away from home?

How did he feel about his new life? **(3)**

(ii) How does this extract show Phatik's longing for home? **(3)**

(iii) What is the significance of Phatik's final words, 'Mother, the holidays have come'? What do they reveal about his emotions? **(3)**

(iv) How did Phatik's uncle treat him in Kolkata?

How was his treatment different from what Phatik had expected? **(3)**

(v) What emotions does the ending of the story evoke in the reader?

Do you think Phatik's fate could have been avoided? Explain. **(4)**

Section (D)

*(Answer **one or more** questions from this section.)*

Poetry

(Treasure Chest – A Collection of Poems and Short Stories)

Question 6

Read the following extract from 'A Work of Artifice' by Marge Piercy and answer the questions that follow.

With living creatures
one must begin very early
to dwarf their growth:
the bound feet,
the crippled brain,
the hair in curlers,
the hands you
love to touch.

(i) What does the poet mean by 'one must begin very early to dwarf their growth'?
What living creature is being compared to humans in the poem? **(3)**

(ii) How does the gardener control the bonsai tree?
How is this a metaphor for the treatment of women in society? **(3)**

(iii) What is the significance of the phrase 'the bound feet, the crippled brain'? How do these phrases relate to traditional gender roles? **(3)**

(iv) The poem uses various literary devices to emphasise its message. Identify the following. **(3)**
(a) A metaphor (b) An example of repetition (c) A contrast presented in the poem

(v) What is the central theme of the poem?
What is the poet's attitude towards societal expectations of women? **(4)**

Question 7

Read the following extract from 'The Night Mail' by W.H. Auden and answer the questions that follow.

Letters of thanks, letters from banks,
Letters of joy from girl and boy,
Receipted bills and invitations
To inspect new stock or to visit relations,
And applications for situations.

(i) What is being described in this extract?
Why is the movement of 'The Night Mail' important? **(3)**

(ii) How does the poet create a rhythmic effect in these lines?
What does this rhythm symbolise in the poem? **(3)**

(iii) What different emotions are associated with the letters mentioned in the poem? Give two examples from the extract that show the range of emotions. **(3)**

(iv) Identify the following poetic devices in the given extract. **(3)**
(a) Alliteration (b) Repetition (c) Enjambment

(v) What is the poet's perspective on the role of the mail train?
How does the poem highlight the importance of communication in society? **(4)**